Productivity in Singapore's
Retail and Food Services Sectors

Contemporary Issues

Productivity in Singapore's
Retail and Food
Services Sectors

Contemporary Issues

Toh Mun Heng
National University of Singapore, Singapore

Shandre Thangavelu
University of Adelaide, Australia

 **World Scientific**

NEW JERSEY · LONDON · SINGAPORE · BEIJING · SHANGHAI · HONG KONG · TAIPEI · CHENNAI · TOKYO

Published by

World Scientific Publishing Co. Pte. Ltd.

5 Toh Tuck Link, Singapore 596224

USA office: 27 Warren Street, Suite 401-402, Hackensack, NJ 07601

UK office: 57 Shelton Street, Covent Garden, London WC2H 9HE

Library of Congress Cataloging-in-Publication Data
Names: Toh, Mun Heng, author. | Thangavelu, Shandre, 1969–   author.
Title: Productivity in Singapore's retail and food services sectors : contemporary issues /
    Mun Heng Toh (NUS, Singapore), Shandre Thangavelu (University of Adelaide, Australia).
Description: New Jersey : World Scientific, [2016] |
    Includes bibliographical references and index.
Identifiers: LCCN 2016035724 | ISBN 9789813142404
Subjects: LCSH: Retail trade--Singapore. | Food service--Singapore. |
    Service industries--Singapore. | Singapore--Commerce.
Classification: LCC HF5429.6.S55 T64 2016 | DDC 381/.1095957--dc23
LC record available at https://lccn.loc.gov/2016035724

British Library Cataloguing-in-Publication Data
A catalogue record for this book is available from the British Library.

Desk Editor: Shreya Gopi

Typeset by Stallion Press
Email: enquiries@stallionpress.com

Printed in Singapore

Preface

The Singapore Productivity Centre (SPC) was established in October 2013 under the auspices of the National Productivity Council. The mandate given to SPC is to be the national productivity centre for services sectors. The initial focus, in 2014, was on the retail and food & beverage (F&B) sectors. Beginning from 2015, the hotel sector was added to SPC's portfolio. SPC aims to help companies in these sectors raise productivity so as to sustain their growth and competitiveness. In executing its mission, SPC supports SPRING Singapore and Singapore Tourism Board in the implementation of their productivity plans for the retail and F&B sectors and for the hotel sector, respectively. In assisting companies, SPC adopts a holistic approach to achieve maximum impact. This approach comprises five major services that are directed specifically at companies. These are consultancy, training and workshops, study missions, benchmarking and conferences. From this range of services, companies obtain direct help through consultancy; receive new knowledge and skills through training and workshops; learn best practices and the latest thinking in productivity through study missions and conferences; and get to understand their performance in the industry through benchmarking.

To support these five services, SPC undertakes applied research studies. The research studies focus on uncovering industry trends, enterprise best practices and productivity solutions that will benefit companies. The findings guide SPC to focus on certain areas for consultancy; determine the topics and contents in training and workshops and conferences; identify the areas of interest in study missions; and scope of the areas to be covered in the benchmarking exercise. They are also disseminated to companies through SPC's website and social media platforms, speeches, collaterals and other channels. Applied research is thus a critical sixth service in SPC's comprehensive suite of services.

Between 2014 and 2015, SPC conducted a total of 36 research studies for the retail and F&B sectors. The principal researchers engaged by SPC for the studies are Professor Toh Mun Heng of the NUS Business School and Professor Shandre Thangavelu of Adelaide University.

Besides the various channels that are already being used to disseminate the research findings, SPC has produced this publication to document them for reference. Unlike the other channels which are able to highlight only selected findings from the research studies, the contents of this publication are more substantive. Hence, companies can turn to them for in-depth insights into key productivity issues.

The topics included in this publication reflect the key issues that are pertinent to productivity improvement in the retail and F&B sectors. They comprise the framework for productivity improvement; entrepreneurism; employment of part-time workers and mature workers; roles of social media and marketing; and financial management. Based on the findings from the research studies, policy conclusions are drawn.

This publication is targeted primarily at companies in the retail and F&B sectors, as well as policy makers responsible for the two sectors. Consultants, trainers and students will also find the substantive contents useful.

Dr Ahmad Mohd Magad
Chairman
Singapore Productivity Centre

Contents

About the Authors

Toh Mun Heng

Dr Toh is an economic professor specializing in the quantitative evaluation and assessment of public policies and programs. He is currently lecturing at the Department of Strategy & Policy, NUS Business School. He had served as Lead Economist at the Ministry of Trade and Industry from 2003 to 2005. He is the recipient of the National Trade Union Congress 'Friend of Labor' Award in 2008, and also awarded Public Service Star in the National Day Award in 2009.

Professor Toh obtained his doctoral degree in Economics and Econometrics from the University of London, London School of Economics. His research interests and publications are in the areas of development strategies of emerging economies in the Asia Pacific, econometric modeling, input-output analysis, international trade and investment, human resource development, and productivity measurement. He has substantive experience as an economic consultant for many international organization, private enterprises and governmental agencies. He has co-authored and edited several titles including *The Economics of Education and Manpower Development: Issues and Policies in Singapore; Health Policies in Singapore; Public Policies in Singapore: A Decade of Changes; Challenge and Response: Thirty Years of Economic Development Board; ASEAN Growth Triangles; Competitiveness of the Singapore Economy; Production Networks and Industrial Clusters: Integrating Economies in Southeast Asia.*

Shandre Thangavelu

Dr Shandre M. Thangavelu is an active researcher on human capital development, technology transfer, foreign direct investment, trade, government infrastructure investment, productivity and economic growth. He has written extensively in technology transfer and economic growth and has published his research in major international journals. His recent publications are in Journal of Economic Development, Empirical Economics, Applied Economics, World Economy, and Journal of Economic Studies. Recently, he was attached as the Head of the Economics Unit, Ministry of Manpower, under the Economist Service to Ministry of Trade and Industry and Ministry of Manpower. He has also worked on several international projects commissioned by Asian Productivity Organization (APO) on the measurement of aggregate productivity for the Singapore economy and the World Bank project on structural changes and skill-mismatch. He is currently working on a government project related to "Returns on CET Training for Singapore Labour Market." He is also assisting as Consultant (Head of Economics Unit, MOM) to the Ministry of Manpower.

Dr. Thangavelu was the Director of SCAPE (Singapore Centre for Applied and Policy Economics) at the Department of Economics, National University of Singapore. He was also the Assistant Dean at the Faculty of Arts and Social Sciences from Jan 2004 to May 2006. He obtained his graduate degrees from Queen's University, Canada.

Acknowledgments

The authors are grateful to the Singapore Productivity Centre (SPC) for commissioning and funding the research studies. Special thanks go to Dr Woon Kin Chung (CEO of SPC), Ms Loo Ya Lee (Director, Planning & Corporate Development) and Ms Lim Sui Lan (Manager, Planning & Corporate Development) for rendering significant assistance in conjunction with the research studies and the production of this publication.

Six Research Assistants contributed to the research studies featured in the publication. They are Lee Wei Xuan (Chapter 4); Tang Jun Huang (Chapter 5); Wee Chong Wei Joshua (Chapter 6); Shen Le (Chapter 7); June Ng Xin Hui (Chapter 8); and Goh Li Ling Rayna (Chapter 9). Their contributions provided the inputs that were critical for the research studies.

The authors would also like to express their gratitude to the companies and the consumers who participated in the various surveys and interviews conducted to support and facilitate the studies.

Chapter 1

Introduction

1. Priority Attention Given to Retail and Food & Beverage Sectors[1]

The productivity growth of the Retail and Food & Beverage (F&B) sectors in Singapore has been low compared to the other sectors and the national average. In 2009, the nominal value added per worker of the Retail and F&B sectors was $37,000 and $22,300, respectively, less than 40% of the national average of $89,800.

Consequently, Retail and F&B are two sectors that are given priority attention by the National Productivity Council (NPC); and SPRING Singapore has been designated as the lead agency for these two sectors. In 2011, SPRING announced two five-year productivity plans to upgrade the sectors, one each for Retail and F&B. Retail was allocated a budget of $86m; and F&B, $75m. This demonstrates the government's commitment to raising the productivity of the two sectors.

2. Establishment of Singapore Productivity Centre

To give focused attention to helping companies in the Retail and F&B sectors, the Singapore Productivity Centre (SPC) was set up in October 2013 under the aegis of the NPC. In executing its mission, SPC supports SPRING in the implementation of the productivity plans.

---

[1]For the purpose of this publication, the standard SSIC nomenclature of "Food & Beverage" is used although SPRING Singapore uses the term "Food Services."

1

SPC offers a comprehensive range of services that span six major areas. These are consultancy services; training and workshops; study missions; conferences; benchmarking; and applied research.

3. Applied Research Studies of Retail and F&B Sectors

SPC's applied research studies cover analyses of industry trends and key issues; identification of best practices; case studies of companies and other productivity-related topics. Besides supporting the other services offered by SPC, the applied research studies shed light on the key issues facing companies; and guide companies and policy makers to take the appropriate actions.

This publication summarizes the major findings of the applied research studies undertaken by SPC in 2014 and 2015. Companies can learn from these findings, benchmark themselves against others and seek assistance from SPC in their productivity journey. Policy makers can also draw conclusions from the findings to help refine and fine-tune policies that are directed at these two sectors.

4. Outline of Publication

The areas covered in this publication reflect the key issues facing companies in the Retail and F&B sectors. Table 1 outlines the various chapters in the publication.

Following the introduction in Chapter 1, Chapter 2 discusses the reasons for the lack of productivity growth and the key challenges in improving productivity in the services sectors, particularly in Retail and F&B. The 8M framework is introduced as an integrated approach to managing productivity growth. The 8Ms comprise Management (leadership and management practices), Manpower (human resources), Material (physical resources and services), Method (appropriate technologies, capital equipment and processes), Money (financial resources), Make (product variety and innovation, and customer experience), Market (domestic and international markets) and Message (branding and communications, both internal and external). The framework enables monitoring,

Table 1: Chapters in Publication and Areas Under the 8M Framework that are Covered

Chapter	Title	Areas Under 8M Framework Covered
1	Introduction	—
2	Analysis of Singapore's productivity performance and proposal for 8M framework to raise productivity growth in the retail and F&B sectors	Introduction to 8M framework
3	Measurement and surveillance of productivity performance based on 8Ms — Application to Retail and F&B Sectors	Statistical application of 8M framework
4	Entrepreneurship, start-ups and productivity: Entrepreneurism in Singapore's retail and F&B sectors	Management
5	Part-time workers' productivity in the F&B sector	Manpower
6	Human capital issues in F&B and retail sectors in Singapore: engagement, retention and usage of mature workers	Manpower
7	Use of social media to raise productivity in the F&B sector	Message
8	Sufficiency of marketing efforts by Singapore SMEs in retail and F&B sectors	Message
9	Cost control and accounting practices: impact on and improvement of productivity in Singapore F&B enterprises	Money, Management
10	Conclusion	—

analysis and planning for productivity improvement at the national, industry and firm levels.

Chapter 3 reveals that the 8M framework has its antecedents in the Total Quality Management approach and the more recent Business Excellence Framework. The central message to companies is that the pursuit of productivity based on a single index can be fraught with difficulties and apparent contradictions in terms of measures to be taken. The 8M framework overcomes this by addressing multiple inputs and multiple outputs that are important for productivity improvement. The statistical application of the framework to the Retail and F&B sectors is elaborated in this chapter.

The next six chapters delve into specific aspects of the Ms. Management is covered in Chapters 4 and 9; Manpower, in Chapters 5 and 6; Message, in Chapters 7 and 8; and Money, in Chapter 9.

Chapter 4 addresses the issue of entrepreneurism in the F&B sector and examines whether it is a boon or a bane for productivity. The prevalence of casual entrepreneurism in the F&B sector is of concern. The reason is that it increases the demand for: (a) labor, thus raising labor cost; (b) shop spaces, leading to higher rental rates and (c) material inputs, leading to higher cost of production.

Chapter 5 deals with the employment of part-time workers in the F&B sector. Since companies in this sector perennially face the issue of manpower shortage, they could tap part-time workers to meet their manpower requirements. The challenge is to use the part-time workers productively and to reduce the high turnover rate of part-time workers. In this respect, there is much room for improvement in the F&B sector.

Another aspect of the augmentation of the manpower supply has to do with the employment of mature workers. This is addressed in Chapter 6. Mature workers offer the potential of a good source of supply of manpower. However, many companies in the Retail and F&B sectors have yet to establish appropriate human resource management practices and job-re-design programs to accommodate the employment of mature workers.

Chapter 7 investigates the use of social media in the F&B sector. Social media has the potential to transform traditional marketing and communication efforts. This is the case even in the F&B sector. However, many F&B companies are slow to embrace social media, and the level of sophistication in the use of social media is generally low.

The broader issue of marketing efforts of SMEs in the Retail and F&B sectors is discussed in Chapter 8. Market segmentation, innovative marketing and social media marketing are strategies that are useful for small businesses. Yet, many companies, especially the micro-businesses, have poor understanding of marketing and perform insufficient market research in the operation of their businesses.

Chapter 9 covers the important domain of cost control and accounting practices in the F&B sector. While a large majority of the companies do use accounting and financial data for decision-making purposes, the frequency of implementation is inadequate. Furthermore, many of them tend to adopt the simpler and traditional techniques. The lack of skilled manpower and resources is a key challenge faced in implementing cost control and management accounting techniques.

Drawing from all the findings, Chapter 10 concludes with a summary of the recommendations.

Chapter 2

Analysis of Singapore's Productivity Performance and Proposal for 8M Framework to Raise Productivity Growth in the Retail and F&B Sectors

1. Introduction

1.1. *Singapore's open economy and consequent challenges*

Singapore's rapid growth from a modest trading post to a developed nation is one of the most notable stories of successful growth and development in the second half of the 20th century. The Singapore economy experienced one of the highest rates of growth in the world over the past three decades with Gross Domestic Product (GDP) appreciating at an annual rate of about 7.2% during the period 1970–2015. The result in turn propelled Singapore's average real per capita income from US$512 in 1965 to US$53,322 by 2015, which surpassed the level of many developed countries. However, long-term averages can hide the vulnerability of the city state to external shocks. Singapore experienced an acute economic contraction in 2001, following the sharp downturn in the global electronics industry and sluggish regional and global growth. A confluence of negative factors exacerbated the recession, including the September 2001 terrorist attack, bird flu and severe acute respirator syndrome

(SARS), tsunami, Middle-east war, oil shocks and dot.com bubble crash.

With manufacturing and services as "twin" engines of the economy, Singapore regained its robust growth over the next decade. Manufacturing provides the export foundation for the economy, with world-class enterprises concentrated in the industrial clusters. However, in the past decade, Singapore has been subjected to several external shocks. The most recent global recession dealt another economic shock to Singapore's economy. This crisis again raised concerns about the challenges facing Singapore's open, trade-oriented policies and how best to manage the nation's essential resources to maintain a sustainable and robust future growth.

The cornerstone of Singapore's economic strategy has been its broad engagement with international trade and investment flows. Singapore has one of the most open economies in the world, with a trade to GDP ratio of around 250%. With few natural resources, the city state must be particularly aware of and responsive to the forces that transform markets and alter ways of doing business, so as to remain "ahead of the game." For example, advances in information systems, communications and related technologies (ICT) have significantly shrunk the economic distances between nations and markets, possibly reducing the demand for some conventional roles for Singapore such as entrepot, overseas headquarters (OHQs) or other ancillary services. Competition for investments, export markets and skilled labor has intensified and, as more economies embrace open door trade and investment policies, some of Singapore's hub roles can be duplicated by lower cost regional rivals. In policy terms, Singapore recognizes that it must maintain a liberal policy environment in both trade and investment in order to retain its attractiveness as a global or regional transnational corporation (TNC) hub.

1.2. Importance of strong productivity growth in the domestic economy

The key driver for the competitiveness and sustained growth of the Singapore economy is productivity growth in the domestic economy. This chapter studies the overall productivity trends of the Singapore economy and identifies the key factors for productivity growth. It also proposes a framework to manage and develop sustainable productivity growth in the domestic economy, of which the retail and food & beverage (F&B) sectors are a key part.

2. Key Macroeconomic Trends of the Singapore Economy

2.1. *Support for liberal trade policy*

With its economic growth and development tied to the global economy, Singapore supports liberal trade policies and maintains almost no applied tariff barriers of its own. As an increasingly service-based economy with strong export interests, Singapore gives particular emphasis to securing greater market access and a transparent rules framework in trading services. While among the most ardent of supporters of the 'global trading system as the preferred approach,' Singapore has also pursued a regional track to liberalization through involvement in both the 10-member Association of Southeast Asian Nations (ASEAN) grouping and the larger 21-member Asia Pacific Economic Cooperation (APEC). Negotiating bilateral trade pacts provides a third-track approach when multilateral and regional progress is slowed by financial crises or the sheer size and diversity of the groupings.

2.2. *Ease of doing business*

Singapore was ranked as the top country for "Ease of Doing Business" in the World Bank's "Doing Business 2014 and 2015" reports. Singapore is ranked sixth in terms of starting a business in 2015. The government provides world-class infrastructure for foreign investments as well as competitive direct and indirect incentives for foreign direct investments (FDI) in key sectors. Incentives normally include concessionary corporate tax rates of between 5% and 15% or corporate income tax exemptions. Non-tax incentives including grants can be offered for particular high value-added sectors, training and research and development (R&D). Among the government's support for R&D-related businesses, Singapore Science Park provides modern infrastructure in its three science parks. The Agency for Science, Technology and Research (A*STAR) also fosters scientific research, among other initiatives, large infrastructure projects such as Fusionopolis (for information and media industries) and Biopolis (for the biomedical sciences industry).

2.3. *More emphasis on small and medium sized enterprises development in recent years*

Singapore's growth has traditionally been driven mainly by its open strategies and by attracting multinational investments complemented by key domestic firms (government-linked companies or GLCs) in targeted industrial clusters. Although there are strong enterprise strategies to develop key industries, the government policies tend to focus more on the activities of large corporations and export-oriented firms. The cluster strategies and enterprise strategies have focused on attracting multinational corporations and developing key industries directly linked to the identified key clusters. In contrast, there was relatively less emphasis on the development of small and medium sized enterprises or SMEs (enterprises with annual turnover sales of not more than S$100 million and/or employing not more than 200 workers) in the past. However, due to lack of local entrepreneurship, the government has now put more emphasis on SME development in terms of government incentives for productivity and SME development strategies in the global environment. This is important as SMEs account for 99% of the total enterprises, employ seven out of 10 workers and contribute to nearly 50% of the GDP. The retail and F&B sectors are two sectors in which policies have been developed for SME development.

2.4. *Weaker growth of economy and most sectors in recent years*

The Singapore economy had a strong output recovery after the Global Financial Crisis. In 2009, the output growth rate was −0.6% due to the financial crisis but it recovered quickly to 15.2% in 2010, before slowing down to 6.2% in 2011 and tapering further to 2.0% in 2015 (see Table 1 and Figure 1). The low growth rate of GDP in 2015 is attributed mainly to the weakness in the externally-oriented

Table 1:   Industrial Structure of Singapore Economy

	2009	2010	2011	2012	2013	2014	2015
GDP at Current Market Prices (S$Billion)	279.9	322.4	346.4	361.5	375.8	388.2	402.5
GDP at 2010 Market Prices (S$Billion)	279.7	322.4	342.4	354.9	371.5	383.6	391.3
Total GDP at 2010 Market Prices (Change in % relative to last year)	−0.6	15.2	6.2	3.7	4.7	3.3	2.0
Goods Producing Industries	−0.7	25.2	7.1	2.1	2.5	2.8	−3.4
Manufacturing	−4.2	29.7	7.8	0.3	1.7	2.7	−5.2
Construction	21.5	7.5	5.7	10.6	5.8	3.5	2.5
Services Producing Industries	−0.8	11.7	6.9	4.4	6.5	3.6	3.4
Wholesale & Retail Trade	−4.4	15.9	6.6	3.4	6.6	2.1	6.1
Transportation & Storage	−9.1	6.0	5.2	4.9	4.0	2.6	0.0
Accommodation & Food Services	−1.9	14.5	11.4	1.8	2.2	1.7	0.2
Information & Communications	5.1	7.9	9.8	6.3	8.0	7.0	4.2
Finance & Insurance	0.3	12.3	8.7	6.0	14.0	9.1	5.3
Business Services	3.8	9.0	7.3	5.5	5.3	1.6	1.5
Other Services Industries	5.6	13.8	4.5	2.6	2.0	2.7	1.6

Source: Department of Statistics, Singapore.

sectors such as manufacturing. The growth in manufacturing declined over the years from 30% in 2010 to 2.7% in 2014 before contracting by 5.2% in 2015. This drastic contraction of the export industries raises important issues on the competitiveness of the domestic economy. The wholesale and retail trade sector also experienced a strong decline from 15.9% in 2010 to 2.1% in 2014 before expanding by 6.1% in 2015. Most sectors in 2015 performed relatively weaker as compared to the previous year, except wholesale and retail sector. The rapid growth of the construction sector after the Financial Crisis had helped little in productivity uplifting but had stimulated property speculation and engendered property price bubble. Property cooling measures by the government have helped to rein in the situation and moderated the construction sector's growth since 2012.

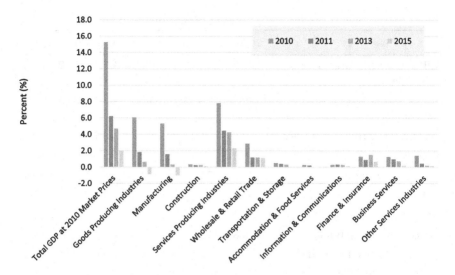

Figure 1:   Contribution of Sectoral GDP Growth to Total GDP Growth

Note: The growth rate of GDP in the current year is the weighted sum of sectoral GDP growth rates. The weights are the shares of sectoral GDP in total GDP in the previous year.

Source: Economic Survey of Singapore, 2015, Ministry of Trade and Industry, Singapore.

2.5. Declining growth contribution of manufacturing to GDP growth

Figure 1 shows the contribution of sectoral GDP growth to the total GDP growth. In 2015, out of the 2.0% total GDP growth, 1.1% is attributed to the wholesale and retail sector. The manufacturing sector was the only sector contributed negatively to real GDP growth in 2015. In fact the contribution of the manufacturing sector has been declining since 2010. The transportation and storage industry as well as the hotels and food services industries made no contribution to the growth performance in 2015. In the last four years, the services producing sector outperformed the goods producing sector in contributing to growth in total GDP.

2.6. Total trade increasing at decreasing rate since 2010

Table 2 provides the growth of trade in the Singapore economy. The total trade volume has exhibited a declining trend since

Table 2:   Total Trade in Singapore (S$Billion)

	2009	2010	2011	2012	2013	2014	2015
Total Trade at Current Prices (S$Billion)	747.4	902.1	974.4	983.4	975.9	977.0	884.1
Imports	356.3	423.2	459.7	474.5	466.8	463.8	407.8
Exports	391.1	478.8	514.7	508.9	509.2	513.2	476.3
Domestic Exports	200.0	248.6	281.3	283.8	270.0	268.1	233.4
Oil	58.7	75.0	104.0	106.8	106.5	107.0	72.5
Non–oil	141.3	173.6	177.4	176.9	163.5	161.1	160.9
Re–exports	191.1	230.2	233.4	225.2	239.2	245.1	242.9

Percentage Change Over Corresponding Period Of Previous Year

Total Trade at Current Prices (Change in %)	−19.4	20.7	8.0	0.9	−0.8	0.1	−9.5
Imports	−21.0	18.8	8.6	3.2	−1.6	−0.6	−12.1
Exports	−18.0	22.4	7.5	−1.1	0.0	0.8	−7.2
Domestic Exports	−19.2	24.3	13.2	0.9	−4.8	−0.7	−12.9
Oil	−34.5	27.9	38.6	2.8	−0.3	0.5	−32.2
Non–oil	−10.6	22.8	2.2	−0.3	−7.6	−1.5	−0.1
Re–exports	−16.6	20.5	1.4	−3.5	6.2	2.5	−0.9

Source: Yearbook of Statistics, Department of Statistics, Singapore.

2011. In fact in 2015, total trade contracted by 9.5% compared to the previous year, and is less than that recorded for 2010. Total exports fell by 7.2% in 2015, while total imports contracted at a even higher rate of 12.1% resulting in a merchandise trade surplus of more than S$70 billion. The weak export performance is reflected in both domestic exports and re-exports. The decline in crude oil prices and vagaries of the international oil market had affected the domestic export of oil related products. In 2015, the domestic export of oil related products contracted by 32%. The decline in trading activities and weakening external demand may have a depressive effects on innovation and productivity improvement effort.

2.7. Levelling off investment commitments in manufacturing sector

The key trends of investment commitments by local and foreign enterprises are shown in Table 3. The same information disaggregated by major industry is also included. Total fixed asset investments (FAI) had increased significantly after the 2008 financial crisis, from S$11.8 billion in 2009 to S$16 billion in 2012. Since then, it had declined to between S$11 billion to S$12 billion in the last three years. The bulk of the FAI, more than 90% in 2015, was made by foreign enterprises. The manufacturing sector accounted for the majority share of the FAI, 72% in 2015, while it is noted that the volume of investment spending in the services cluster comprising of regional & global headquarter activities and professional services has increased over the years.

The chemicals cluster attracted most of the fixed asset investments with a value of S$3.6 billion in 2015. FAI in the computer and electronic industry, S$3.3 billion, is no less significant than that of the chemicals. Though it is a relatively mature industry, its scope of expansion and importance in supporting the production and innovation activities of incumbent and emerging industries in the digital age is not likely to diminish but enhanced. Stagnating inflow of foreign capital may be inimical to the effort expended in uplifting the productivity and competitiveness of the economy.

Table 3:   Investment Commitments in Manufacturing and Services

	2009	2010	2011	2012	2013	2014	2015
Total FAI (S$Billion)	11.8	12.9	13.7	16.0	12.1	11.8	11.5
Local	*3.4*	*2.1*	*1.9*	*1.8*	*3.1*	*1.9*	*1.1*
Foreign	*8.4*	*10.8*	*11.9*	*14.2*	*9.0*	*9.9*	*10.4*
Manufacturing (S$Billion)	10.1	10.0	11.3	14.3	8.0	6.8	8.3
Petroleum & Chemicals	*2.8*	*1.6*	*2.5*	*6.5*	*2.5*	*2.6*	*3.6*
Computers. Electronic Pdts	*4.9*	*5.7*	*7.4*	*6.3*	*3.3*	*1.7*	*3.3*
Transport Equipment	*0.2*	*1.1*	*0.3*	*0.3*	*0.6*	*0.7*	*0.5*
Services Clusters (S$B)	1.7	2.8	2.5	1.7	4.2	5.1	3.2

Source: Yearbook of Statistics, 2015, Department of Statistics, Singapore.

2.8. *Higher labor force growth and lower labor productivity growth*

The employment trends are given in Table 4. The labour force had expanded, but at a diminishing rate over the years to reach 3.6 million in 2015. Between 2010 and 2012 the labour force grew at an average rate of 3.5% per annum, and this decreased to 2.4% in the period 2013 to 2015. In 2015, total employment created was 31.8 thousand much lower than the 130 thousand in 2014. The substantial decline in the job creation is a reflection of the slower growth of the domestic economy amidst restricted inflow of foreign labour, uncertain global economic condition and lower economic growth performance in the major trading partners. Furthermore, the jobs created are mainly attributable to the services industries. Employment in the manufacturing sector has declined every year since 2013, while the construction sector still registered positive growth in the years after the 2008 Financial Crisis.

Table 4:   Key Labour Market Statistics for Singapore Economy

	2009	2010	2011	2012	2013	2014	2015
Labour Force ('000)	3030	3136	3237	3362	3444	3531	3611
Employed Person ('000)	2906	3047	3150	3275	3353	3440	3516
Manufacturing	*506*	*509*	*510*	*521*	*520*	*509*	*496*
Construction	*366*	*375*	*394*	*432*	*459*	*468*	*482*
Services	*2011*	*2142*	*2224*	*2299*	*2350*	*2439*	*2514*
Unemployment Rate (%)	4.1	2.8	2.7	2.6	2.6	2.6	2.6
Change in Employment ('000)	37.6	115.9	122.6	129.1	136.2	130.1	31.8
Manufacturing	*−43.9*	*−0.8*	*3.4*	*11.4*	*5.3*	*−4.4*	*−22.1*
Construction	*24.0*	*3.4*	*22.0*	*39.1*	*35.2*	*14.3*	*8.6*
Services	*58.6*	*112.6*	*96.1*	*77.0*	*94.1*	*119.7*	*45.5*
Change in Average Monthly Earning (%)	*−2.6*	*5.6*	*6.0*	*2.3*	*4.3*	*2.3*	*2.6*
Labour Productivity (% Change in VA per worker)	−3.3	11.6	2.3	−0.3	0.5	−0.5	−0.1

Notes: The unemployment rate is computed = 100*(Labour Force − Employed)/Labour Force.
Source: Singapore Department of Statistics and Ministry of Manpower.

Services was the only sector that experienced positive annual employment growth throughout the period 2009 to 2015. The overall unemployment rate of 2.6% has been unchanged since 2012. Nominal wages rose by 2.6% in 2015, while the growth rates were 5.6% and 6% in 2010 and 2011, respectively. Labour productivity, measured by the real value-added per worker, fell by 0.1% in 2015, a slight improvement relative to negative 0.5% recorded for the previous year.

3. Decomposition of Productivity Growth

3.1. *GDP growth decomposition*

To understand the overall labour productivity trend in the Singapore economy, a decomposition of GDP into productivity and employment contributions is undertaken (see Chia *et al.*, 2004). In Table 5, the GDP growth is decomposed into components attributed to labour productivity and changes in local and foreign employed manpower.

3.2. *Slower productivity growth since post-Asian crisis period of 1997–2002*

In 1992–1997, the Singapore economy experienced an average annual GDP growth of around 11.7%, which is well above the economy's

Table 5: Growth Decomposition in Terms of Productivity & Labor Growth from 1992 to 2008 (%)

| Period | GDP | Average Annual Growth in Percentage | | |
		Productivity	Local Labor	Foreign Labor
1992–1997	11.7	4.4	2.8	4.5
	100.0	37.2	24.3	38.6
1997–2002	3.0	2.0	1.0	0.1
	100.0	64.1	32.8	3.1
2002–2008	6.0	1.5	2.3	2.2
	100.00	24.3	39.0	36.7

Source: Decomposition from 1992–2002 is from Chia *et al.*, 2004.

potential growth of 4 to 5%. The decline in labor productivity is quite visible in the post-Asian crisis period of 1997–2002 as the GDP growth rate decelerated to around 3% due to several negative external shocks such as SARS, terrorism and slump in global electronics demand. In 2002–2008 as the economy grew around 6%, the labor productivity declined significantly to around 1.5%.

The contribution of labor productivity growth to GDP rose from 37% in 1992–1997 to 64% in 1997–2002. This increase could be attributed to rising capital intensity and wider use of information technologies. However, in recent years, the labor productivity is showing a declining trend. The contribution of labor productivity to GDP growth declined from 64% in 1997–2002 to only 24% in 2002–2008. This indicates that GDP growth in the recent years is driven more by labor input growth, in particular foreign labor, as compared to growth from capital intensity and innovative activities.

3.3. Continued declining trend of productivity growth since 2009

Recent evidence also indicates that labor productivity is showing a declining trend since the recovery from the Global Financial Crisis (see Table 6). The large improvements in labor productivity after the recovery from the Global Financial Crisis are not sustainable in the domestic economy, as labor productivity has been declining since 2010.

3.4. Too few industries drive productivity growth

Singapore's productivity challenge exists on a nationwide scale in both the manufacturing and services sectors. Conceivably, there is a greater vulnerability in the services sector due to large employment share and low capital investment and technology intensity. In the digital age, information communication technology (ICT) and innovation in transaction using electronic platforms can possibly be exploited to power both revenue growth and productivity. ICT, many believe is a general purpose technology, should be pervasively

Table 6:   Contribution to National Productivity Growth by Industry, 2010–2015

	Within Sector Effect			% Contribution		
	2010–2013	2010–2014	2010–2015	2010–2013	2010–2014	2010–2015
	(a)	(b)	(c)	(d)	(e)	(f)
Total Economy	**3.53**	**2.72**	**2.25**	**100.0**	**100.0**	**100.0**
Goods Producing Industries	*1.59*	*1.28*	*0.94*	*45.0*	*47.1*	*41.6*
Manufacturing	1.52	1.25	0.90	43.2	45.8	40.2
Construction	0.06	0.03	0.03	1.8	1.3	1.4
Services Producing Industries	*2.01*	*1.54*	*1.34*	*57.2*	*56.6*	*59.4*
Wholesale & Retail Trade	0.93	0.70	0.74	26.3	25.6	32.8
Transportation & Storage	0.14	0.10	0.06	4.0	3.8	2.5
Accommodation & Food Services	0.05	0.03	0.01	1.3	1.0	0.6
Information & Communications	0.05	0.06	0.04	1.5	2.1	1.6
Finance & Insurance	0.53	0.54	0.49	15.0	19.8	21.6
Business Services	0.17	0.02	−0.04	4.8	0.9	−2.0
Other Services Industries	0.15	0.09	0.05	4.2	3.5	2.2
Total Within Sector Effect	**3.60**	**2.82**	**2.27**	**102.2**	**103.7**	**101.0**
Total Reallocation/Shift Effect	**−0.08**	**−0.10**	**−0.02**	**−2.2**	**−3.7**	**−1.0**

Note: The growth in productivity can be decomposed into 3 components: within sector effect, static shift effect and dynamic shift effect. The within sector effect for each industry is the product of its productivity growth and the industry share of total GDP. The other two effects, collectively referred to as re-allocation or shift effect, are usually relatively small. See Goh (2013) for further detail.
Source: Computed by Author.

used in all industries to support innovation and fine tune strategies to scale higher growth in output and productivity.

In Table 6, the productivity growth of the economy is decomposed into components contributed by major industries. For instance in column (c), the economy wide average productivity growth between 2010 and 2015 is 2.25% per annum. Out of this total, 0.94% was contributed by the goods producing industries, and 1.34% by the services producing industries. The same information is depicted in column (f) where the goods producing industries accounted for 41.6% of the total productivity growth.

The information in Table 6 clearly indicated the secular decline in productivity growth after financial crisis. With the exception of the wholesale & retail sector, and the finance & insurance sector, all sectors bark the overall trend of declining productivity growth in the period 2010 to 2015. Another observation, is the preponderance on a few industries to contribute materially to the overall productivity growth. The sectors are: wholesale & retail, manufacturing, and finance& insurance. Unavailability of data had disallowed closer scrutiny and investigation of productivity performance in the sub-sectors or industries of these sectors.

3.5. *Negative total factor productivity growth of Singapore economy from 2011*

The growth in GDP can be attributed to the growth of factor inputs such as capital equipment and labour resources, and the growth in total factor productivity (TFP).[1] Table 7 presents the decomposition of the GDP growth for the years 2009 to 2015. The contributions of the factor inputs had remained relatively stable, with contribution of capita input about twice that of labour input. The same cannot be said of TFP growth. Throughout 2012 to 2015, TFP growth was negative (about −1.0%), reflecting the lack

Table 7: Total Factor Productivity Contribution to Real GDP Growth*

	2009	2010	2011	2012	2013	2014	2015
Percentage Change in Real GDP	−0.6	14.2	6.0	3.6	4.6	3.2	2.0
Percentage Contribution to Growth in Real GDP of:							
Capital Input		2.9	3.0	3.0	3.2	3.1	2.6	2.2
Labour Input		1.2	1.4	1.5	1.7	1.8	1.7	1.0
Total Factor Productivity		−4.7	9.7	1.5	−1.2	−0.3	−1.0	−1.2

Source: Yearbook of Statistics, Department of Statistics, Singapore.
*All growth rates are expressed in log terms.

---

[1] See Jayaram and Lee (2010) for an alternative approach.

of innovative and productivity improvements in the domestic economy. Government assistance to private companies in the form productivity and innovation credit (PIC) can be an effective scheme to encourage enterprises to adopt technology and innovative strategies to improve productivity (Enterpiseone.gov.sg (2013)). There are several other public grants and schemes that private companies, especially the small and medium enterprises (SMEs) can access to improve their innovation capabilities and productivity. However, due diligence is required of them to be familiar with the assistance scheme or grant that best suited to their operational condition and constraint.

3.6. *Unhealthy situation of rising unit-labour cost coupled with low productivity growth*

In addition, business cost over the years driven mostly by unit-labour cost (ULC) and rental for business properties. Indeed, as shown in Figure 2, ULC and rental are rising at a faster rate than labour productivity in the years after 2011. Rising labor cost is due largely to the restriction on inflow of foreign labour into the economy, pushing up the average wages in the labor market. Bullish sentiment in the real estate market had stoke industrial/commercial property owners chasing for higher yield and exerted upward pressure on rental. With rising labor and rental cost, sustainability of business and economic growth has to rely on reversing the declining labor productivity trend, increasing innovation and competitiveness.

4. A Holistic Approach to Tackling Productivity Improvement — 8M Framework

The above analysis suggests that there are multiple factors that determine the productivity growth of the Singapore economy, the sectors and the individual companies. Clearly, an ad hoc approach

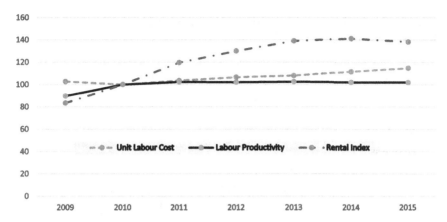

Figure 2: Indices for Unit-Labor Cost, Rental, and Productivity (2010 = 100)

Source: Computed & prepared by author.

Data on ULC and Labour Productivity from Economic Survey of Singapore 2012-2015, Ministry of Trade and Industry, and data on rental index for industrial properties from Jurong Town Corporation, Singapore.

will not work well. Rather, a holistic approach at both the micro level and the macro level addressing all the key factors is critical. Further detail of the approach is considered in Chapter 3 of this volume and also in Toh (2010), Thangavelu and Toh (2013).

4.1. *8M framework at company and sector level*

Given the critical need to improve the productivity of SMEs and the service sector, an effective approach to sustain productivity is needed. The SMEs and the service sector do not have the scale or the incentives to invest in technologies due to barriers in terms of large fixed cost in investment in technologies. Thus, there is a need to tackle productivity growth at the company level effectively.

There are many available frameworks for productivity improvement at the company level. However, they do not address the various productivity improvement factors comprehensively. An 8M framework is proposed to address the various factors systematically. The 8Ms comprise:

- Management (leadership and management practices);
- Manpower (human resources);
- Material (physical resources and services);
- Method (appropriate technologies, capital equipment and processes);
- Money (financial resources);
- Make (product variety and innovation and customer experience);
- Market (domestic and international markets) and
- Message (branding and communications, both internal and external).

Improvements in these factors are, in turn, the manifestation of a change in mindset that underlies the "bottom-up" approach to productivity improvement. The 8M framework is shown diagrammatically in Figure 3.

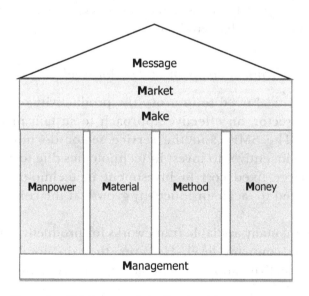

Figure 3: 8M Framework for Productivity Improvement

To achieve the goals of higher productivity, there is need for convergence of views and mindset in considering the importance of productivity. From the companies' perspective, productivity is not the primary objective to ensure the ultimate goal of survival and profitability, at least in the short run. The day-to-day running of a company can be summarized by the 8Ps: Physical presence; Productivity and quality; People (managers and workers); Process (customers' experience); Place (locational advantage); Promotion (marketing); Price (competitiveness) and Product (relevance and varieties). Productivity is just one of the eight daily concerns for the companies. In what ways are the company's offering a good deal for the customer? It is about the business improving its productivity for cost management and how the company can retain its customers. Ideally, it should be more about how the company passes the benefits of productivity improvement onto its customers. Also, productivity always needs to be tied with quality; the company supplies the best and uses the best intermediate products, procured fairly at the lowest cost. These various important issues can be addressed systematically through the 8M framework.

4.2. 8M framework at economy level

At the economy level, a coherent strategy is needed to achieve the key productivity goals and objectives. Conceptually, this comprises the strategic vision — what is the nation going to do? — and the strategic thrust — how is the nation going to do it? Singapore has identified productivity improvement as a strategic thrust to sustain the competiveness of the economy and further build the nation's capabilities.

The 8M framework, with appropriate interpretation, is applicable at the economy level as well. Improving productivity requires Singapore to take concrete action on the 8Ms — Management (government leadership), Manpower (human capital), Material (primary resources including energy, land space, etc.), Method (appropriate technologies and capital infrastructure), Money (finance for investment and upgrading), Make (excellect products and services),

Market (access to the world market) and Message (Singapore branding). Improvements in these areas are, in turn, the manifestation of a change in mindset with regard to productivity improvement.

4.3. Applying 8M framework systemtically at various levels

Table 8 shows a productivity matrix based on applying the 8M framework at various levels. The important point is that the same framework can be used at different levels and it is necessary to use this framework to address all the key factors determining productivity holistically.

4.4. Example of application of 8M framework: F&B sector

A successful program for productivity improvement requires the objectives of the stakeholders, namely, the companies and the government, to be aligned. Taking the case of the F&B sector as an example, the 8M framework can be used to assess the alignment of challenges and responses.

In terms of Management, the government has demonstrated willingness to champion the productivity drive of the sector, supported by a productivity plan and various schemes and incentives. The industry association could play an important role in improving

Table 8:   Productivity Matrix Based on 8M Framework

	Company	Industry	International	Role of Government
Management				
Manpower				
Material				
Method				
Money				
Make				
Market				
Message				

the productivity of the sector. However, a fairly large number of F&B enterprises is not represented by the Restaurant Association of Singapore (RAS). The RAS, in its website, reported its membership base to be more than 300 members, accounting for over 1,500 restaurant outlets. According to the Service Sector Survey Report,[2] there are 6,668 establishments in the F&B sector of which 2,426 are restaurants. Hence, there could be a large segment of F&B outlets who are unaware of the many initiatives and programmes for productivity improvement.

Manpower shortage is an important issue for the F&B enterprises. The manpower crunch is worsened when there is relatively low adoption of technology and poor human resource practices in the sector.[3] Furthermore, the inflow of less skilled and less expensive foreign workers is targeted for inflow curb and higher levies. To lessen the impact of this manpower challenge, the government has responded by pushing programs in the other M's: Method (appropriate technology), Market (accessing the world market), and Money (finance for investment and upgrading).

Companies are encouraged to mechanize where possible. Information and practices of F&B companies at the forefront of technologies and best practices in the country and overseas are made available for reference and enquiry. Efforts made by Singapore Tourism Board (STB) to establish Singapore as a gourmet center in Southeast Asia are possibly helpful in getting more foreign clients to local F&B outlets. Consultants and several financial schemes are available to companies which are willing to adapt and adopt. A budget of $75 million was committed by SPRING Singapore to boost productivity in the F&B sector for five years (2010–2015).

However, the transition from a low productivity state to a high productivity state is a difficult one. Government help and subsidies is not a long-term solution. When an enterprise is under constant

---

[2]Department of Statistics: Services Survey Series: Report on Food and Services 2013.
[3]SPRING Factsheet on the Food and Beverage Sector.

pressure from erosion of profit due to rising cost of rentals and wages, cost cutting and 'perverse' productivity measures may be adopted. Such measures include demanding workers to work longer hours, or more tasks and duties are loaded onto incumbent workers with minimal monetary compensation.

The F&B sector is a relatively space-demanding business. Rising rental together with rising wage costs can only be met with higher prices in the final output — adding inflationary pressure to the macro economy (see Figure 4). The final outcome may not be a desirable one. The F&B sector may be polarized into one that is offering an expensive experience that most will only visit infrequently and only during special occasions. The practice of cooking one's own food and buying pre-packed cuisine may have bright prospects for growth.

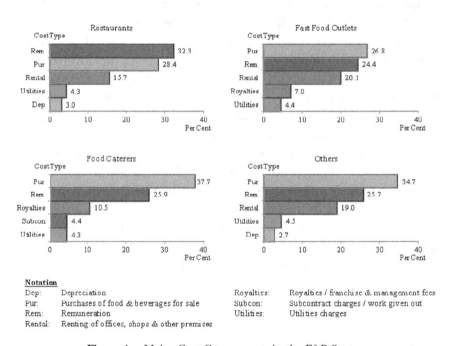

Notation

Dep:	Depreciation
Pur:	Purchases of food & beverages for sale
Rem:	Remuneration
Rental:	Renting of offices, shops & other premises

Royalties:	Royalties / franchise & management fees
Subcon:	Subcontract charges / work given out
Utilities:	Utilities charges

Figure 4:   Major Cost Components in the F&B Sector

Source: Department of Statistics: Report on the Food and Beverage Sector, 2012.

The basic lesson is that productivity improvement should not be simply an exercise of getting a ratio (such as value added per worker) as large as possible. What is needed is a comprehensive understanding of the value chain associated with each company using the 8M framework. The improvement at each link of the chain contributes to productivity improvement, while failure at one of the links will adversely affect the overall performance of the company.

5. Recommendations — Examples Based on Application of the 8M Framework to the Retail and F&B Sectors

From the preceding analysis, some recommendations can be drawn. These are illustrative of what can be derived from the application of the 8M framework. They are dealt with in more detail and substantiated in the subsequent chapters.

5.1. *Management*

To increase productivity, one of the key areas for improvement is in business operations and management. Many of the companies in the retail and F&B sectors are small businesses. They are not well versed in the most effective management techniques that managers in the larger companies have adopted. Besides the many upgrading programs already available, a program that could be considered is the establishment of networks between the SMEs and the larger companies. Managers from the larger companies could be assigned to mentor SMEs to impart skills to their local staff. This will ensure that the best practices trickle down to SMEs. To facilitate improvement in management skills, the government could extend its existing productivity and workforce programs and schemes to cover more management courses.

5.2. *Manpower*

There is a need to continue managing the inflow of less skilled foreign workers so that companies in the two sectors will have the incentive to invest in innovation and capital. This inflow should be regulated carefully rather than curtailed drastically.

To encourage companies to train and develop their local staff, the government should continue to provide adequate incentives to improve their investment in human capital. This is a huge concern especially for the SMEs who have short-term marginal cost issues as their top priority. To prevent short-term cost considerations from affecting long-term human capital gains, the government can fine-tune the provision of financing and subsidies as a way to incentivize companies to engage in training and development.

5.3. Material

While companies look for productive gains, they should also attempt to reduce their material cost. Though it is tough for an SME to negotiate and reduce material cost, there are solutions at the sector level. Firstly, the SMEs can be represented by an industry consortium which will have greater bargaining power due to its aggregated mass. Secondly, the government can enable the SMEs to purchase directly from the GLCs at favorable rates. While this does not directly contribute to the latter's bottom line, it will count towards increased financial flexibility for the SMEs.

5.4. Method

Another important aspect of productivity growth in the retail and F&B sectors is the continued need to introduce the most efficient machinery and technology. As technology develops, companies in the two sectors will experience new production possibilities. They could either increase the intrinsic value of their products, or increase their production capacity. To achieve this, the companies must first refrain from replacing machinery with foreign labor.

5.5. Money

While the SMEs are not as well financed as larger companies, they can increase the efficacy of their monetary purchases and become more productive. One possibility is for the SMEs to pool resources together for training and development. Doing so will help them to reap economies of scale, thus decreasing the training cost per unit of labor. Furthermore, they can avoid the overlapping administration cost. As for the government, it can facilitate by helping the SMEs to decrease business cost. This does not entail subsidizing their business operations. Rather, it can increase the efficiency and decrease the unit cost of infrastructural services. Taking electricity cost as an example, the government need not subsidize fuel cost but can help companies by decreasing non-fuel cost, which takes up a significant proportion of the total electricity bill. By providing more efficient infrastructure, the government can help the SMEs alleviate cost pressures without making them reliant on subsidies.

5.6. *Make*

To meet the challenges of increasing competition, companies in the retail and F&B sectors need to increase their emphasis on product innovation. This diverges from their current cost orientation and will require them to take on more risk. However, this risk can be minimized and managed by providing them with various incentives.

5.7. *Market*

Given their relatively weak market power, SMEs in the retail and F&B sectors often have difficulties penetrating new markets. The government could play a greater role in forming consortia and providing incentives for them to expand both locally and internationally. This will help them establish a firm footing in new markets.

5.8. *Message*

SMEs in the retail and F&B sectors must be in a position to receive the most up-to-date information about the industry and labor market. To this end, the industry associations and other organizations providing supporting services to the SMEs can play a greater role in gathering and disseminating critical information. Furthermore, many SMEs in the two sectors have raised the issue that they could not hire sufficient local graduates as they prefer to work in Multinational corporations (MNCs). To increase information symmetry in the labor market, the SMEs should make extensive use of university hiring platforms such as National University of Singapore (NUS) TalentConnect. Through these platforms, the SMEs can forge a strong relationship with their interns so that they will return as full-time employees. The government could also realign the incentives for graduates by providing incentives if they are to work for local SMEs.

6. Conclusion

The analysis of Singapore's productivity performance affirms that a holistic approach must be taken to sustain productivity growth. An 8M framework is proposed to address the key factors determining productivity growth, at various levels of the economy. Examples of policy conclusions emerging from the application of the framework to the retail and F&B sectors are given.

The subsequent chapters will delve into the various parts of the 8M framework that are applied to the retail and F&B sectors and make specific recommendations to raise the productivity of the two sectors.

References

Chia, B., Thangavelu, S. M. and Toh M. H. (2004). "The Complementary Role of Foreign Workers in Singapore", *Economic Survey of Singapore*, First Quarter 2004, Ministry of Trade and Industry, Singapore.

Department of Statistics (2013). *Services Survey Series: Report on Food and Services 2013*. Ministry of Trade and Industry, Singapore. Available at: http://www.singstat.gov.sg/statistics/browse_by_theme/economy/findings/summary_findings_fnb.html

Department of Statistics (2016). *Yearbook Statistics of Singapore 2015*. Ministry of Trade and Industry, Singapore.

Enterpriseone.gov.sg (2013). *EnterpriseOne — Productivity and Innovation Credit (PIC)*. Available at: http://www.enterpriseone.gov.sg/en/Government%20 Assistance/Tax%20Incentives/Product%20Development%20and%20 Innovation/gp_iras_pic.aspx [Accessed on 7 Feb 2015].

Goh T. W. (2013) "A Shift-Share Analysis of Singapore's Labour Productivity Growth, 1998–2013", *Economic Survey of Singapore 2013*, pp. 70–77, Ministry of Trade & Industry Singapore."

Jayaram, S. and Lee, T. (2010). Singapore's Productivity Puzzle: Estimating Singapore's Total Factor Productivity Growth Using the Dual Method. *Economic Survey of Singapore*, Third Quarter 2010, pp. 14–24, Ministry of Trade and Industry, Singapore.

SPRING (2014). Factsheet on the Food and Beverage Sector. Available at: http://www.spring.gov.sg/NewsEvents/PR/Documents/Fact_Sheet_ on_food_services_productivity_plan.pdf [Accessed on 25 March 2015].

Toh M. H. (2012). "A Comprehensive Approach in Evaluating & Uplifting Productivity: 8Ms Approach", *mimeo*, NUS Business School Research Paper.

Thangavelu, S. and Toh M.H. (2013). "Productivity and Singapore: Where is the Productivity?", paper presented at SCAPE Forum: *Illusive productivity and SMEs in Singapore*, organized by Singapore Centre for Applied and Policy Economics (SCAPE), National University of Singapore, 9 December 2013. The Shaw Foundation Building, NUS, Singapore.

World Bank (2013). *Doing Business 2014: Understanding Regulations for Small and Medium-Size Enterprises*, Report of the World Bank Group. Washington D.C.

World Bank (2014). *Doing Business 2015: Going Beyond Efficiency*, Report of the World Bank Group. Washington D.C.

Chapter 3

Measurement and Surveillance of Productivity Performance Based on 8Ms — Application to Retail and Food & Beverage Sectors

1. Introduction

The concept of productivity appears deceptively simple when it is interpreted as the ratio of total output to total inputs associated with production. A relatively high value of the ratio is considered desirable as it connotes efficiency in the utilization of scarce resources (Kendrick, 1977; Kuznets, 1966; McConnell, 1979). In fact, productivity is a complex performance variable comprising of many interacting components. Production and operation managers are responsible for the actual productivity of the process with which they deal on a day-to-day basis. They could improve productivity if they knew how to cope with the organizational constraints that seem to tie their hands. Financial planning that integrates marketing and distribution with production considerations is essential for a systems capability to maximize productivity. Learning how to attain both expected and improved performance as a continuing, dynamic managerial effort is an unending, challenging task.

This chapter aims to highlight the limitations of conventional productivity measures like output per worker, value added per man-hour and to suggest that a more comprehensive framework such as the 8M be used to monitor and manage productivity efforts made in the enterprises. The main suggestion is to adopt managerial control ratios and financial ratios that decision makers at the enterprise level can understand and leverage on to make improvement in the performance of their enterprises. In the identification of drivers that contribute to the productivity performance, the method of data envelopment analysis (DEA) is recommended. This method recognizes the contribution of multiple inputs as well as outputs in more than one dimension. An empirical exercise is undertaken, using two samples of data, consisting of about 130 observations from the food & beverage (F&B) Sector and Retail Sector each.

The past several decades have been characterized by an extraordinary surge of concern about low productivity and continued growth of the economy. Many authors have supported the viewpoints that increase in productivity growth may lead to benefits such as higher standard of living, improved balance of trade, higher productivity growth, more leisure time, better support for an ageing population and even environmental improvements and inflation control. Such benefits could indeed result from advances in productivity and technology, but not without any accompanying costs and seldom without extended gestation. Moreover, these relationships are not universally accepted. For instance, Gold (1955, 1975) points out that most of the authors rely on aggregate economic studies and many of the analyses are based on 'production functions'. For some schools of thought, the costs of the efforts for increasing productivity, the changes required in the industrial structure, the immediate or short-term implications for social and environmental conditions, or the time lags involved are factors that are sometimes weighted differently. Such factors lead to differences in the attractiveness of alternative solution strategies.

Improvements in productivity and in technological capabilities are primarily the result of decisions by particular groups and their decisions tend to give much heavier weight to the specific criteria representing their own interests and responsibilities than to the amorphous aspirations of society at large. Accordingly, one set of useful insights into causes of the absence of productivity increases may be provided by considering differences in the evaluative profiles of the key groups influencing such decisions.

Actual changes in industrial productivity and technological capabilities take place in individual plants and enterprises and they are initiated by management decisions. In the private firms, the basic objective of such decisions is neither to increase productivity nor to improve technology, but rather to increase profitability or simply the returns to capital invested. Profitability may be increased through a variety of means, including improvement in product design, marketing, pricing, financing, manpower upgrading and re-scheduling, and procurement. Hence, managements are likely to commit resources to programs for improving productivity or technology only up to whatever level seems to offer greater returns than these other alternatives relative to the costs, risks, and time delays involved. In fact one may perceive that a manager chooses the right level of productivity such that the company can achieve objectives as in market penetration (e.g. Merlitz model in international trade), pre-empting and deterring new competitors entering into the industry and capitalizing on prevailing market condition to enjoy higher profitability. Efficiency is a much desired objective, but its attainment is not cost-free. A highly efficient product or service may not be something that the clients and customers want especially when it is out of sync with other components and sequential services required in their business. In short, managements are prepared to leave productivity levels unchanged or even to reduce them, if that should appear to be more profitable.

The next groups to be affected by managerial decisions involving changes in productivity and technology are the suppliers of the inputs and materials, with labor usually the foremost. Their primary objectives tend to center around increasing wage rates, maintaining employment, improving fringe benefits and working environment, and reducing job hazards and discomforts. Their responses to such productivity improvement measures and technological innovations in the form of demands for higher wage rates, employment levels, working conditions and fringe benefits may significantly alter managerial evaluations of prospective benefits of seeking to develop or to adopt particular improvements. Such decisions may also be influenced, of course, by the availability and prices of other inputs affected by particular innovations, especially capital.

Consumers may also react more favorably to some improvements in productivity and technology than to others. They tend to applaud those yielding more durable, more service-free, safer and lower priced products. But they are often less favorable to those that reduce variety in products responsive to wide differences in need and tastes. In such product categories, management cannot help comparing the cost benefits of prospective innovations with possibly offsetting market penalties.

The most important of the remaining possible sources of influence on managerial decisions concerning possible improvements in productivity and technology is government. Over the long-run, the government seeks to promote a wide array of objectives, including reasonable economic growth, rising standard of living, development and effective utilization of resources, high employment level, the maintenance of a strongly competitive position in international trade and an attractive destination for foreign investments. It is recognized that productivity improvement in productivity and technological capabilities may offer major contributions towards achieving such objectives. It is also apparent that such improvements may entail negative effects on some of these objectives, at least in the short run. Government policies can affect prospective profitability of enterprises. Among the most influential of these are tax policies, regulatory restrictions, and, in some industries, the prevention of unfair competition from foreign producers.

2. Revisions of Basic Concepts

Among the most widely prevailing elements of the mythology relating to productivity, the following five may be the most important:

(a) Productivity measures reflect changes in the 'efficiency' of production.

(b) Changes in productivity are reasonably well measured by output per man-hour.
(c) Increases in output per man-hour or output per unit of other inputs are invariably desirable because they yield decreases in unit costs and hence, tend to increase profitability.
(d) Cost accounting analyses and management efforts to improve performance can be significantly improved by reliance on productivity measures that purport to compare the quantity of all inputs combined with the quantity of all output combined.
(e) Prevailing productivity measures permit reasonably effective comparisons of productivity performance among all firms within an industry and even among different industries, as well as comparisons with performance levels in the past.

2.1. *Productivity and 'efficiency'*

In contrast to physical science, there is lack of an economic concept of physical efficiency. There is absence of physical common denominators for combining the input contributions of labor energy and skills, various materials and suppliers and a wide array of technical and managerial activities. Nor are there important physical common denominators for combining the wide range of quality characteristics and service characteristics of output.

Lacking an economically significant concept of 'physical efficiency', managerial efforts to improve operation must be refocused on appraising the effects of changes in various input–output relationships on specified performance objectives subject to management control. Thus, management needs a productivity analysis framework.

2.2. *Output per unit of labor input as productivity measure*

Output per worker, value added per man-hour are popular partial measures of productivity. However, outside of service activities, labor inputs usually account for only a limited proportion of total input contributions and hence changes in labor input requirements per unit of output tend to play only a modest role in accompanying output changes. Other inputs can play comparably significant roles. It does not follow that decreases in any input per unit output necessarily represent an increase in its productivity, or even that such a change is necessarily advantageous from the management's point of view. Instead of reflecting an increase in a given factor's productivity, a decrease in its input per unit of output may result from shifting some of its former tasks to other inputs. For example, output per man-hour may rise for a variety of reasons other than increased efforts by direct labor: (1) It may actually result from a reduction in labor's contribution through the purchase of more highly fabricated components, the replacement of manual tasks by machinery and (2) it may result despite no change in labor's contributions through increasing out of machinery without changing the numbers tending such equipment, either by utilizing machine capacity more fully or by increasing such capacity through technical improvements.

Whether such reductions in any given input per unit of output are advantageous or not depends on their effects on total unit costs relative to the cost effects of associated changes in the other inputs affected and also on the effects of the given set of changes on the quality and revenue-producing potentials of product affected by these productivity changes. Apparent increases in 'productivity' often lead to increases rather than decreases in total unit costs. One of the most widespread examples of this involves the mechanization (or computerization) of manual tasks. Often, resulting increases in output per man-hour have been offset by accompanying increases in wage rates, thus eliminating the expected reduction in unit wage costs, but have also entailed increases in capital charges, thereby resulting in higher total unit costs than before the innovation. The effect of apparent productivity improvements on profitability is not clear as well. It is also necessary to assess possible changes in quality of products, which may affect the quantities that can be sold and the prices that can be obtained for them. Profitability is also affected by how prevalent the same innovation is adopted by competitors in the industry. On the whole technological capability and adoption have improved but profitability may not.

Advances in productivity analysis can strengthen existing managerial guides for planning, controlling and evaluating operating performance within the firm by providing deeper penetration into sources of changes in costs, investment requirements, revenues and profits. Such contributions require an analytical framework that would enable management to work backward from changes in the aggregate performance of the plant or firm to uncover the positive and negative contributions to that outcome of each organizational unit; to identify productivity and other changes responsible for alterations in each unit's performance; and, furthermore, to determine the extent to which such changes were caused by departmental innovations *vis-à-vis* plant level decisions, such as changes in product designs, product-mix or capacity utilization. Such a framework would also facilitate working in the other direction to trace the effects of past or prospective productivity-improving innovations on inputs, processing methods and product-mix through successive linkages — from procurement through the various stages of production and distribution — that engender changes in overall operating performance and profitability.

To fulfill the decision making requirements of management, productivity analysis must reach beyond customary simplified approaches in order to cover:

(a) Changes in the level of each category of input requirements per unit of output, including materials, facilities investment and salaried inputs as well as direct labor.
(b) Changes in the proportions in which inputs are combined, both in order to take account of substitutions and in order to differentiate productivity from different inputs.
(c) Utilization rate of inputs.
(d) Changes in prices of input attributed to changes in quality.
(e) Changes in composition of output attributable to changes in relative prices.
(f) Interactions among input volumes, qualities and prices as well as among product volumes, relative prices and mix.
(g) Interactions between resulting changes in total unit costs, total revenue and investment to determine effects on profit rates.

3. Productivity Management Approach for F&B and Retail Enterprises

This section dwells more deeply into the use of the 8M framework (as introduced in the previous chapters) in measuring and analysis of productivity in the F&B and Retail sectors. The 8M Productivity Advantage Framework (8M_PAF) is an adapted and enhanced version of the Total Quality Management (TQM) model focusing on productivity issues.

3.1. *8M productivity advantage framework — an enhanced TQM model*

In the following, we adapt the TQM or the more recently revamped version known as Business Excellence Framework (BEF) which is one of the management tools recommended by the Asian Productivity Organization and SPRING Singapore[1] for SME to 'plot' the path towards higher productivity in the enterprise.

BEF helps organizations to assess their strengths and areas for improvement and guide them on what to do next. BEF provides senior managers with a holistic method with which to manage their business and get buy-in to key decisions that will lead to sustainable and measurable success. In a sense, the BEF serve as the organization's own internal business consultant — ensuring that business decisions incorporate the needs of all stakeholders, are aligned to the organization's objectives and take into account current thought on international best practices.

The 8M_PAF is adapted from the approaches used in TQM models and the BEF. The gist of the framework can be discerned from Figure 1.

---

[1]More details are available at: http://www.spring.gov.sg/QualityStandards/. Companies which adopted the BEF have reported good results. In one report, the overall performance of productivity is higher by about 11% for companies which are users of BEF relative to those which are not users of BEF. See also Asian Productivity Organization (2002a, 2002b).

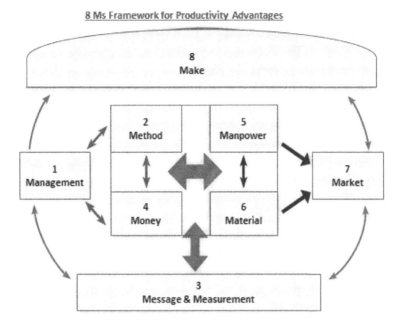

Figure 1: Productivity Advantages Framework based on 8Ms

The 4Ms (Method, Manpower, Money and Material) in the middle of the diagram depict the core activity of production of the commodity or service which the organization 'Make' to sell to in the 'Market.' The 'Management' is the driver of the system. It must have the capability to sell what is being made and also able to use 'Messages and Measurement' derived from customers in the market to feedback into the production process to achieve higher level of quality of product and efficiency in the use of resources.

3.2. *Undertaking productivity quantification and improvement assessment*

Assessments not only track an organization's progress but, more importantly, identify an organization's strengths and weaknesses. From this information, management can make decisions on plans that can deliver the desired results. Figure 2 show the seven steps

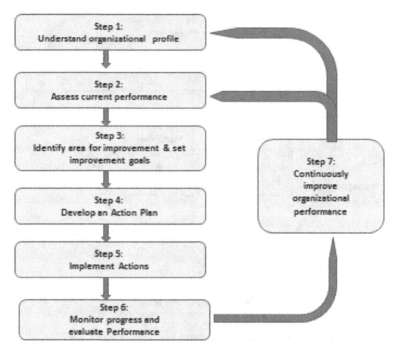

Figure 2:   Seven Steps to Improve Organizational Productivity

that can be adopted to improve organizational performance towards higher productivity and profitability level.

To assist in the conduct of Step 2, the organization can make use of the scorecard like the one shown in Table 1. Each M is partitioned into two sub-categories. Each sub-category is evaluated from a (Likert) scale of 0 (minimum effectiveness) to 60 (maximum effectiveness). There is also an item to capture the overall reinforcement effects of the 8Ms, with zero for absence of effective interactive effect to a score of 40 to measure maximum interactive effect. The establishment under study has scored 690 out of a maximum of 1,000 points. The dimensions in which the establishment is being assessed conformed to the 8Ms framework. For each M there can be two or more areas of assessment to provide more refined quantification.

Table 1:   8Ms Productivity Advantages Score Card for an Establishment: An Example

	Categories and Items	Actual Score	Max Score
1	Management		120
	1.1 Leadership	50	60
	1.2 Strategic Planning	50	60
2	Method		120
	2.1 Processes of Production	30	60
	2.2 Technological Innovation	30	60
3	Message and Measurement		120
	3.1 Media Presence and Branding	30	60
	3.2 Benchmarking	30	60
4	Money		120
	4.1 Working Capital and Investment Fund	60	60
	4.2 Credit Worthiness	60	60
5	Manpower		120
	5.1 Work Force Engagement and training	50	60
	5.2 Working Environment	40	60
6	Material		120
	6.1 Supply Chain of Inputs	35	60
	6.2 Physical Resources	35	60
7	Market		120
	7.1 Market Share	45	60
	7.2 Locality Advantages	45	60
8	Make		120
	8.1 Product Diversity and Quality	20	60
	8.2 Customer Satisfaction Feedback	50	60
	Interactive Effect of 8Ms	30	40
	Total	690	1000

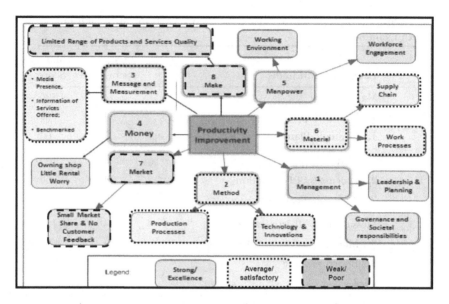

Figure 3:   Example of Potential Main Areas of Improvement

Whilst scores are important for monitoring progress, the main value from the 8Ms is that they help companies to clearly understand their strength and opportunities for improving the productivity relating to each category. This information helps companies to identify areas for improvement (Step 3), which can be facilitated by performing a mind-mapping exercise. An example for an establishment under study is provided in Figure 3.

In the example, the establishment has identified that it is weak in "Make" and "Market". It has limited range of products offered and its service quality has room for improvement. The patronage is not up to the expectation of the management, though it has a niche segment of the market. Feedback from customers could possibly help to expand the range of services and market reach. The company has little worry about escalating rental payment constraining its working capital and bottom line as the shop was bought and fully paid-up a few years ago.

Productivity is reckoned to be multifacets involving multiple inputs and multiple outputs. Measurement of performance based on the ratio of weighted outputs to weighted inputs can be assessed by the method of DEA.

3.3. Data envelopment analysis

Message and Measurement is one of the eight factors in the Productivity Advantage Framework. Measurement, in particular, is an important activity that provides objective quantitative assessment on efficiency of enterprises and the relative competitiveness in the market. A method that yields useful information on the performance of an enterprise among its peers is the DEA.

Traditional performance measurement system provides a very unbalanced picture of performance that can lead managers to miss important opportunities for improvement. The most common methods of comparison or performance evaluation were regression analysis and stochastic frontier analysis. These measures are often inadequate due to the multiple inputs and outputs related to different resources, activities and environmental factors. DEA provides a means of calculating apparent efficiency levels within a group of organizations. In DEA study, efficiency of an organization is calculated relative to the group's observed best practice.[2] *Effectiveness* is the extent to which outputs of service providers meet the objectives set for them. *Efficiency* is the success with which an organization uses its resources to produce outputs — that is the degree to which the observed use of resources to produce outputs of a given quality matches the optimal use of resources to produce outputs of a given quality. This can be assessed in terms of technical, allocative, cost and dynamic efficiency. Improving the performance of an organizational unit relies on both efficiency and effectiveness.

---

[2]The method of DEA is often credited to seminal work of Charnes *et al.* (1978). Since then, there are several good books on the technical aspects and application of DEA published in recent years. An example among many others is Zhu (2009).

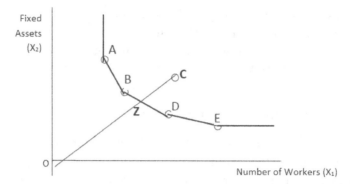

Figure 4: Efficiency Frontier for Case of One Output and Two Inputs

The mathematical formulation and solution of the DEA model is relegated to Appendix 2. However, the methodology of DEA is best discerned using an example. We consider the case where there are five companies in the F&Bs sector. Each company is called a decision making unit (DMU) and is assumed to project itself as productive (efficient) as possible among its peer. There is one output measure, sales revenue (y_1.) and there are two inputs: number of workers (x_1.), and fixed assets investments (x_2.).

A simple visualization of the problem in a two-dimensional diagram may be helpful. If every DMU were to produce one standard unit of output with two inputs, we can represent each of five DMUs in the diagram as points A, B, C, D and E in Figure 4.

The line joining points A, B, D and E provides an efficient frontier (envelope) — a unit isoquant. DMU C is obviously inefficient relative to the other four DMUs. In fact, the efficiency of C can be measured relative to Z which is on the frontier joining B and D. The efficiency of DMU C is measured as the *ratio* OZ/OC which is less than unity. DMU C is less efficient than some other DMUs. The optimization exercise is repeated for each of the five DMUs; hence, there are five efficiency scores in this example.

The knowledge of the score is not simply for academic interest. Each participating DMU can be informed of the its score. This will enable a DMU to know its performance relative to its peer. Furthermore, the inefficient DMU can be informed of the attributes in which it is lagging behind its peer so that targeted improvement can be made. If

Table 2:   Efficiency Scores of DMUs and Benchmarks

	Eff (%)	λ_i		λ_j	
DMU 1	85.9	0.257	DMU 2		
DMU 2	100.0	1.000	DMU 2		
DMU 3	55.7	0.445	DMU 2		
DMU 4	39.2	0.277	DMU 2	0.350	DMU 6
DMU 5	59.0	0.345	DMU 2	0.038	DMU 6
DMU 6	100.0	1.000	DMU 6		

confidentiality is not an issue, DMU can be informed of the efficient DMUs in which the inefficient DMU can used as benchmarks. These are the organizations in which other DMUs can strive to emulate. As an illustration using a small section of the empirical results, six DMUs (restaurants) are highlighted in Table 2.

For example, a benchmark for DMU 1 and DMU 3 is DMU 2 (note that DMU 2 is efficient). A benchmark for DMU 4 and DMU 5 are two restaurants, DMU 2 and DMU 6. This means, to become efficient, DMU 4 and DMU 5 must use a combination from both DMU 2 and DMU 6 (a virtual restaurant) to become efficient. How much of DMU 2 and how much of DMU 6 (what combination) are calculated to achieve efficiency and reported next to each Benchmark restaurant. These are λ weights obtained from the dual version of the linear program that is solved to estimate these values. More detail analysis can be done like DMU 4's weak performance is largely due to higher than normal floor space per unit sale, and excessive advertisement expenditure relative to its peer.

In our measurement exercise, we have 128 DMUs for the F&B Sector, and 127 DMUs from the Retail Sector. The data comes from a survey conducted by SPC in the year 2012 for the purpose of a benchmarking project. The variables measured and constructed with information of the survey together with other variables (under-lined variables) not currently available are cross tabulated as input/output variables and categories associated with the 8Ms in Table 3.

In the evaluation of DMUs in the retail sector, a single output is measured by the value added per worker is used. The input variables include material (measured by expenditure on goods and services,

Table 3:   Input and Output Variables Associated with the 8Ms.

	Output Variables	Input Variables
Management	PROFIT; VALUE ADDED	SEAT
Method		$MACH; $ITCAPEX
Message and Measurement		AREA; ADVERT
Money	SALES; CHEQUE	LOANS
Manpower		TRAINHR; LABCOST
Material		COGS; INVENTORY
Market	TRANSACT; MKT-SHARE	
Make	MENU	FEEDBACK

Note: SALES: Sale revenue ($'000) per worker, CHEQUE: Payment ($) per cheque per worker, TRANSACT: Number of transaction per worker, PROFIT: Profit ($'000) per worker, VA: Value Added ($'000) per worker, COGS: Cost ($'000) of goods and services per worker, SEAT: Number of seats per worker, LOANS: Loans from banks and financial institutions, MENU: Number of items in the menu, FEEDBACK: Number of feedback reported by customers, LABCOST: Labor cost ($"000) per worker, $CAPEX: Capital expenditure ($'000) per worker, $MACH: Expenditure ($'000) on machinery per worker, $ITCAPEX: IT ($'000) capital expenditure per worker, TRAINHR: Number of Training Hours per worker, AREA: Area (sq m) of biz premise per worker, INVENTORY: Stock of inventories, MKT-SHARE: Market share, ADVERT: Advertisement expenditure.

COGS) per worker, Machinery per worker, IT capital expenditure ($ITCAPEX) per worker, Training Hour (TRAINHR) per worker; space (AREA) per worker. For the F&B sector, number of transaction (TRANSACT) per worker[3] is the additional output, and the number of seats (SEAT) per worker is the additional input. The DEA efficiency score is computed for each DMU.[4] The DEA Efficiency Score for the F&B sector and the retail sector are shown in Tables A.1 and A.2, respectively in Appendix A. Basic Statistics of the two sectors are presented in Tables A.1 and A.2 in the Appendix A.

---

[3]The number of transactions is computed as the quotient of SALES revenue and the average payment (CHEQUE) per transaction.

[4]The LP problem can be solved using the solver available in the Excel spreadsheet. There are also several specialized software for DEA available for commercial and academic use. A good example is the DEA-Frontier, a menu driven add-in software based on the Excel Solver developed by Joe Zhu. A demo version is available at http://www.deafrontier.net/.

Table 4: Comparing Productivity Scores of Sub-Sectors in the F&B Sector

	Value Added Per Worker	Overall DEA Efficiency (%)	Sectoral DEA Efficiency
ALL			
Average	41.96	50.91	
Std dev	31.81	28.69	
CAFÉ			
Average	36.91	54.64	77.94%
Std dev	30.65	33.86	32.23%
RESTAURANT			
Average	46.26	51.82	53.92%
Std dev	31.17	26.61	26.70%
FAST FOOD			
Average	29.05	70.10	#
Std dev	16.30	42.53	
FOOD CATERER			#
Average	24.48	36.95	
Std dev	15.97	12.73	
PUB			
Average	51.48	46.83	89.62%
Std dev	42.99	21.51	21.52%

Note: The number of observations is too small for meaningful computation.

In Tables 4 and 5, the DEA Efficiency Scores for sub-sectors in the F&B and retail sectors are presented together with the standard productivity measure, value added per worker.

Pub outlets have the highest average value added per worker, followed by the restaurants. However, in terms of DEA efficiency scores, restaurants outperformed the pubs, but they are behind the fast-food establishments and cafes. In the final column of Table 3, the DEA efficiency scores computed among establishments of each sub-sector are shown. Pubs and cafes do have significantly higher average efficiency scores among their peers.

It shows there are few highly efficient establishments and each sub-sector is dominated by the low efficiency establishments.

Table 5:   Comparing Productivity Scores of Sub-Sectors in the Retail Sector

	Value Added per Worker	Overall DEA Efficiency (%)	Sectoral DEA Efficiency (%)
ALL			
Average	78.6	44.4	
Std dev	97.0	34.3	
Personal Accessories			
Average	120.4	59.7	65.7
Std dev	141.9	35.6	35.6
Beauty, Fashion and Sport			
Average	70.5	40.0	67.7
Std dev	71.3	30.7	27.3
General Groceries			
Average	47.8	37.3	50.7
Std dev	57.3	34.2	39.0

Table 6:   Incremental Efficiency for F&B Services

	Base	+ ITCAPEX	+ TRAINHR	+ Area	+ Seat
ALL					
Average	2.8%	28.4%	34.7%	44.0%	50.9%
Std dev	9.1%	24.4%	25.6%	29.5%	28.7%
RESTAURANT					
Average	23.0%	31.6%	35.1%	45.2%	53.9%
Std dev	24.9%	25.6%	26.4%	29.0%	26.7%
CAFÉ					
Average	59.9%	62.6%	71.2%	73.0%	77.9%
Std dev	31.8%	31.6%	33.1%	33.2%	32.2%

For the retail sector, establishments dealing in personal accessories have the highest average value added per worker. It is more than 70% higher than the overall Retail sector average. In terms of DEA efficiency score, the overall average score is merely 44% and the situation is not very different in the sub-sectors.

Table 7: Incremental Efficiency for Retail Sector

	Base	+ ITCAPEX	+ TRAINHR	+ Area
ALL				
Average	5.2%	6.3%	12.7%	37.3%
Std dev	19.7%	23.1%	28.1%	34.2%
Personal Accessories				
Average	5.4%	25.5%	40.1%	65.7%
Std dev	17.9%	27.0%	33.8%	35.6%
Beauty, Fashion & Sport				
Average	26.7%	45.8%	57.9%	67.7%
Std dev	26.0%	32.0%	30.8%	27.3%
General Groceries				
Average	6.4%	6.4%	13.4%	50.7%
Std dev	23.1%	23.1%	27.9%	39.0%

In Tables 6 and 7, the increment in the average DEA efficiency score attributable to additional inputs are shown. Starting from the "base" model where only material (COGS) and Machinery per workers are included as inputs, the DEA efficiency score is computed with the addition of input consecutively: IT capital expenditure; training hours, working area and seat availability (for F&B sector). The results indicate that the additional inputs do contribute to higher average DEA efficiency score.

4. Conclusion

This chapter reviews the limitations associated with the partial productivity measures such as value added per worker. Analysis and management of productivity can be effected by 8Ms framework of productivity advantages model. The latter framework is proposed as a comprehensive approach that managerial decision makers can follow to achieve excellence in productivity improvement. A close scrutiny will reveal that the 8Ms framework has its antecedent from the TQM approach as well as the more recent BEF. Regardless of TQM or BEF, the central message to SME executives is the importance of an articulate operational procedures to be executed to strive for better management results and productivity performance.

Pursuing good productivity performance based on a single index or measure can be fraught with apparent inconsistencies and confusing remedial actions. A systems view of productivity issues can be beneficial for better comprehension and appreciation among stake holders; this can enable suggested solutions to have greater probability of success. Measurement of performance is critical and essential. The method of DEA enables weak companies to be identified and factors responsible for the unsatisfactory performance in such entities can also be enumerated and remedial measures be suggested.

Tracking the productivity of each DMU over time is feasible when information of the cross section of DMUs are collected as time series. The Malmquist Index which is closely associated with the total factor productivity (TFP) index in the standard growth accounting exercise can be computed.

References

Asian Productivity Organization (2002a). *Understanding Business Excellence.* An Awareness Guidebook for SMEs. Tokyo: Japan. Available at: http://www.apo-tokyo.org.

Asian Productivity Organization (2002b). *Implementing Business Excellence.* A Guidebook for SMEs. Tokyo: Japan. Available at: http://www.apo-tokyo.org.

Charnes, A., Cooper, W.W. and Rhodes, E. (1978). Measuring the efficiency of decision making units. *European Journal of Operational Research*, 2, 429–444.

Charnes, A., Cooper, W.W., Lewin, A.Y. and Seiford, L.M. (1994). *Data Envelopment Analysis: Theory, Methodology, and Applications.* Springer, New York.

Cook, W.D. and Zhu, J. (2008). *Data Envelopment Analysis: Modeling Operational Processes and Measuring Productivity.* York University, Canada and Worchester Polytechnic Institute, USA.

Dogramaci, A. (1981). *Productivity Analysis: A Range of Perspective.* Martinus Nijhoff Publishing, Boston.

Fabricant, S. (1969). *A Primer on Productivity.* Random House, New York.

Fabricant, S. (1981). Issues in Productivity Measurement and Analysis, Chapter 2, 24–38. In Dogramaci, A. (Ed.), *Productivity Analysis: A Range of Perspective.*

Gold, B. (1955). *Foundation of Productivity Analysis.* University of Pittsburgh Press, Pittsburgh USA.

Gold, B. (1971). *Explorations in Managerial Economics: Productivity, Costs, Technology and Growth.* Basic Book, New York and Macmillan, London.

Gold, B. (1975). *Technological Change: Economics, Management and Environment.* Pergamon Press, Oxford.

Gold, B. (1979). *Productivity, Technology and Capital: Economic Analysis, Managerial Strategies, and Government Policies.* Dc. Heath and Company, Lexington, Lexington Books, Massachusetts.

Kendrick, J.W. (1977). *Understanding Productivity.* John Hopkins University Press, Baltimore.

Kuznets, S. (1966). *Modern Economic Growth.* Yale University Press, New Haven, Connecticut.

McConnell, C.R. (1979). Why is US productivity slowing down?. *Harvard Business Review*, March–April Issue, 16–25.

Shang, J. and Sueyoshi, T. (1995). A unified framework for the selection of a flexible manufacturing system. *European Journal of Operational Research*, 85, 297–315.

Sherman, H.D. and Gold, F. (1985). Bank branch operating efficiency: Evaluation with data envelopment analysis. *Journal of Banking & Finance*, 9(2), 297–315.

SPRING. *Business Excellence Framework*, Singapore Quality Award. Available at: http://www.spring.gov.sg/QualityStandards/.

Sueyoshi, T. (1994). Stochastic frontier production analysis: measuring performance of public telecommunications in 24 OECD Countries. *European Journal of Operational Research*, 74, 466–478.

Zhu, J. (2009). *Quantitative Models for Performance Evaluation and Benchmarking: DEA with Spreadsheets*, 2nd edn. Springer, New York.

Appendix A

Table A.1:   Basic Productivity Statistics for F&B Sector

	OBS	SALES	CHEQUE	TRANSACT	PROFIT	VA	COGS	LABCOST	$CAPEX	$MACH	$ITCAPEX	TRAINHR	AREA	SEAT
0 ALL														
Average	128	60.44	31.03	4254	27.27	41.96	18.48	14.69	7.36	3.59	0.732	1.437	2.811	0.284
Std dev	128	42.84	30.98	5659	29.45	31.81	17.42	11.51	14.75	4.25	1.221	2.826	4.118	0.472
1 CAFÉ														
Average	24	56.54	13.25	6991	24.99	36.91	19.63	11.92	4.53	3.76	0.676	2.426	2.878	0.432
Std dev	24	50.98	12.87	7237	25.72	30.65	25.48	7.61	6.13	5.29	0.945	5.117	5.217	0.511
2 RESTAURANT														
Average	69	65.17	35.19	3847	30.05	46.26	18.91	16.21	8.76	4.26	0.693	1.421	2.221	0.249
Std dev	69	41.84	33.04	5662	26.77	31.17	14.35	8.61	15.69	4.53	1.003	2.083	2.955	0.504
3 FAST FOOD														
Average	5	44.84	17.80	4741	21.09	29.05	15.79	7.96	6.10	0.97	0.356	0.326	0.149	0.051
Std dev	5	26.05	13.55	3779	12.52	16.30	11.88	4.89	2.98	0.69	0.186	0.605	0.255	0.020
4 FOOD CATERER														
Average	7	37.84	13.29	4728	13.15	24.48	13.35	11.33	5.05	1.72	0.731	0.633	0.612	0.133
Std dev	7	21.25	13.43	4328	8.67	15.97	6.91	9.96	5.09	1.21	0.407	0.739	0.553	0.085
5 PUB														
Average	14	66.57	49.64	1536	40.11	51.48	15.09	11.37	2.76	2.43	0.593	0.518	8.117	0.431
Std dev	14	48.16	34.67	829	39.72	42.99	6.62	5.55	2.62	1.41	0.750	0.997	5.269	0.505

Note: OBS: Number of observations, SALES: Sale revenue ($'000) per worker, CHEQUE: Payment ($) per cheque per worker, TRANSACT: Number of transaction per worker, PROFIT: Profit ($'000) per worker, VA: Value added ($'000) per worker, COGS: Cost ($'000) of goods and services per worker, LABCOST: Labor cost ($'000) per worker, $CAPEX: Capital expenditure ($'000) per worker, $MACH: Expenditure ($'000) on machinery per worker, $ITCAPEX: IT ($'000) capital expenditure per worker, TRAINHR: Number of training hours per worker, AREA: Area (sq m) of Biz premise per worker, SEAT: Number of seats per worker.

Table A.2: Basic Productivity Statistics for Retail Sector

	OBS	SALES	VA	PROFIT	COGS	LABCOST	$CAPEX	$MACH	$ITCAPEX	TRAINHR	AREA
0 ALL											
Average	127	178.5	78.6	57.1	99.9	21.5	38.6	1.7	41.5	2.7	7.8
Std dev	127	231.0	97.0	93.5	184.8	16.4	102.0	7.7	443.6	8.8	36.4
1 Personal Accessories											
Average	36	303.6	120.4	95.5	183.1	24.9	69.4	3.3	3.8	1.4	3.7
Std dev	36	316.3	141.9	140.3	275.6	19.0	152.2	13.9	13.8	3.1	13.2
2 Beauty, Fashion and Sport											
Average	47	126.4	70.5	46.7	55.8	23.8	21.9	1.0	108.2	1.6	10.0
Std dev	47	182.7	71.3	65.0	119.6	16.7	51.2	2.8	729.1	3.6	33.4
3 General Groceries											
Average	36	128.5	47.8	32.4	80.8	15.4	35.1	1.1	1.1	6.1	1.1
Std dev	36	153.1	57.3	53.5	131.7	12.8	96.3	2.5	1.5	15.4	3.9

Note: OBS: Number of observations, SALES: Sale revenue ($'000) per worker, PROFIT: Profit ($'000) per worker, VA: Value added ($'000) per worker, COGS: Cost ($'000) of goods & services per worker, LABCOST: Labor Cost ($''000) per worker, $CAPEX: Capital expenditure ($'000) per worker, $MACH: Expenditure ($'000) on machinery per worker, $ITCAPEX: IT ($'000) capital expenditure per worker, TRAINHR: Number of training Hours per worker, AREA: Area (sq m) of Biz premise per worker.

Table A.3:   DEA Efficiency Score for Each Company in F&B Sector

	Eff (%)		Eff (%)		Eff (%)		Eff (%)
DMU 1	85.9	DMU 33	30.7	DMU 65	100.0	DMU 97	28.4
DMU 2	100.0	DMU 34	48.7	DMU 66	48.7	DMU 98	100.0
DMU 3	55.7	DMU 35	24.8	DMU 67	82.8	DMU 99	100.0
DMU 4	39.2	DMU 36	57.6	DMU 68	48.5	DMU 100	22.2
DMU 5	59.0	DMU 37	29.4	DMU 69	100.0	DMU 101	53.0
DMU 6	100.0	DMU 38	21.3	DMU 70	44.2	DMU 102	100.0
DMU 7	49.4	DMU 39	32.7	DMU 71	45.6	DMU 103	61.9
DMU 8	42.1	DMU 40	75.3	DMU 72	37.5	DMU 104	19.2
DMU 9	18.5	DMU 41	86.8	DMU 73	46.8	DMU 105	43.7
DMU 10	5.3	DMU 42	0.3	DMU 74	57.3	DMU 106	54.0
DMU 11	59.2	DMU 43	11.5	DMU 75	36.1	DMU 107	12.9
DMU 12	11.4	DMU 44	7.3	DMU 76	49.3	DMU 108	49.7
DMU 13	100.0	DMU 45	100.0	DMU 77	36.6	DMU 109	25.7
DMU 14	36.2	DMU 46	62.8	DMU 78	74.2	DMU 110	59.2
DMU 15	100.0	DMU 47	21.0	DMU 79	51.4	DMU 111	29.8
DMU 16	9.9	DMU 48	65.9	DMU 80	47.4	DMU 112	25.5
DMU 17	69.3	DMU 49	49.4	DMU 81	10.2	DMU 113	100.0
DMU 18	77.4	DMU 50	25.2	DMU 82	100.0	DMU 114	30.5
DMU 19	16.3	DMU 51	81.1	DMU 83	17.3	DMU 115	45.0
DMU 20	28.2	DMU 52	34.2	DMU 84	50.3	DMU 116	45.2
DMU 21	15.2	DMU 53	37.7	DMU 85	44.7	DMU 117	51.7
DMU 22	35.5	DMU 54	78.3	DMU 86	59.6	DMU 118	76.1
DMU 23	100.0	DMU 55	41.2	DMU 87	19.9	DMU 119	100.0
DMU 24	97.7	DMU 56	35.5	DMU 88	38.5	DMU 120	49.6
DMU 25	100.0	DMU 57	62.0	DMU 89	65.8	DMU 121	38.2
DMU 26	41.6	DMU 58	52.3	DMU 90	74.4	DMU 122	21.3
DMU 27	8.9	DMU 59	9.1	DMU 91	38.7	DMU 123	22.9
DMU 28	100.0	DMU 60	34.3	DMU 92	100.0	DMU 124	24.1
DMU 29	100.0	DMU 61	54.9	DMU 93	49.0	DMU 125	24.2
DMU 30	42.3	DMU 62	100.0	DMU 94	72.8	DMU 126	47.4
DMU 31	28.9	DMU 63	22.7	DMU 95	24.1	DMU 127	18.7
DMU 32	25.7	DMU 64	100.0	DMU 96	34.7	DMU 128	77.4

Table A.4:   DEA Efficiency Score for Retail Companies

	Eff (%)		Eff (%)		Eff (%)		Eff (%)
DMU 1	11.2	DMU 33	52.2	DMU 65	1.2	DMU 97	34.1
DMU 2	100.0	DMU 34	72.0	DMU 66	9.0	DMU 98	48.7
DMU 3	84.5	DMU 35	9.7	DMU 67	23.5	DMU 99	4.7
DMU 4	0.8	DMU 36	21.8	DMU 68	24.4	DMU 100	0.1
DMU 5	100.0	DMU 37	24.4	DMU 69	63.6	DMU 101	71.3
DMU 6	6.5	DMU 38	15.1	DMU 70	12.1	DMU 102	91.4
DMU 7	29.5	DMU 39	100.0	DMU 71	100.0	DMU 103	100.0
DMU 8	97.4	DMU 40	28.7	DMU 72	84.3	DMU 104	31.1
DMU 9	69.7	DMU 41	47.8	DMU 73	60.1	DMU 105	5.7
DMU 10	31.7	DMU 42	46.4	DMU 74	44.8	DMU 106	6.5
DMU 11	32.9	DMU 43	100.0	DMU 75	30.9	DMU 107	40.9
DMU 12	39.3	DMU 44	13.2	DMU 76	19.0	DMU 108	1.0
DMU 13	51.1	DMU 45	3.5	DMU 77	16.7	DMU 109	0.5
DMU 14	33.8	DMU 46	47.4	DMU 78	23.8	DMU 110	8.2
DMU 15	80.0	DMU 47	100.0	DMU 79	18.8	DMU 111	5.6
DMU 16	41.8	DMU 48	9.0	DMU 80	15.7	DMU 112	100.0
DMU 17	17.0	DMU 49	5.5	DMU 81	63.8	DMU 113	15.7
DMU 18	100.0	DMU 50	63.8	DMU 82	31.2	DMU 114	15.8
DMU 19	1.3	DMU 51	55.1	DMU 83	3.1	DMU 115	13.3
DMU 20	100.0	DMU 52	24.9	DMU 84	48.9	DMU 116	100.0
DMU 21	93.3	DMU 53	64.1	DMU 85	28.1	DMU 117	5.9
DMU 22	100.0	DMU 54	4.5	DMU 86	20.3	DMU 118	20.2
DMU 23	82.7	DMU 55	11.1	DMU 87	12.9	DMU 119	34.0
DMU 24	100.0	DMU 56	65.1	DMU 88	4.5	DMU 120	13.6
DMU 25	100.0	DMU 57	17.4	DMU 89	46.0	DMU 121	4.6
DMU 26	100.0	DMU 58	100.0	DMU 90	3.5	DMU 122	61.7
DMU 27	53.1	DMU 59	45.9	DMU 91	100.0	DMU 123	2.5
DMU 28	59.1	DMU 60	37.6	DMU 92	51.3	DMU 124	100.0
DMU 29	63.3	DMU 61	22.5	DMU 93	31.2	DMU 125	47.0
DMU 30	100.0	DMU 62	100.0	DMU 94	66.7	DMU 126	57.8
DMU 31	14.4	DMU 63	48.4	DMU 95	100.0	DMU 127	29.7
DMU 32	100.0	DMU 64	33.7	DMU 96	22.4		

Appendix B: Data Envelopment Analysis

DEA is a linear programing based technique for measuring the relative performance of organizational units where the presence of multiple inputs and outputs makes comparisons difficult. We consider the case where there are 30 companies in the F&B sector. Each company is called a DMU, and is assumed to project itself as productive (efficient) as possible among its peer. There two output measures: sales revenue ($y_{1.}$) and number of transactions ($y_{2.}$); and there three inputs: number of workers ($x_{1.}$), fixed assets investments ($x_{2.}$) and floor area of business premise ($x_{3.}$). Without loss of generality, let's focus on the first DMU. The DMU consider the productivity ratio (h_1) of weighted output to weighted inputs.

$$h_1 = \frac{U_1 y_{11} + U_2 y_{21}}{V_1 x_{11} + V_2 x_{21} + V_3 x_{31}}.$$

The second subscript for the variables x and y is used to denote the company, hence y_{21} is the amount of output 2 (transactions) in the first company, and x_{31} is the amount of the third input (floor area) utilized by the first company. The first company will like to determine the values of the weights, U's and V's so that the productivity ratio, h_1 is maximized subject to constraints. The DEA mathematical model is as follows:

Max h_1

s.t.

$$h_1 = \frac{U_1 y_{11} + U_2 y_{21}}{V_1 x_{11} + V_2 x_{21} + V_3 x_{31}} \leq 1.$$

$$h_2 = \frac{U_1 y_{12} + U_2 y_{22}}{V_1 x_{12} + V_2 x_{22} + V_3 x_{32}} \leq 1.$$

$$h_{30} = \frac{U_1 y_{1,30} + U_2 y_{2,30}}{V_1 x_{1,30} + V_2 x_{2,30} + V_3 x_{3,30}} \leq 1.$$

The U's and V's are variables of the problem and are constrained to be non-negative. The solution to the above model gives a value h_1, the efficiency of the first DMU. If $h_1 = 1$ then this unit (first DMU) is efficient relative to the others. But if it is less than 1 then some other DMUs are more efficient than this unit, which determines the most favorable set of weights.

To solve the model, convert it into linear programming formulation:

$$\text{Max } z_1 = U_1 y_{11} + U_2 y_{21}$$

s.t.

$$V_1 x_{11} + V_2 x_{21} + V_3 x_{31} = 1,$$

$$U_1 y_{12} + U_2 y_{22} - V_1 x_{12} - V_2 x_{22} - V_3 x_{32} \le 0.$$

$$U_1 y_{1,30} + U_2 y_{2,30} - V_1 x_{1,30} - V_2 x_{2,30} - V_3 x_{3,30} \le 0.$$

The exercise is repeated for each of the 30 DMUs; hence there are 30 efficiency scores in this example. The efficiency scores enable the DMUs to be ranked accordingly.

Since DEA was first introduced by Charnes *et al.* (1978), this methodology has been widely applied to the efficiency measurement of many organizations. Sherman and Gold (1985) used DEA model for evaluating bank branch operating efficiency. Shang and Sueyoshi (1995) applied the model to the selection of flexible manufacturing systems. Sueyoshi (1994) developed a model for evaluating the efficiencies of 24 public telecommunication companies in 23 countries.

Chapter 4

Entrepreneurship, Start-ups and Productivity: Entrepreneurism in Singapore's Retail and Food & Beverage Sectors

1. Introduction

Entrepreneurship refers to the process of starting up and taking risks in a new business, while entrepreneurism refers to the state of mind of constantly looking out for opportunities and business potential. Entrepreneurism can thus be manifested both in existing businesses and in the setting up of new businesses. This study examines not only the process of starting up new businesses (entrepreneurship) but also the intentions behind the process (entrepreneurism).

Entrepreneurial activities directly affect the productive performance of firms and hence, the overall productivity in the domestic economy. The dynamism of economic growth is in the process of creative destruction of creation and destruction: the creation of new firms, new investments and new methods of production that replaces the redundant and less productive firms and methods of the past (Schumpeter, 1934). Entrepreneurs create new businesses and new investments. These investments create new jobs, intensify competition and can increase productivity by introducing new technologies or working practices. Although, key factors such as institutions, efficient financial systems, and human capital are important for productive activities of firms, it is the individual's entrepreneurism and initiative that bring all the various elements of factor inputs, management processes of production, investment in the innovative activities together to drive the production activities of the firm. Without the entrepreneur to bring these factors together, to utilize and deploy them efficiently and to seek out new ways of conducting business and undertaking new investments, the economic churn that drives productivity growth would be likely to be subdued and in most case it will not take place.

The relationship between the entrepreneurial activities and the innovator is highlighted by Schumpeter (1934): "The entrepreneur is the innovator who implements change within markets through the carrying out of new combinations. The introduction of a new good, the introduction of a new method of production, the opening of a new market, the conquest of a new source of supply of new materials or parts or the carrying out of the new organization of any industry". Thus we can define entrepreneurial activities as any individuals who identify market opportunities and moves to take advantage of it, whether they are starting up a new firm or innovating and creating new products in an established firm.

There are several ways in which the average productivity of firms in the economy can increase. We should expect the productivity levels of individual firms to grow as they improve their production methods through the introduction of more capital, skilled labor and new innovative ideas. However, even if individual firms' productivity levels do not increase, the process of economic churn pushes up the average level of productivity in the economy: poorer-performing firms experience decreasing market share or exit the market and more productive firms increase their market share or enter the market. An OECD study highlights that the process of entry, exit and changing market shares improves productivity and economic growth of the economy (Ahn, 2001). The entrepreneurial activities to start-up a new business and to improve an existing one are the key mechanisms for productive performance of the economy.

However, several studies have highlighted that not all entrepreneurial activities are productive and desirable (Baumol, 1990, 1993; Dallago, 1997). Although we should expect the engine of entrepreneurial activities of creative destruction to improve the average productive activities in the economy, entrepreneurial activities to purely generate profits, power and prestige do not necessarily lead to improvements of the average productive performance of firms in the economy. Thus, Baumol (1993) defines the importance of distinguishing between "positive" and "negative" activities of entrepreneurs, which is the productive, unproductive and destructive entrepreneurship. Several studies by Baumol (1990, 1993) and Dallago (1997, 2000) and Foss and Foss (2002) highlight that activities that are rent seeking in the form of litigation, lobbying, takeovers, tax evasion and avoidance efforts as well as 'use of the legal system'; illegal and shadow activities and activities that generate prestige and power are often mentioned among unproductive or destructive entrepreneurship activities. Job generation and innovativeness, if not used for rent seeking purposes, are mainly associated with a 'productive value' on societal and economy levels (e.g. Baumol, 1990, 1993; Foss and Foss, 2002; Dallago, 2000).

In this chapter, we examine the creative destruction of entrepreneurial activities on the average productive performance of industries in the Singapore economy. The study uses the business formation and cessation data to measure the creative destruction in the economy. In particular, the chapter also studies the creative destruction at the disaggregated industry level including the services sector. The second part of the chapter develops the concept of entrepreneurial activities in the form of the 8M framework that affect food & beverage (F&B) profitability and productivity: manpower, material, methods, message, make, market and management. An effective entrepreneur needs the skills and vision to effectively use the 8Ms to create productive and successful business activities. In the second part of the chapter, we undertake a qualitative survey of F&B companies to understand their key constraints and challenges to effectively undertake entrepreneurial activities in Singapore under the 8M principles.

Recent studies also highlight the role of small and medium-sized enterprises (SMEs) in the process of productive, unproductive and destructive entrepreneurship (Sauka, 2008; Baumol, 1990, 1993; Davidsson, 2004; Warren, 2003; Wiklund and Shepherd, 2005; Aidis and Van Praag, 2007; Fadahunsi and Rosa, 2002; Sobel, 2006). The chapter also examines the size of business in the productive entrepreneurial activities in the Singapore economy. Several studies have highlighted that some SMEs tend to be very "casual" and short-run in perspectives regarding entrepreneurial activities. They do not pursue all elements of effective entrepreneurship in terms of effective innovation and investment decisions and risk taking activities of the firm (Aidis and Van Praag, 2007; Fadahunsi and Rosa, 2002; Sobel, 2006). Such "casual" activities tend to be more unproductive and tend to "explore" business ventures without effective business plans and long-terms sustainable objectives.

"Entrepreneurial activities cannot be casual", as highlighted by several CEOs in our survey. Several young entrepreneurs funded by 'daddy venture capital' are making rapid in-roads into the F&B sectors, by setting up cafes and bistros that appear hip and fancy but are often ephemeral in existence. The CEOs highlight that although competition is welcomed, they bring along serious problems to the whole industry. Firstly, they are competing for the shrinking pool of workers, hence driving up wage rates and overall business costs. Secondly, such new enterprises do not appear to care much about profitability and long-term survival. They are willing to pay much higher rental and yet are not too worried about selling their products at prices much higher than similar incumbent players in the industry. They make losses and quit in a short time but their intrusion has caused the landlords and mall owners to increase rents. Rents have been raised, making profit margin ever thinner and disappearing for those that continue to stay in the industry.

The results of the empirical study highlight that business formation and creative destruction in Singapore could have negative impact on the average productive performance of business in Singapore. There is greater creative destruction and lower productivity in the retail and F&B sectors. The results also indicates that the size of the firms directly affects the productive performance of firms. In particular, smaller firms (with less than 1 million in operating receipts) tend to experience very low productivity as compared to larger ones. This indicates that SMEs do not have economies of scale and scope to undertake effective entrepreneurial activities. This might also suggest that smaller business tend to be more "causal" in their entrepreneurial activities as compared to larger ones.

2. Entrepreneurship and Creative Destruction in Singapore: Business Formation and Cessation

In the Global Entrepreneurship Monitor 2012 Singapore Report, it has been found that more than one-fifth of respondents (21%) reported to have intentions to start a business within the next three years, ranking Singapore 2nd behind Taiwan among 24 other selected economies. However, only one-fourth of respondents (26%) felt they had the knowledge, skill and experience to start a business, which was considerably lower than the average of 38%, ranking Singapore 23rd out of 24 other countries. Also, Singapore ranked 17th with less than a quarter of respondents (22%) reporting that there would be good opportunities to start a business in Singapore. Singapore is also ranked among the highest when it comes to entrepreneurial intention but is ranked 3rd lowest among perceived skills for new ventures. This shows that more Singaporeans were considering entrepreneurship but lack the skills and experience to be an effective entrepreneur.

The formation and cessation by sectors is given in Figures 1 and 2. Figure 1 shows the business formation by sectors from 2007 to 2013. The general trends indicate that wholesale and retail trade tends to have experienced the largest number of business formation of over 7,000 business entities from 2007 to 2013. This accounts for nearly 30% share of the total business formation from 2007 to 2013. This was followed by professional, scientific and technical services with over 3,000 business entities from 2007 to 2013, which accounts for nearly 15% share of total business formation. The accommodation and food services activities only account for 6% share of the total

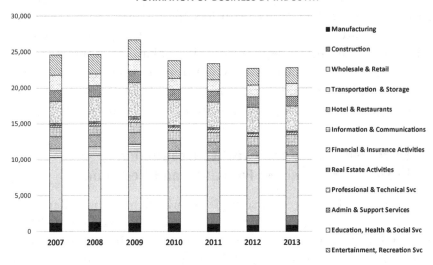

Figure 1: Business Formation in Singapore 2007–2013

Source: Department of Statistics, Singapore.

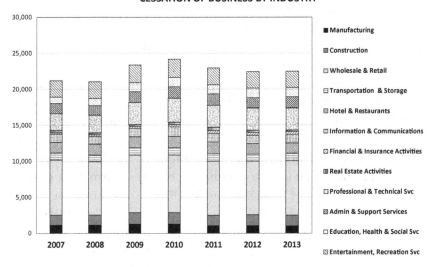

Figure 2: Cessation of Business in Singapore 2007–2013

Source: Department of Statistics, Singapore.

business formation from 2007 to 2013. The large share of business formation for the retail and wholesale suggests the ease to start-up business activities with little capital and business planning.

The cessation of business from 2007 to 2013 is given in Figure 2. Again, we observe that wholesale and retail services trade tend to experience large number of cessations across the sectors from 2007 to 2013 with over average cessation of 7,000 business entities. The wholesale and retail sector accounts for nearly 35% share of total business cessation in Singapore from 2007 to 2013. We also observe that professional, scientific, and technical services experienced business cessation of nearly 12% in 2007–2013. The accommodation and food services activities experienced nearly 6.2% business cessation in 2007–2013. The high cessation (exit) of business in wholesale and retail indicates that ease of exit and "casual" business activities in this sector.

The creative destruction of business (formation less cessation of business) in Singapore is given in Figure 3. The wholesale and

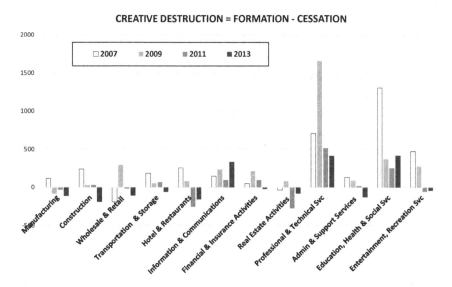

Figure 3: Creative Destruction in Singapore — Formation Less Cessation of Businesses: 2007–2013

Source: Department of Statistics, Singapore.

retail services and real estate activities experienced largest number of creative destruction with a net exit of nearly 534 and 557 business entities respectively for 2007–2013. The professional, scientific and technical services and education, health & social services experienced more business formation with net entry of around 5,000 and 3,500 business entities from 2006 to 2007.

The high number of business formation and cessation (high creative destruction) in the wholesale and retail sector indicates that ease of entry and exit and "casual" nature of entrepreneurship in this sector. This high rate of entry and exit directly creates negative externalities in a resource constraint economy such as a Singapore that drives rental, labor cost and capital available for productive investment. This clearly could indicate an inefficient allocation of productive resources in the economy.

2.1. *Productivity of retail and F&B services sectors by size*

The inefficient allocation of productive resources is clearer by segmenting by size of the business, which is defined by the annual operating receipts. The number of establishments and value-added activities of retail services sector is given in Figure 4 for 2012. It is clear that business with less than 1 million in operating receipts account for nearly 76% share of total retail establishments and only 25% share of the total retail value-added activities in 2012. A similar trend is also observed for the F&B services sector where business with less than 1 million in operating receipts account for nearly 76% share of total F&B services establishments and contributing to around 16% share of total value added in the sector 2012 (see Figure 5).

The productive performance of establishments for retail and F&B services sector by value added per establishment by size of the business is given in Figure 6. The productive performance of services sector highly dependent on the size of the business. Large business has both the economies of scale and scope to fully exploit

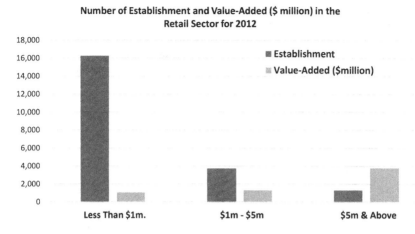

Figure 4: Establishments (Operating Receipts) and Value Added (S$M) for Retail Sector 2012

Source: Department of Statistics, Singapore.

the productive returns of their activities as compared to the smaller firms. We also observe that F&B services sector with large firms are more productive per establishment as compared to the retail services sector. The high share of establishments of SMEs (less than 1 million of operating receipts) and very low value-added activities in the retail and F&B services sector is clearly an important concern and not a healthy trend. SMEs (Smaller-sized firms) are not very productive as their activities do not have the economies of scale, likely to be short-term with little investment in innovative activities and "casual" in nature.

2.2. Empirical analysis of impact of creative destruction on productive performance of business in Singapore

We further explore the impact of creative destruction of business on the productive performance of industries by creating a panel study by sectors from 2007 to 2012. The data for formation and cessation

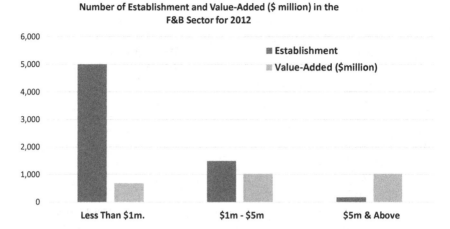

Figure 5:   Establishments (Operating Receipts) and Value Added (S$M) for F&B Sector 2012

Source: Department of Statistics, Singapore.

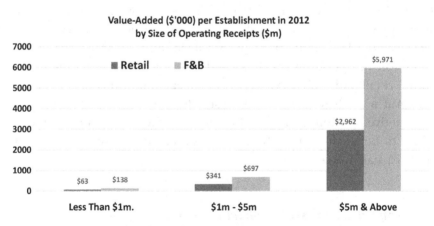

Figure 6:   Comparison of Singapore F&B and Retail Sector Value Added per Establishment for 2012

Source: Department of Statistics, Singapore.

of business is obtained from Department of Statistics, Singapore. All the data in the study is based to 2010 prices. The following panel data empirical model is implemented:

Ln (Labor productivity$_{it}$)
   = f(Ln(electricity consumption per worker$_{it}$),
   Ln (business formation$_{it}$), Ln (business Cessation$_{it}$),
   Ln (Creative Destruction$_{it}$), time dummy,
   industrial dummies) (1)

The labor productivity variable is defined as real gross output to number of workers. Electricity by sectors is given as kilowatts per hour and this captures the overall capacity utilization of the business. The formation and cessation of business is given in number of establishments. We also introduced the time dummy to account for the global financial crisis in 2008–2009. We cover 10 aggregated sectors including manufacturing, construction and service sectors.

The scatter plots of business formation and cessation on labor productivity for Singapore industries is given in Figures 7 and 8. As indicated from Figure 7, we observe a positive relationship between

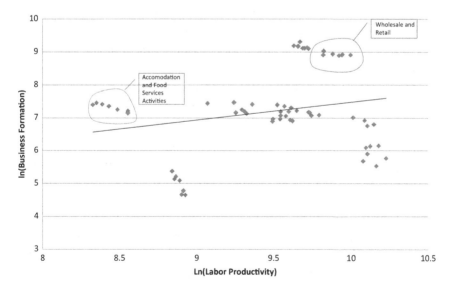

Figure 7: Impact of Business Formation on Labor Productivity for Singapore Industries 2007–2013

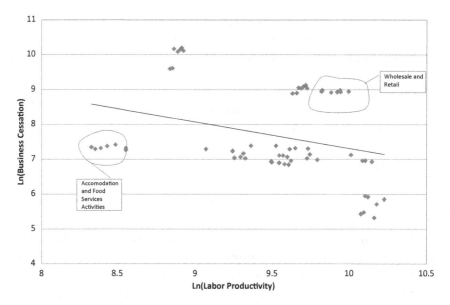

Figure 8: Impact of Business Cessation on Labor Productivity in Singapore Industries 2007–2013

business formation and labor productivity for the industries in Singapore. The retail sector and business services sector experience high level of business formation. The high level business formation indicates that there might be less barriers to entry into these sectors as compared to other sectors such as accommodation and food services activities.

Figure 8 indicates the business cessation effects on labor productivity for Singapore industries. As expected we observe a negative relationship between business cessation and labor productivity. As with business formation, we also observe high level of business cessation for wholesale and retail services sector as compare to other sectors. The high level of business formation and cessation might suggest the low entry barriers and also short-term investment planning of entrepreneurial activities (casual activities) in this sector.

The scatter plots of creative destruction (business formation less cessation) of business by sectors are given in Figure 9. In Figure 9, we observe a marginally positive relationship (trend line) between creative destruction and labor productivity for the sectors in

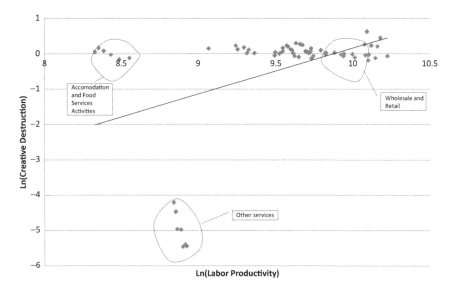

Figure 9: Impact of Business Creative Destruction on Labor Productivity in Singapore Industries: 2007–2013

Singapore. However, there are several outliers represented by "other services" sector in the data that greatly influence the positive trend between labor productivity and creative destruction. If these outliers are removed, there is likely to be no significant trend of creative destruction on labor productivity of the sectors. It is also observe that exited business entities are equally productive as the entry of new business entities. It is expected that the new business formation should be more productive than the exit business entities based on the creative destruction literature. However, we observe equally productive business entities exiting the industrial activities.

The general observation from the scatter plots suggests that there is no clear trends between creative destruction of business and labor productivity. However, the results of the empirical analysis indicate that creative destruction in Singapore has a negative impact on labor productivity. The results of the empirical analysis are given in Table 1. This might suggests that entry of new firms might not be making positive contribution to productivity from their investment and risk taking activities in the Singapore economy. The results indicate that

Table 1: Empirical Analysis of Creative Destruction on Labor Productivity in Singapore: 2007–2013 (Panel Data by Sectors)

	Ln (Labor Productivity) (1)	Ln (Labor Productivity) (2)	Ln (Labor Productivity) (3)	Ln (Labor Productivity) (4)	Ln (Labor Productivity) (5)
Ln(Business Formation$_{it}$)	-0.212** (-2.150)	-0.184* (-1.860)	-0.189* (-1.900)	—	—
Ln(Business Cessation$_{it}$)	-0.023 (-0.220)	-0.014 (-0.131)	—	—	—
Ln(Creative Destruction$_{it}$)	—	—	—	-0.182** (-2.350)	-0.158* (-1.980)
Ln(Electricity$_{it}$)	0.159** (2.530)	0.164** (2.590)	0.165** (2.640)	0.194** (2.940)	0.198** (3.050)
Constant	10.850** (9.990)	11.295** (7.280)	11.211** (10.110)	8.947** (58.370)	8.945** (58.890)
Time(Global Financial Crisis)	-0.068** (-2.120)	-0.061* (-1.870)	-0.060* (-1.920)	—	—
Interactive Term: Creative Destruction*Time (Global Financial Crisis)	—	—	—	-0.008 (-0.390)	-0.005 (-0.050)
Ln(Business Formation$_{it}$)* Retail,F&B dummy		-0.397 (-1.100)	-0.400 (-1.160)		
Ln(Business Cessation$_{it}$)* Retail,F&B dummy		0.011 (0.020)			
Ln(Creative Destruction$_{it}$)* Retail,F&B dummy					-0.512 (-1.460)
Industry	Yes	Yes	Yes	Yes	Yes
Observations	63	63	63	63	63
R-Square	0.346	0.366	0.366	0.247	0.277

* 10% statistical significance, ** 5% statistical significance.

the business formation coefficient is negative and statistically significant. It is also robust and stable to different estimation specifications. In contrast, the business cessation variable is not statistically significant. It is also interesting to observe that the creative destruction variable has a negative impact on labor productivity, thereby suggesting that net effect of the entry and exit of firms have a negative impact (see columns 4 and 5). This suggests that new entrance might not be making positive contributions as compared to those that are exiting the business activities. If we account for the economic shocks such as the global financial crisis (see the interactive time variable), we still observe a negative impact of creative destruction on labor productivity but not a statistically significant variable.

The negative coefficient of the creative destruction variable suggests that new business formation has no significant impact on labor productivity after accounting for the business destruction through the cessation variable. We further explored this effect by adding an interactive dummy for retail, F&B and accommodation services with business formation business cessation, and creative destruction variables. Firstly, the interactive dummies for business formation and creative destruction for retail sector are negative. However, these variables are not statistically significant. This likely indicates that business formation is not adding much to productivity improvements in the retail, F&B and accommodation services sectors. The overall results indicate that 1% increase in business formation in the retail, F&B and accommodation services sector, leads to a fall of around 0.5% fall in the labor productivity in this sector. Conversely, if we observe a 1% increase in creative destruction, we will observe a fall of 0.6% decline in labor productivity. This result has important implications for improving the productive performance of domestic industries, especially those in wholesale, retail, and F&Bs services sector. The importance of investment based activities in the wholesale, retail and F&B services sector is very crucial to improve the productivity in these sectors. In addition, the negative coefficients of the creative destruction and business formation indicates that the new business are not adopting new technologies and management practices, which will have direct impact on the productivity of these industries. However, we do need further analysis of the data at more detail and disaggregated micro level to establish the impact of innovation on productive performance of the service sectors.

3. 8M Framework for Effective Entrepreneurship in F&B Sector

An entrepreneur is someone with the personal skill set and vision to identify potential market opportunities and the willingness to bear risk. They require a personal skill set including some or all of the management, financial, business and communication skills to identify opportunities and succeed, depending on whether they are a start-up or part of a larger firm. They need access to the necessary resources to take advantage of that opportunity: access to capital, skilled labor, research resources and information. The entrepreneur chooses the mix of these factors of production to best suit the opportunity. These actions occur within a framework that can impose or help mitigate barriers to activity and provide incentives or disincentives for entrepreneurial actions. We explore these qualities of entrepreneurship in the 8M framework.

As identified by Schumpeter, entrepreneurs have special skills to identify new opportunities and drive productivity growth. The entrepreneur needs a range of skills to be successful: the vision to identify potential opportunities and the ability to analyze the likelihood of success or failure, the communication skills to sell that idea to managers, manage human resource, understand and control production process, raise funds for investment activities and the managerial talent to access and control the resources required to make it work. However, these qualities are difficult to identify from the data and thus we undertake a qualitative survey of selected F&B businesses in Singapore. We interviewed 17 F&B businesses.

The summary of the interview is as follows:

(a) Most business ranked manpower supply, manpower cost and rental as the top challenges in the F&B sector.

(b) Business also highlighted that message in terms of marketing and networking is important. They highlight the role of trade and business associations playing a bigger role in the network process.

(c) There is no career path for labor in F&B sector. Thus, business associations could play a bigger role in changing the perceptions of the public in terms of understanding the career path in the sector. The role of the government is also important to create this awareness and formally create the career path structures at the training institutes.

3.1. *Discussion of 8M framework*

3.1.1. *Management*

Management was a category that was consistently ranked important for success. However, it was not a factor that the respondents have an issue with or require government support. This could be because management practices might be generally viewed as the responsibility of the entrepreneur.

3.1.2. *Manpower*

Manpower on the other hand was consistently ranked highest for all three questions. It was seen as the most important factor for success (50%, ranked as 1st) and it was also the factor most respondents had issue with (94%, ranked as 1st) and would require government support (77%, ranked as 1st).

The common issue among the owners and managers is related to labor shortages. Most of the owners and managers observed that the F&B sector jobs are not jobs that most locals desire (various reasons like locals preferring cushy office jobs were cited). This meant that they had difficulties hiring local workers to work in their establishment. They also pointed out that some young local workers were asking for high pay with little to no working experience. The problem was compounded when they were unable to hire foreign workers to make up the numbers due to the foreign workers quota.

The labor crunch in the F&B sector can have significant implications on productivity. One of the ways the labor crunch can have an adverse effect on productivity was how the lack of manpower can keep the workers' schedule too tight. As a result, the owners and managers had trouble sending the workers for training. They were aware of the various training schemes and subsidies provided by the Workforce Development Agency but there were not enough manpower to free up time for the workers to be sent for these training. Thus, productivity gains from learning and training was limited by the labor crunch.

The other impact was more specific to certain food establishments that have more complex and less modular operations (e.g. cafes and fine dining restaurants). They preferred full-time workers over part-time workers as they found them more productive and committed. Full-time workers tend to have more training and experience on the job and would be able to perform a wider variety of tasks as well as carry them out in a more efficient manner. More in-depth analysis on part-time workers is covered in Chapter 5.

Overall, the lack of manpower has led firms to experience lower productivity for some food establishments. It restricted the amount of training employers can give. It also forced them to employ the type of worker not of their preference (this issue pertains to non-Taylors establishments where they would prefer full-time over part-time workers).

3.1.3. *Material*

The category 'Material' was not an issue that most of the establishments have 5% of respondents ranked it as the 2nd most challenging issue they face while 16% ranked it as 3rd. Most of them recognize ingredients cost as a result of market forces while a handful of them pointed to the lack of transparency.

The issue highlighted was that there was no centralized information center for the cost of ingredients in Singapore. Owners and managers were unable to compare prices of the ingredients. As a result, owners and managers have to approach suppliers individually for quotation. The current system was not as transparent and this may promote monopolistic activities. This was contrasted with the system in Australia where there were large-scale wholesale markets. F&B owners and managers can then compare the prices to have a reliable sense of how much the ingredients should cost them.

Due to the lack of transparency in ingredients prices, potential entrants were also unable to conduct a proper feasibility study on the ingredients costs before starting up. It could be worth investigating in future studies if having a reliable sense of the ingredients costs can help alleviate the high turnover rates in the F&B sector.

3.1.4. *Method*

11% of the respondents ranked 'method' as the 3rd most important for success. 6% of them ranked it 2nd and 17% ranked it 3rd in terms of how challenging of an issue 'method' is. Lastly, 5% ranked 'method' as the 1st category they would like to receive government support while 11% ranked it 3rd.

Some owners were not able to get reimbursement on their equipment after purchasing them as they were not covered under the Productivity and Innovation Credit (PIC) grant. There were certain equipment which were more productive and efficient that could not be claimed while some equipment that were less productive could be claimed by the PIC grant. On top of that, it caused cash flow issues as they only found out that the equipment cannot be reimbursed after they purchase it. Identifying what equipment was claimable was also a lengthy and complex process. The PIC IT and Automation List provided broad categories on what was claimable. They commented that this caused ambiguity problems which might translate to more time and money spent.

3.1.5. *Money*

11% of the respondents ranked 'money' as the 2nd and 3rd most important factors for success. The results for issues that were the most challenging were as follows: 6% for 1st, 43% for 2nd and 6%

for 3rd. As for receiving government support, 'money' was ranked in the following manner: 17% for 1st, 38% for 2nd and 6% for 3rd. Although the issue of financial resources is not consistently ranked 1st, it still remained at the top of our respondents' minds by having most of them ranking it as the 2nd most important.

One of the obstacles they consistently faced when it comes to financial resources was with their rental. Some respondents reported that the increase in rental every year was higher than the annual inflation rate. Few of businesses in our interview experienced more than 10% increase in rent every year. Furthermore, they were unable to increase the prices of their food as they fear customer backlash. As the rental increased much faster than their menu prices, their profits suffered. When profits are lower, less of them can be reinvested back into the business in terms of better equipment and training. Productivity gains may be limited as a result.

There were also some respondents who highlighted the rise of "hit-and-run" entrepreneurs who got their capital from their parents or their previous high-paying jobs. They might not have the same passion nor the equivalent experiences and skills in the F&B business as they do. These "hit-and-run" entrepreneurs proceeded to open new cafes and restaurants only to close them down within six months to a year. They commented that these entrepreneurs could have contributed partly to the rise in rental by driving up the demand for rental spaces.

Rental increase could also have adverse effects on workers' salaries as the food establishments lower salaries to balance the increase in rental.

3.1.6. Make

11% of the respondents ranked 'make' as the 2nd most important category for success and 17% of them ranked it as 3rd. 6% of them ranked it as the 2nd most challenging issue they faced while none of them ranked it as a category they would like to receive government support.

A few of them acknowledge that 'make' was one of the few most important factors for success, emphasizing on product innovation and quality assurance. However, the majority of them believe that with a good team of people and management, they would ensure that the best product and customer experience will be delivered to the customer. One of the issues the respondents faced with 'make' was closely related to the factor 'manpower' as well. They had difficulties delivering the consistency in the customer experience as the turnover rate of their serving crew was high. This meant that the service quality fluctuated according to the quality of their service crew.

This issue seemed to pertain only to service quality and not food quality. This could be because most of the head chefs in the kitchen were full-timers or the owners themselves.

3.1.7. Market

17% of the respondents ranked 'market' as the 3rd most important factor for success. They highlighted the importance of a product market fit. However, 'market' was usually ranked after manpower and management. 11% of the ranked it 2nd and 6% of them ranked it 3rd in terms of issues faced. The issues faced were pertaining to the expansion of their customer group. One of them faced issues with expanding his franchise business overseas and would like to receive larger franchise grants for overseas expansion. The others faced issues extending their targeted customers to other groups in the domestic market.

3.1.8. Message

17% of the respondents ranked 'message' as 1st in terms of importance for success, 6% ranked it at 2nd and 27% ranked it at 3rd. Branding and marketing were deemed important in differentiating themselves from their competitors, especially in a competitive industry like F&B.

Majority of the respondents see the importance of 'message' but did not find it too much of an issue compared to the other categories. However, 6% of them ranked it 2nd and 27% of them ranked it 3rd in terms of receiving government support.

Some owners commented that the branding of Singapore's food could be focused less on prominent brand names and celebrity chefs etc. They felt that a food sector without independent and smaller establishments would be "boring". Large fast-food chains and restaurant groups meet certain needs in the market. However, vibrancy and diversity in culture and food could be nurtured through the many different individual F&B entrepreneurs. One of their reasoning was that, small independent food establishments will need to innovate and find their own niche in the market to survive. Many such small independent F&B entrepreneurs will then help make up a more vibrant and diverse food culture in Singapore.

4. Recommendations

While entrepreneurism should be encouraged and could manifest in both existing and new businesses, the act of entrepreneurship should be better supported and considered before entrepreneurs start new businesses. The empirical results indicate that business formation has a negative impact on labor productivity of Singapore industries. In addition, the creative destruction variable (number of business formation number of less business cessation) also indicates a negative impact on labor productivity. This suggests that new business formations are not undertaking investment based activities that are adding new technologies and new management structures. The results for the retail, F&B and accommodation services sector indicates that 1% increase in business formation leads to 0.5% fall in labor productivity, which is higher than the average decline for the industries as a whole. The lack of investment activities and increasing the human capital is also highlighted by the survey undertaken by the study. The current drive by the government to increase investment activities through tax credits is in the right direction to increase investment and productivity activities in the Singapore industries.

The rapid entry and exit in the retail sector indicates that there are lower barriers to entry and investment decisions on innovative activities might not be effectively undertaken. It is also likely that investment decisions might be short-term in nature and thereby might be "casual" that might not serious implications for productive activities. These short-term and "casual" entrepreneurial activities will have serious implications on the cost of resources and production in the domestic in terms of increasing the demand for labor and rising the labor cost; and also increasing the demand for shop spaces leading to rising rental rates; and increasing the demand for other material inputs raising the cost of production.

Entrepreneurship is the key for productive performance of businesses and creating the effective environment for undertaking such activities becomes crucial for sustaining and improving productivity in the Singapore economy.

The empirical results indicate that the rapid formation and cessation of SMEs tend to have negative impact on the labor productivity in the domestic economy. In particular, the large business formation and cessation of wholesale and retail industry indicates that it is easy for entry and exit of the business in the sector. The rapid entry and exit indicates that there are lower barriers to entry and investment decisions on innovative activities might not be effectively undertaken. It is also likely that investment decisions might be short-term in nature and thereby might be "casual" and detrimental to long run industrial development and business performance. These short-term and "casual" entrepreneurial activities will have serious implications on the cost of resources and production in the domestic in terms of increasing the demand for labor and rising the labor cost; and also increasing the demand for shop spaces leading to rising rental rates; and increasing the demand for other material inputs raising the cost of production.

The empirical results suggest that new business formations do not add much to the average productive activities of the industries as compared to the ceasing business entities. This requires more coordination of information and management of new formation of firms in terms of investment planning, human resource management, and networking the domestic economy and global activities.

There are several policy implications for the relevant government agencies, business associations and other stakeholders within the ecosystem.

(a) Business associations could play an important role in coordinating and providing information to new starts-ups in terms of risk, networking and human resource management. The results suggest that SMEs do not have the economies of scale and scope to effectively manage the human capital and technology investment in their business activities. There are little agglomerative effects and externalities for the SMEs. The business associations could play an important role in providing the platform for more information sharing in the economy.

(b) There could be more seminars and workshops conducted to improve the understanding of entrepreneurial activities in retail and F&B sectors. Dissemination of key information of new business opportunities and changing global business environment will be useful for SMEs to plan their investment and marketing strategies for long-term investments in technologies and human capital.

(c) More information on the types of businesses that are exiting and type of new businesses that are created in the domestic economy could be made available. This information will be useful to manage the risk of new businesses that will be entering the sectors. This could be done as case studies of success and failures of business.

(d) Agencies, associations and companies could collaborate to improve the career opportunities and to create a progressive career path for those in retail and F&B services sector. The public perceptions of the career and professionalism of jobs in the retail and F&B services sectors could also be improved. It was noted by the F&B players that the perception of chefs generally improves with celebrity chefs like Jamie Oliver and Gordon Ramsay in the limelight recently. However, more can be done for workers in the serving crew. The transferable skills (wine-picking, selling techniques and etc.) picked up from serving customers could be highlighted as well. Portraying the working conditions in the kitchen more accurately could also help with the recruitment of kitchen staffs (some respondents observed that young culinary students have unrealistic expectations of the kitchen working environment). This approach would require a longer time horizon to address the labor crunch. The younger generation's perception of career path in the F&B services sectors have to change if Singaporeans wish to have a stake in the vibrant sector.

(e) One possible way to improve the agglomerative effects for SMEs is to create a common pool of human resources, management resources, and innovation resources. This could be created by the business associations and public agencies of developing a retail academy, and establishing Singapore as a regional culinary and gourmet hub where model companies and talents assemble to champion best business models and management practices.

References

Ahn, S. (2001). Firm dynamics and productivity growth: A review of micro evidence from OECD countries, OECD Economics Department Working Papers No. 297.

Aidis, R. and Van Praag, M. (2007). Illegal entrepreneurship experience: Does it make a difference for business performance and motivation? Analyzing the effects of illegal entrepreneurship experience in Lithuania. *Journal of Business Venturing*, 22(2), 283–310.

Baumol, W. (1990). Entrepreneurship: productive, unproductive and destructive. *Journal of Political Economy*, 98, 893–921.

Baumol, W. (1993). *Entrepreneurship, Management and the Structure of Payoffs*, MIT Press, London.

Davidsson, P. (2004). *Researching Entrepreneurship*. Springer, New York.

Fadahunsi, A. and Rosa, P. (2002). Entrepreneurship and illegality: Insights from the Nigerian crossborder trade. *Journal of Business Venturing*, 17(5), 397–427.

Global Entrepreneurship Monitor 2012 Singapore Report. Nanyang Technological University. Available at: http://www.ntu.edu.sg/nieo/Pages/GEM.aspx.

McMillan, J. (2004). Quantifying creative destruction: Entrepreneurship and productivity in New Zealand, MOTU Economic and Public Policy Research, 04/07.

Ministry of Trade and Industry (2012). Food and Beverage Work Group Report. Available at: https://www.mti.gov.sg/ResearchRoom/Documents/app.mti.gov.sg/data/pages/507/doc/ERC_DOM_MainReport_Part%203.3a.pdf.

New Zealand Treasury (2008). Enterprise and productivity: Harnessing competitive forces, New Zealand Treasury Productivity Paper 08/04, April 2008.

Sauka, A. (2008). Productive, unproductive and destructive entrepreneurship: A theoretical and empirical exploration, William Davidson Institute Working Paper Number 917 March 2008.

Sobel, R. (2006). Testing Baumol: Institutional Quality and the Poductivity of Entrepreneurship, Econ Papers, No. 06-06. Available at: http://econpapers.repec.org. Storey.

Schumpeter, J. A. (1943). *Capitalism, Socialism and Democracy*. New York: Harper and Row.

Warren, E. (2003). Constructive and Destructive Deviance in Organizations. *Academy of Management Review*, 28(4), 622–631.

Wiklund, J. and Shepherd, D. (2005). Entrepreneurial orientation and small business performance: a configurational approach. *Journal of Business Venturing*, 20, 71–91.

Chapter 5

Part-Time Workers' Productivity in the Food & Beverage Sector

1. Introduction

Since 2006, Singapore has been experiencing a steady increase in sales performance in the food & beverage (F&B) sector as seen from the F&B Index at constant prices (Yearbook of Statistics Singapore, 2013). However, the sector is still lagging behind in terms of productivity growth. Currently, the Singapore F&B sector is one-fifth of Hong Kong's in terms of productivity growth (Singapore Budget Speech, 2013).

The F&B businesses in Singapore have traditionally relied heavily on manpower in their operations. They faced challenges in attracting and retaining locals, especially for frontline and laborious jobs, and depended on foreign manpower. In order to curb the surge in foreign manpower dependency in the Singapore economy, the government has tightened the number of foreign workers in the labor market. Concurrently, businesses are encouraged and incentivized to adopt measures to improve their productivity.

The F&B sector is the 2nd largest employer of part-time workers (Labor Force Singapore, 2013). 16.1% of the total part-time workers employed in Singapore are in the F&B sector. Overall, part-time workers also constitute 24.4% of the total employed in the sector, the highest among all sectors. According to Nelen *et al.*, (2011), the prevalence of part-time workers in the workplace is due to the flexibility of scheduling part-time workers to cushion and complement the fluctuating demand in the F&B sector. The flexibility of part-time workers creates higher productivity because they can be utilized during peak periods where there might not be sufficient full-time workers to handle the crowd. The dependence on part-time workers would mean that the productivity of part-time workers is crucial in ensuring the performance of the sector in the midst of manpower crunch.

To assist small and medium-sized enterprises (SMEs) to better leverage on part-timers, SPRING Singapore piloted a three-year Part-time Pool Programme (PTP) in 2011. Under the PTP, SMEs from the Retail and F&B sectors would engage the services of appointed recruitment agencies to provide them with a reliable stream of trained part-time workers based on their requirements. The part-time workers deployed to the F&B sector were required to attend basic courses conducted by the Restaurant Association of Singapore (RAS). Besides the PTP, the demand for part-timers and the manpower crunch experienced by the F&B sector have also led to the development of part-time job-matching portals, mobile applications and services by private sector players, specifically targeting at the sector.

This chapter attempts to understand the impact of part-time workers on the productivity and profitability of F&B businesses, through a qualitative survey of 19 restaurant owners and managers.

2. Productivity of Part-Timers

Despite several studies highlighting the differences in wages between part-time and full-time workers, there are only few studies that focus on the productivity differences between them. A recent study by Cataldi *et al.,* (2013) on the impact of part-time workers on firm productivity highlights that a marginal increase in the share of "short" part-time workers does not affect the overall average firm's productivity. However, the study also highlights that there seems to be productivity improvements if there is a marginal increase in the share of "long" part-time workers. Overall, there is no strong detrimental effect of the use of part-time workers on a firm's average productivity.

The study by Vandenberghe (2013) describes the differences between "long" part-time workers and "short" part-time workers. The study highlights that sectors such as retail and trade where flexibility is crucial, part-time workers do help in productivity gains unlike other sectors. "Long" part-time workers are found to have higher educational status, much like their full-time counterparts, as compared to "short" part-time workers. Hence, "long" part-time workers seem to be more active in industries where their additional job-related experience matters for productivity, which is not the case for the F&B sector. In this case, productivity gains of "long" part-time workers are not as significant as compared to "short" part-time workers.

Other than the innate differences in productivity between full-time workers and part-time workers, there are also other factors that affect the productivity gains pertaining to part-time workers. For example, the scheduling of part-time to full-time workers also affects the overall average productivity gains in the firms. Efficient scheduling allows for optimal productivity of a firm along with choosing the right type of part-time worker for the job. Vakharia *et al.*, (1992) highlights that an efficient scheduling system of part-time workers incorporates employees' time preferences. Thus in efficient scheduling, there would be some trade-offs between the employees' satisfaction versus minimizing the cost of wages. The findings also suggest a possible reason for the high turnover rates of part-time workers in service establishments, which is the overemphasis on cost minimization of wages.

There are also several theories revolving around part-time workers and their productivity. One such theory claims that due to start-up effects, productivity rises slowly at the beginning of the workday and since part-time workers work less hours, their productivity levels might be below the average productivity of a full-time worker (Barzel, 1973). Another theory contests the previous model as working longer hours might cause fatigue that lowers productivity, and hence part-time workers who work lesser hours are more likely to be productive (Brewster *et al.*, 1994). Research has also shown that part-time workers might not be always easily managed unless they are in a Taylorist organization — one that embraces a production efficiency methodology that breaks every action, job, or task into small simple segments, which can be easily analyzed and taught. Restaurants and cafés require more human interaction and customer relationship. These skill sets have a longer learning curve, which makes substitution of part-time workers with each other disruptive to the continuity of customer relationships (Edward and Robinson, 2004).

There is also a need to define how productivity in the F&B industry is perceived. On one hand, productivity can be seen as a reduction of labor costs while maintaining sales, and this might help to achieve short-term productivity targets (Reynolds, 2004). On the other hand, such narrow perception of productivity might not last in the long run if no emphasis is placed on the *service quality* of the part-time workers. Good service quality can help create returning customers and generate increased long-term profits per employee (Bates *et al.*, 2003).

3. Methodology

The study undertakes a qualitative survey by conducting interviews with 19 restaurant and café owners and managers, to gather opinions and feedback regarding their views on part-time employment. The focus of the interview questions are largely based on the 8M Framework, focusing on four key Ms: Manpower, Management, Method and Money, as these will directly affect the performance of part-time workers in restaurants and cafés.

Phone interviews with the service providers appointed for the PTP was conducted to understand more about the use of part-timers in the F&B sector.

4. Research Findings

The interviews ranged from big established restaurants to smaller individual cafés. Although our sample includes restaurants of different sizes (in terms of monthly sales turnover), the overall results of the survey indicate certain common factors affecting part-time workers across the sample.

4.1. Pessimism about the F&B industry

In the sample, most of the interviewees expressed certain pessimism about the F&B industry. One of the common findings includes a general consensus on the shortage of manpower in the F&B sector in Singapore. However, only 9 out of the 19 interviewed expressed their concern over lack of supply of part-time workers.

4.2. Employment of students

Another common finding reveals that those who employed part-time workers all had students as their part-time workers and only one restaurant did not employ student as part-time workers. This suggests that the pool of part-time workers in F&B sector mostly consists of students. The interviewees are generally not satisfied with the performance of their part-timers, with none of them indicating a satisfaction level above 3 (where 3 indicates "satisfied", 4 as "Quite satisfied", and 5 as "Very satisfied"). One common problem faced by most of the interviewees was the level of commitment of the part-time workers to the restaurant. For example, they highlighted problems such as "no show" and the lack of commitment to the assigned work schedule. The other factor that is of concern to the interviewers is the inconsistency in service quality, and the ability of part-time workers to communicate with the customers effectively and fluently. Several restaurant owners highlighted that human interaction and service quality are critical for service sector productivity. Table 2 summarizes the advantages and disadvantages of using full-time workers over the part-time workers.

Table 1:   Advantages and Disadvantages of Full-Time and Part-Time Workers

	Full-Time Workers	Part-Time Workers
Advantages of full-time over part-time workers	Better consistency in food quality.	High turnover resulting in varying food quality.
	Better consistency in service quality and allows for improvement in standard.	High turnover resulting in re-training and "back to square one" service levels.
	More committed due to career advancement.	Less commitment due to "quick cash" attitude.
Disadvantages of full-time over part-time workers	Lower productivity per worker during non-peak period.	Provides flexibility in using manpower more effectively during peak periods and corporate events.

Table 2:   Summary of Issues and Solutions

Issues	Recommended Solutions
Spillover effects of shortage of full-time workers	Increase permanent part-time pool of workers via incentives like decreased levy on foreign workers.
Infeasible training	Restaurants and cafés around the vicinity can group together and register under an on-site joint training program where training is conducted in the restaurant rather than at the training facility.
Versatility of student part-time workers	Extend training subsidy for courses like Food Hygiene to students.
Informational problem	Regular updates on available schemes to firms via mail or electronic means.
Importance of work-Life balance	Having more non-monetary benefits might help to change the composition of part-time workers as the composition now consists of mainly students wanting fast cash in the short term.
Perception of F&B as a viable career option	Campaigns and better transparency on career progression pathways, to improve the image and perception of the F&B sector as a viable career option.

4.3. Administration of PTP

The interviews with the PTP service providers revealed that they faced problems in administering the Program. The problems could be classified into demand-side and supply-side problems.

On the demand side, there was a problem of inconsistency in the demand of smaller firms, where they used the service provider only as a back-up supplier of part-time workers. Therefore, these smaller companies would not stay long with them once they have gotten their intended supply. Thus only bigger companies with many branches would stay with the providers, as they would be constantly searching for part-time workers due to high turnover.

On the supply-side, service providers had little control over the performance of the part-timers as the quality and training of the workers were left to the discretion of the restaurants and the external training agencies. The providers also faced difficulties in trying to schedule training dates for the part-time workers with the external training agencies.

Another supply-side problem was the low take-up rate of the part-time workers to training. The transaction cost of the additional traveling time for training was one of the key deterrence for the part-time workers. Secondly, there was a 10% upfront payment for training as required by the external training providers, which added to the transaction cost of training. Since the bulk of the part-time workers were students, they could not afford the extra cost of training. The service providers also expressed more concern over the supply-side problems as there is always demand for part-time workers.

Even though there were challenges faced in implementing the PTP, the program has helped to raise awareness and encourage industry players to start their own initiatives to better tap and manage part-timers. Examples of these initiatives include websites and mobile applications that gather and match part-timers with companies that are looking for part-timers; and internal PTP within a F&B conglomerate that helps to recruit and schedule part-timers to meet their own requirements.

5. Analysis of Results

5.1. *Spill over effects of shortage of full-time workers*

Bigger companies with monthly sales turnover of more than $100,000 have expressed concerns on the lack of supply of part-time workers. Firstly, bigger companies are more likely to attract and recruit full-time workers as their established brand name give job seekers the perception of better career progression. Part-time workers are used to complement full-time workers, to increase the productivity of the large companies. Hence, a lack of part-time workers will impede their growth and hence, their ability to allocate resources productively.

On the other hand, smaller firms have problems hiring full-time workers and hence, part-time workers are used as substitutes to handle the work of full-time workers. This results in a mismatch of interest that causes the use of part-time workers to be less productive. Smaller firms would then want to find full-time workers, instead of more part-time workers, which suggest why smaller firms mostly did not express a lack of supply of part-time workers.

The results of the survey indicate that larger firms with full capacity of full-time workers are able to handle and ensure the continuity of customer relations in the restaurant, and thus able to use part-time workers like that of a Taylorist organization to improve productivity. Smaller firms, however, with low employment of full-time workers have to use more part-time workers, which disrupt the continuity of customer relations and hence leading to lower productivity in the restaurants.

Recent trends could have a role to play in the rise of this problem. Firstly, F&B is becoming less and less of a preferred career path due to the difficult working environment (oily and greasy environment in the kitchen; handling of tough customers in service work). With recent foreign manpower tightening, the manpower problems at the restaurants have increased. The smaller restaurants are not able to leverage on their economies of scale or scope to effectively use the part-time workers.

Finally, an initiative or service that works like the PTP might not be adequate to address the above situation, as smaller firms do not wish to shift their dependency towards part-time workers, unless the part-time workers are able to commit as much as full-time workers.

5.2. Constraints of training and job scope

The interviews also show that most managers and owners are not able to send their employees for training as they do not have sufficient manpower to cover their duties when they are away. This would mean that incentives for manpower training would do little to help with the situation.

Majority of the part-timers engaged by the interviewers are deployed to front-of-house duties. Only six establishments had part-time workers working in the kitchen. Smaller firms are very vulnerable to the high turnover of part-time workers if they were to invest in training of part-time workers in kitchen work. In addition, most of the part-time workers are students and the current subsidy for hygiene courses are not extended to students. Hence, there is a limit to the job scope that could be undertaken by the current pool of part-timers available to businesses.

5.3. Informational problem

We also observed a lack of awareness among the restaurants and cafes with regard to the PTP. Out of the sample, only one restaurant knew of the Program. This directly affected the take-up of such schemes with the restaurants and cafes.

5.4. Importance of work–life balance

Employers who have participated in the survey also indicated that work–life balance is important for part-timers to perform well on the job, though in varying degrees ranging from 'a little important' to 'very important'. There could be more emphasis on the type of benefits that part-time workers are entitled to that can help them attain more work–life balance. These benefits can potentially attract part-time workers and retain them for a longer period of time.

6. Recommendations

6.1. *Spillover effects of shortage of full-time workers*

Since the smaller companies are the ones who are most affected by the manpower crunch, they are the group that requires most help in ensuring that they are able to use part-time workers more productively. Based on the findings, students are the main source of part-time workers and one main characteristic of students is that students are mostly able to commit only during school holidays. As such, we can further differentiate part-time workers into two types: permanent part-time workers and temporary part-time workers. Students belong to temporary part-time workers, as they are only able to commit between 1 and 3 months as compared to housewives and retirees who are able to commit longer periods of time. Housewives and retirees are generally permanent part-time workers that companies hire.

More emphasis could be placed by the business associations and government to increase the supply of permanent part-time workers like housewives and retirees through incentives. Permanent part-time workers have lower turnover rates and function more like full-time workers less the benefits but with more flexibility. The concern of disruption of the continuity of customer relationships can then be mitigated. An example of an incentive scheme could be to decrease foreign workers levy incurred by companies for every few retirees who are hired as part-time workers. This will also help to expand the pool of part-time workers in Singapore.

6.2. *Perception of F&B as a viable career option*

However, such an incentive scheme is more of a short-term demand-side solution to the problems relating to the part-time worker population in Singapore. Companies, business associations and government agencies could play a bigger role in projecting F&B as a viable career option. As mentioned by most managers and owners interviewed in the study, locals do not wish to work in the F&B industry due to the working conditions and the wages. Locals would rather sit in an air-conditioned room to work as compared to working in the kitchen or put up with customers' demands. A long-term supply-side solution would be to improve the perception towards the F&B industry as a viable career path. Information on career progression can be more clearly articulated by the business associations in Singapore. For example, to work as an assistant restaurant manager, one has to go through the life of an ordinary service staff and slowly rise up to the ranks of a managerial role. Better information would allow proper planning by workers who wish to pursue an F&B job position and also to reduce the level of turnover apparent in the industry.

6.3. Versatility of part-time workers

Subsidies to attend courses such as Food Hygiene could be extended to students to increase the versatility of part-time workers, which can then help to alleviate the situation of shortage of full-time workers in the F&B sector.

6.4. Informational problems

Programs and schemes once implemented can be better articulated and communicated to the F&B community through mail or electronic means on a regular basis. This helps to ensure that needy firms will be able to make use of the schemes intended for them. Furthermore, this reduces the risk that underlying problems related to the programs and schemes are disguised by informational problems.

6.5. Job redesign by business

Businesses could redesign the job scope of certain occupations and processes to suit the needs of part-time workers, and to more effectively use part-time workers to fit and complement the work of the full-time staff. The effective engagement of part-time workers is crucial to increase the productive performance of business.

7. Conclusion

This chapter has identified the supply-side issues pertaining to part-time workers in the F&B sector. These issues arise due to two key factors. The first is the shortage of full-time workers in the F&B sector and the second is the bulk of the composition of part-time workers in the restaurants and cafés are students. Since the focus here is part-time workers, the recommended solutions are directed towards the second factor, such that a more permanent-oriented part-time pool can be built.

Recommended solutions both offer a short-term perspective as well as a long-term perspective. The short-term perspective revolves around rectifying the current situation of a student-dominated part-time pool of workers while the long-term perspective revolves around improving the image and perception of the F&B industry as a viable career path.

References

Bates, K., Bates, H. and Johnston, R. (2003). Linking service to profit: The business case for service excellence. *International Journal of Service Industry Management*, 14(2), 173.

Barzel, Y. (1973). The determination of daily hours and wages. *Quarterly Journal of Economics*, 87(2), 220–238.

Brewster, C., Hegewisch, A. and Mayne, L. (1994). Flexible Working Practices: The Controversy and the Evidence. In Brewster, C. and Hegewisch, A., (Eds.), *Policy and Practice in European Human Resource Management: The Price Waterhouse Cranfield Survey*. Routledge, London.

Cataldi, A., Kampelmann, S. and Rycx, F. (2013). Part-time Work, Wages and Productivity: Evidence from matched panel data. Available at: http://www.sole-jole.org/12382.pdf.

Services Survey Series (2012). Department of Statistics. Food & Beverage Services. Available at: http://www.singstat.gov.sg/statistics/browse_by_theme/economy/findings/fnb.pdf.

Trends in Productivity and Value-added by Industry. Department of Statistics. Available at: http://www.singstat.gov.sg/statistics/visualising_data/visualiser/productivity/productivity.html.

Yearbook of Statistics Singapore (2013). Department of Statistics Singapore. Available at: http://www.singstat.gov.sg/publications/publications_and_papers/reference/yearbook_2013/yos2013.pdf.

Edwards, C. and Robinson, O. (2004). Evaluating the business case for part-time working amongst qualified nurses. *British Journal of Industrial Relations*, 42(1), 167–183.

Budget Speech (2013). Ministry of Finance. Available at: http://www.mof.gov.sg/budget_2013/pc.html.

Labour Force Singapore (2013). Ministry of Manpower. Available at: http://stats.mom.gov.sg/Pages/Labour-Force-In-Singapore-2013.aspx.

Kum-Nelen, A., De Grip, A. and Fouarge, D. (2011). Is part time employment beneficial for firm productivity. Discussion Paper Series. IZA DP No 5423. Available at: http://ftp.iza.org/dp5423.pdf.

Vandenberghe, S (2013). Is part-time employment a boon or bane for firm productivity? Available at: http://perso.uclouvain.be/vincent.vandenberghe/Papers/Part_time_Belgium.pdf.

Vakharia, A., Selim, H. and Husted, R. (1992). Efficient scheduling of part-time employees. *Omega*, 20(2), 201–213. doi:10.1016/0305-0483(92)90074-H.

Chapter 6

Human Capital Issues in F&B and Retail Sector in Singapore: Engagement, Retention and Usage of Mature Workers

1. Introduction

For the past two decades, the Singapore economy is experiencing rapid aging population. The impact of aging population and workforce is already felt in the Singapore labor market. In 1990, the median age of the resident population was around 29.8 years of age, which increased to nearly 39.8 years of age in 2014. In addition, the age support ratio of residents continued to fall since 1970s. In 2014, there were 6.0 residents aged 20–64 for each resident aged 65 years and above, which was a decline from 13.5 in 1970. As of 2014, the share of employed workers aged 40 and above (mature workers) is around is around 46% of the labor force and the number is close to 975,000 (Department of Statistics, Singapore). As the working population ages, the effective retention and utilization of the mature (40 years of age and above as defined by Ministry of Manpower, Singapore) and older workers in the labor market will be crucial to maintain the productivity of workers as well to manage the labor constraints in the labor market.

The impact of this aging labor force is expected to have profound impact on the supply and quality of the Singapore workforce.

Thus, it is imperative that the effective utilization of aging labor force in the labor market will be important to maintain the competitiveness of the workforce. In this chapter, we examine the needs and concerns of mature workers in the retail and food & beverage (F&B) sectors. In particular, we study the key challenges in terms of employment of mature workers in the retail and F&B sector in Singapore. The study focuses on the challenges of mature workers from the perspective of the workers as well as that of firms. Further, the chapter focuses on mature workers in the labor force from 40 years of age and above (as defined by Ministry of Manpower, Singapore), as opposed to older workers aged 50 and above.

The current study is similar to the study by Tripartite Alliance for Fair Employment Practices (TAFEP) (2013) in terms of examining the challenges of employing mature workers in Singapore from the perspective of employers. In this study, we explore the challenges from both employers and also the mature workers, as oppose to the study by TAFEP. It is important to capture the key challenges and opportunities from the workers' perspective as mature workers tends experience more displacement of jobs and longer unemployment due to their deprecation of skills, and also weaker work and wage bargaining power due to depreciation of their intrinsic (industry specific-skills) and extrinsic skills. In our study, we interviewed mature workers to identify the key challenges and opportunities they face in the labor market.

However, the results of the current study on the challenges and opportunities faced by employers are similar to the results obtained by TAFEP (2013). As in their study, we also found employers are very positive with regard to the employment of mature workers. Employers also have strong expectations that mature workers do bring strong values to the firms in terms of experience, higher loyalty, commitments and also stronger work maturity and ethics.

Several studies highlight the importance of retaining mature workers to improve the productivity of the firms. In particular, developing successful organization strategies such human resource management to increase the productivity of mature workers in the labor market (Kroeger, 2010). Retaining mature workers allows firms to benefit from intrinsic accumulated skills, experience, loyalty and training (Boomer Authority, 2009). In order to optimize the skills of mature workers, organizations have to develop retention strategies that will enhance and accommodate the needs of mature workers (Eisen, 2005). It is important for organization to capitalize on the abilities and qualities of mature workers as compared to younger workers who have less experience and on the job skills.

Several studies have also highlighted the economic values of mature workers and suggested strategies on how they can be gainfully utilised such economic values (Wee and Kwek, 2002; Wee *et al.*, 2002). For example, promoting and supporting lifelong employability of mature workers have positive impact on the productivity of firms. Contrary to the belief that mature workers have less capacity to learn, several studies highlighted that mature workers can actually learn new skills under the right environment. The study by Bertschek and Meyer (2008) highlights that accounting for the interactions between IT intensity and the proportion of older workers, their results do not show any significant effect from mature workers thereby indicating mature workers do not lower IT-enabled productivity. Their study found that workers older than 49 years of age are not significantly less productive than prime age workers, whereas workers younger less than 30 years are significantly less productive than prime age workers. Older workers using a computer are significantly more productive than older non-computer users. In fact, the positive and significant relationship between labor productivity and IT intensity is not affected by the proportion of older workers. There are also studies that have shown that mature workers, if given the right working environment, are able to mentor, lead and coach younger employees, employ creative and innovative ways to solve problems and impart wisdom to younger workers (McCartney and Worman, 2014).

Apart from conventional ways such as giving the option of part-time work, many retail and F&B chains around the world have designed innovative methods to keep mature workers engaged. One example will be the global fast food chain McDonalds in Singapore. About 50% of its workforce consists of workers aged 50 and older. McDonalds has implemented two key adjustments namely adding visual and graphics to the food station and touch screen cash registers. The former was implemented so as to make it easier for the mature workers to understand the requirements of their job, while the latter was implemented so that the workers need not squint to read texts on the register.[1]

One country that has a thriving population of mature workers is the United States of America. In a study by Tishman and Van Loo (2012),[2] it was shown that companies in the United States have designed range of strategies such as ergonomic design of workspace to tailor to older workers, doing regular job analysis for matured workers so that their risks of injuries will be minimized and having a culture of wellness and integrated health promotion within the workplace.

Recent study by the Australian Institute of Management (2013) highlight that businesses must be able to increase productivity by ensuring critical parts of the business are not affected by retirement and older workers' experience is spread all over the organization, move beyond stereotypes, invest in flexibility and train for the future growth by developing suitable training programs for older workers.

This study focuses on two key issues: (a) identifying the key opportunities and challenges facing both mature workers and firms and (b) identifying the conducive environment for mature workers to contribute positively to the productivity and efficiency of the firms. In this respect, the study undertakes a survey of employees and firms at retail and F&B sectors in Singapore.

2. Mature Workers in Retail and F&B sectors in Singapore

Typically, in most global settings, mature workers are defined as workers who are working past their retirement age. In some countries, mature workers are defined as workers that either at or are nearing the age of retirement or crossed the halfway mark of their working life. For instance, in the US, mature workers are defined as workers above the age of 40.[3] In other countries such as Australia

---

[1] Available at: https://www.tafep.sg/mcdonald-s-restaurants.

[2] Available at: http://www.dol.gov/odep/pdf/NTAR_Employer_Strategies_Report.pdf.

[3] Available at: http://www.eeoc.gov/laws/types/age.cfm.

and Japan, mature workers are defined as workers above 50 years of age[4] and 65 years of age[5] respectively. In Singapore, mature workers are defined as 40 years and above and older workers are defined as 50 years and above (MOM, 2007). As indicated earlier, it is important to focus on mature workers (workers aged 40 and above), as the vulnerability of workers could be addressed earlier as their displacement and retrenchment effect increases as they get older. This allows policy makers to increase the resilience and skills of workers as they get older rather than addressing such issues when workers are already at the stage of older workers (50 years and above).

The key trends of mature workers are given in Figures 1 and 2. In Figure 1, the median age of workers has been increasing over the years in Singapore, where the median age is over 43 years of age

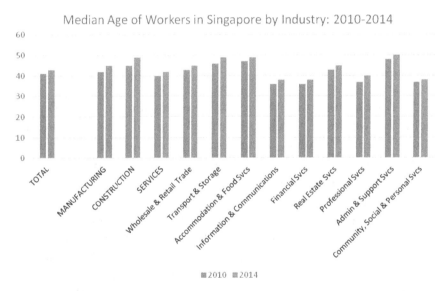

Figure 1:   Median Age of Workers in Singapore by Sectors
Source: MRSD, MOM.

---

[4]Available at: http://www.business.gov.au/business-topics/employing-people/diversity-in-the-workplace/Pages/employing-mature-aged-workers.aspx.
[5]Available at: http://www.bloomberg.com/news/articles/2012-08-26/willing-wrinkled-workers-help-defuse-pension-time-bomb-in-japan.

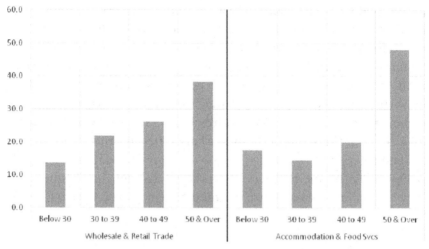

Figure 2: Employment by Age Group in Wholesale & Retail and Accommodation & Retail in Singapore

Source: MRSD, MOM.

in 2014. By sectors, we observe that the median age of workers is higher for wholesale & retail (nearly 45 years of age), transport & storage (nearly 50 years of age), and accommodation and food services (nearly 49 years of age) sectors have the larger share of mature workers across the industry.

The employment by age groups in wholesale & retail and accommodation is given in Figure 2. It is also interesting to observe that the share of mature workers account for a larger share of workers at wholesale and retail and accommodation and services. In wholesale and retail, the share of mature workers is nearly 68% and nearly 70% in accommodation and services sectors. This clearly reflects younger workers prefer not to work at these sectors and these sector have a greater reliance on mature workers for their manpower.

Since mature workers include older workers, we also observe greater share of older workers in these sectors. The accommodation and food services sector tend to have a higher share of older workers compared to wholesale & retail sector. In the retail trade, almost 40% of the workforce is aged 50 and over. Likewise, in the

F&B we observe that more than half of the workforce is aged 50 and above.

3. Survey Framework

A qualitative survey of mature workers and companies was done to understand the key opportunities and challenges facing the workers and firms in retail and F&B sectors in Singapore.

The survey covered nearly 50 mature workers and 26 retail and F&B companies. In summary, the survey captures mature workers aged 40 years and above. The sample accounts for nearly 40% is within the age of 40–50 years, 50% within the age of 50–60 years and rest in for workers aged 70 and above. Most of the mature workers have only secondary and primary and lower education. The major share of the mature workers in our sample are also not at the front-line occupations but jobs as supporting staff (60%) such as chefs, cooks, dishwashers, etc. There is only around 40% of our sample has frontline mature workers such as cashiers (20%), supervisors (10%), and rest as managers and assistant managers. The company inter-views were conducted directly and internet surveys were conducted with mature workers. In terms of gender, we have nearly 50% who are male. Most of our mature workers have secondary and below education that accounts for nearly 90% of our sample. The sample also consist of 50% employed in retail and 50% employed in F&B.

4. Research Findings

The surveys covered two sample groups: (a) mature workers and (b) the employers. The results of the qualitative survey are elaborated below.

4.1. *Findings from mature workers*

From Figure 3, it is evident that most mature workers continue to work as they need to earn income for their daily expenses.

The need to earn income for daily expenses including cost of medications are the key reasons for mature workers seeking

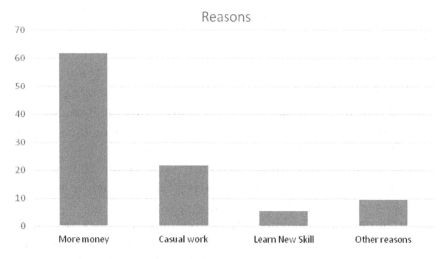

Figure 3: Reasons for Mature Workers seeking Employment

employment. In most cases, the expense includes day-to-day meal allowances and money to pay for their medications. The need to have temporary employment to keep them occupied is also indicated as the other key reasons for seeking employment for the mature workers. This is indicated by nearly 20% of the workers surveyed. The need to acquire skills tends to account for less than 5% of the sample.

It is indeed noteworthy that most of them stated that they do not face any major challenges at work, albeit there were some that brought up issues such as lack of support and health benefits as reasons (see Figure 4). However, nearly 20% of the mature workers indicated that hectic work environment as one of the key challenges in Singapore. This was followed by the need for healthcare, demanding bosses and age-based discrimination which were not highlighted as the key factors faced by mature workers.

Figure 5 indicates the key considerations that will be important to retain mature workers at the workplace. About 30% of the mature workers highlighted that having flexibility in the workplace creates good incentive for mature workers to participate in the labor market. In particular, the option to work as "permanent" part-time workers could be one of the senior friendly initiative that could be provided

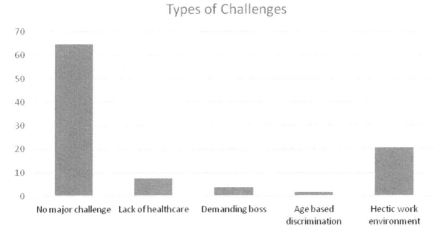

Figure 4:   Challenges Faced by Mature Workers

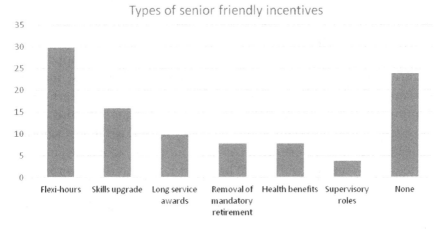

Figure 5:   Key Consideration for Retaining Mature Workers at Workplace

by the employers that could increase the labor market participation of mature workers. Another 24% of mature workers in our sample indicated that there are no special incentives that are specifically catered towards mature workers (as indicated as "None") that could increase their incentive to participate in the labor market. This indicates that mature workers do not see the special need for senior-friendly incentives to increase their labor market participation.

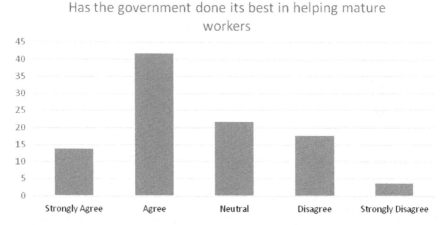

Figure 6: The Role of Government in Encouraging and Supporting Mature Workers

The sample also indicated that most companies do not really have a supportive environment for mature workers other than giving them the option of part-time work.

As to the role of government in encouraging and supporting mature workers to participate in the labor market, most mature workers actually either agree or strongly agree that the government has done its utmost best in helping them integrate into the workforce (see Figure 6). Only about 20% of the workers in our sample indicated that the government could do more to encourage employers to employ mature workers. When asked on what the government can do better, most mature workers indicated that they prefer to have more financial support and skills upgrade opportunities from the government.

4.2. Findings from employers

Most of the mature workers of the participated companies are between the ages of 40–70 years. The companies indicated that it is quite rare to find workers aged 70 years and above in accommodation and services and wholesale and retail sectors as these sectors have irregular working hours and mostly require some level of physical strength. In the sample, most of the mature workers are deployed

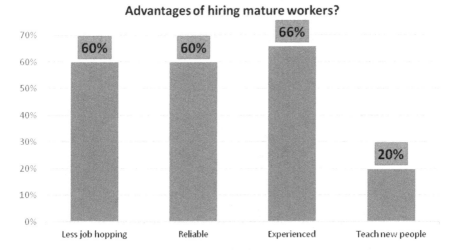

Figure 7: The Advantages of Hiring Mature Workers

mostly at the supportive role such as cashiers as oppose to the service frontline. A small minority of the workers are holding on to managerial positions as most of them have either primary or at most a secondary school education.

Figure 7 highlights the advantages of hiring mature workers. Generally, what most employers like about mature workers is their reliability and their experience. In the sample, nearly 66% indicated that mature workers are important in terms of their knowledge and skills. Also, nearly 60% indicated that mature workers are more reliable and dependent as compared to younger workers. The employers also indicated that there is more loyalty and less job hopping with mature workers as compared to younger workers. However, with regard to new knowledge, only 20% indicated that mature worker bring new technologies to the workplace. These results are in line with the TAFEP (2013) study on perception firms to mature workers.

The employers are also surveyed on the challenges of mature workers in the workplace. The results are given in Figure 8. When asked about the problems/disadvantages faced by mature workers at work, most employers cited their inability to learn and unwilling to change to the new environment as the key challenges. This could be attributable to their low level of education and older workers are less

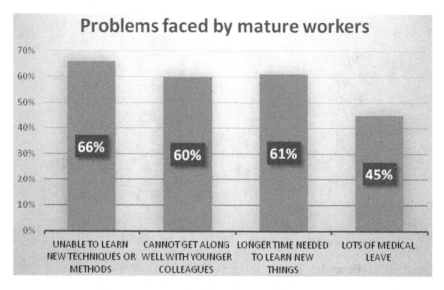

Figure 8: The Challenges of Mature Workers in Workplace

adaptable to working under younger managers and supervisors. We also observed that the large share of employers also indicated that the mature workers take a much longer time to learn new things. They also have difficulty in working as a team and difficulty in get along well with their younger colleagues. This response was reflected by both younger and older employers. Again, this was also observed in the TAFEP (2013) study. We also observe that nearly 45% of the employers indicated that mature workers take more medical leave as compared to younger workers.

Figure 9 shows the problems faced by employers in hiring mature workers. Most cited the shortage in numbers and high healthcare costs. The high healthcare costs can be attributed to the fact that most of them have at least one if not more chronic illness such as diabetes, high blood pressure, etc.

Indeed, the above mentioned are issues faced globally by older workers. However, in countries like the US, employers have taken a different perspective when looking at mature workers. They choose to focus on their strengths such as loyalty, not having parental

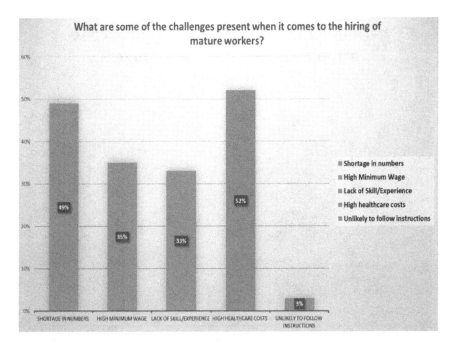

Figure 9:   Challenges in Hiring of Mature Workers

obligations (i.e. thus more flexibility), being more responsible and being able to think on their feet.[6]

The survey also sought the views of employers in attracting and retaining mature workers in the workplace. Figure 10 indicates the various strategies employers could adopt to attract and retain mature workers in the workplace.

Most employers indicated that flexible working conditions are crucial to retain mature workers in the work place. The employers also highlighted that giving simple instructions for mature workers to follow is also an effective way to keep mature workers in their company. From the survey, it is heartening to know that most companies are aware of the physical and educational limitations that

---

[6]Available at: http://www.halogensoftware.com/blog/the-gray-wave-why-companies-refuse-to-hire-older-workers.

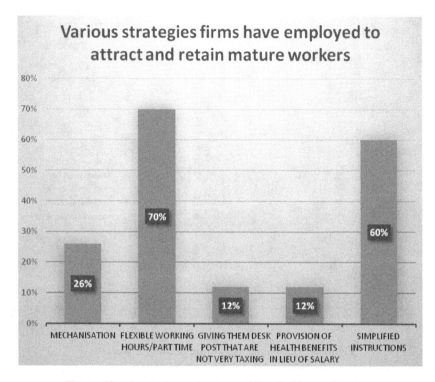

Figure 10:   Strategies to Attract and Retain Mature Workers

most mature workers. To manage this, firms indicated that they have adopted measures such as giving simplified instructions and the option of part-time work so as to create a conducive work environment for them.

In Figure 11, the results of types of incentives that could be effective to retain mature workers is given. Respondents were further given a set of probable senior-friendly initiatives and asked if they feel that the initiatives will be able to help retain mature workers.

From the results, we can see that the general perception amongst Singapore employers is that jobs having routine and non-strenuous part-time work is the best way to keep mature workers given their limitations in age and education. About half feel that giving incentives for good performance may help. This may be so for those mature workers who have dependents to support. However, if the mature workers are working on a temporary employment, then it

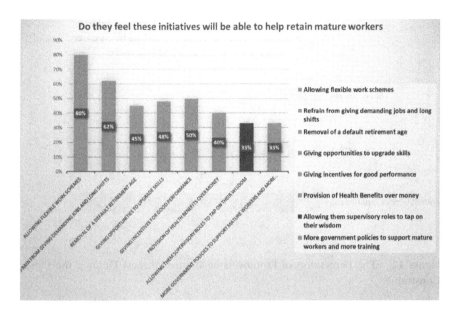

Figure 11:   Incentives to Retain Mature Workers in the Workplace

may not be effective. A significant minority also indicated that provision of health benefits over money, giving them supervisory roles and effective government policies may be useful. However, this might not be applicable widely as mature workers need a certain qualification attainments. Giving supervisory roles can only be appropriate for mature workers with post-secondary education, have minimally pre-university education and have held leadership positions before. Even if the government invests in training these mature workers, it is not certain there will be a suitable return on the capital spent given the shorter working lifespan of a mature worker compared to a younger worker.

A further question was posed to the respondents on whether they would like to employ mature workers on a full-time or a part-time basis. About 70–80% indicated that part-time as their main preference. They cited reasons such as their inability to work for long hours on the floor and possible health limitations as reasons. For those who preferred to hire mature workers on a full-time basis, reasons such as less disruption to the scheduling and better familiarity were cited.

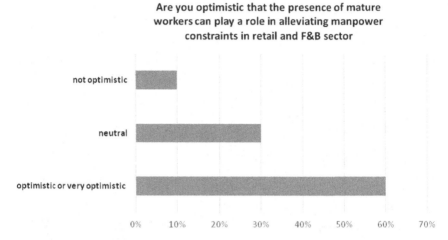

Figure 12:   The Perception of Employers of Mature Workers Helping the Labor Constraints

Overall, it is heartening to know that most Singaporean employers in the retail and F&B sector are moderately optimistic that the presence of mature workers can play a role in alleviating manpower constraints. About 60% either indicated optimistic or very optimistic while another 30% indicated neutral. Only about 10% indicated that they were either unoptimistic or very unoptimistic about having more matured workers. The optimistic observation in our survey is also observed at the TAFEP (2013) study on the mature workers in Singapore.

5. Recommendations

The study highlights that it is important to develop labor market policies earlier at the mature stage so that the retention and training of workers in terms of tooling and re-tooling workers with skills will be more effective when workers reach the older stage of employment.

From the above results, it is evident that the idea of having an active pool of mature workers in the workforce is still relatively nascent. Given the severe manpower shortages in retail and F&B sectors, retention and attraction of mature workers to these industries seems to be crucial to sustain the flow of labor supply in these sectors. From the survey results, both workers and employers indicated that the main incentives that entice the mature workers are flexible working conditions and environment such as part-time and temporary employment. The results of the survey also indicate that mature workers usually are willing to take up this job, sometimes at pay below the market wage rate and with employment terms that may not be very favorable to them as they need to earn income for the daily sustenance. Unfortunately, by just giving part-time work or temporary employment, the companies might not address the key issues faced by mature workers as they need flexibility in the workplace and also their inability to work for long hours. This is in spite of the fact that the government has implemented schemes such as the Special Employment Credit (SEC)[7] and WorkPro Scheme.[8] It might be important to emphasize the need for an active business environment whereby mature workers can be gainfully used in a company that can bring about real productivity improvements.

Given the aging population, it is important to create the environment for employability of mature workers as they will form an important component of the Singapore labor market. Thus, the following policy discussions are important to improve and create the appropriate environment for employing mature workers.

5.1. *To improve work environment for mature workers for businesses*

5.1.1. *Job redesign: minimize physical exertion*

Often in F&B or even retail sectors, the workers that are employed are usually required do the whole spectrum of jobs. Like in the F&B sector, they do the whole gamut of tasks ranging from taking reservations from customers to getting them ready for the meal and serving

---

[7]Employers who hire Singaporean employees aged above 50 earning up to $4,000 a month receive SEC of up to 8% of the employee's monthly wages. The Government has committed to provide the SEC for a five-year period until 31 December 2016.

[8]Details can be found in the Appendix at the end of this chapter.

them food. In the case of the retail sector, their jobs can range from guiding customers, to managing new stocks and ensuring the neatness of the display of the food items and condiments. It might be important to redesign the job such that mature workers could handle less physically demanding part of the job. For example, firms should let the mature workers focus on work such as the management of stock inventory in the retail sector and less strenuous and physically demanding frontline serving and clearing of food in the F&B industry such as cashiering and managing the ordering from customers.

Given the labor constraints in Singapore, most mature workers, if employed will probably be deployed to do labor-intensive tasks given their lack of education. Due to their age, many of them may not be able to withstand the long hours on the floor. Even for those who have been employed, the prolonged periods of standing and doing manual work will take a toll on their health to some extent given their age, thereby increasing the healthcare cost of workers.

Germany, like Singapore, is also facing similar aging problems in their labor market, a rapidly shrinking pool of younger workers and aging workforce. Job redesign is an important way to retain older workers in the labor market. For example, a recent article in Financial Times highlighted that a person where his employer offered him a deal that allowed him to swap 13% of his salary for an additional nine weeks of holiday. This form of job redesign that suits the needs and ability of mature workers will have productive impact on firms as well as better retention of mature workers in the workforce. The article also highlighted that firms have made changes to the working environment, (i.e. providing ergonomic chairs) to accommodate the older workers.[9]

Most retailers and F&B operators do not have the knowledge or the funds to re-design the job scope of their operations that allow effective employment of mature workers. More effort could be placed in assisting companies to redesign their jobs and improving

---

[9]Available at: http://www.ft.com/cms/s/0/7678f538-883e-11e3-8afa-00144feab7de.html#axzz3hO2sb3cr.

their human resource (HR) practices. This could be done through training, consultancy, and profiling and rewarding companies that have re-designed their jobs-successfully. Further, the employment of mature workers also requires improvements in HR practices.

5.1.2. *Allocate some time for exercise and promote healthy lifestyle in the companies*

Often, the reason for lack of hiring mature workers is their health. The workplace and job could be re-designed such that mature workers be given time-off to do joint exercise and even providing subsidized membership to health clubs. This could be part of subsidy that could be supported by the government. By giving the mature workers time during work hours, be it an hour or even half an hour to do light workouts and simple exercise, firms can actually help the mature workers to maintain their fitness level. Higher fitness level will have positive impact on productivity at the workplace.

5.1.3. *Adopt more flexible employment policies*

Often, many mature workers sign standard employment contracts. Employers can look into working around their constraints rather than taking a "one size fits all" approach. For those who cannot work for long hours, the employers can give them hourly breaks or extended lunch breaks with some adjustments in their salary. For those who may not want to be tied down to work too much, or want to work on an *adhoc* basis, the employers can give them more leave for less pay or even engage them on "pay as you work scheme". Ultimately, the employment contract must be tailored to the needs of both the company and the individual worker.

Interestingly, Finland, Norway and the UK have a project entitled "Working life changes and training of older workers" (Worktow), in which 73% of the older workers participated in it.[10] The job learning subsequently followed a similar pattern, 52.2% of people in the

---

[10] Older worker is considered to be a worker above 45 years of age in this instance.

service line applied the new skills while 45% of people in the office line applied the new skills. It was subsequently established that some less formal types of learning seem to suit older workers as compared to classroom learning.[11]

5.1.4. *Create a better working environment for mature workers: improve the perception*

Many recruiters and companies have very negative pre-conceived notions on mature workers. When the term "mature workers" comes to their mind, they often associate them as less educated, inflexible and physical incapacities. The relevant government agencies and business associations can help by emphasizing the strengths of mature workers such as their loyalty, job experience and ability to respond to situations much better and less family related cost such not having parental obligations. They can also conduct courses and seminars from time to time on how to keep mature workers engaged and occupied.

5.1.5. *Extending the re-employment age*

The Singapore Government will be extending of the re-employment age from the current 65 years old to 67 by 2017 to encourage the employment of older workers. The extension of re-employment age could provide strong supply-side effects on the labor market and also increase the incentive for older workers to participate in the labor market. It should also be aligned with stronger institutions to protect the rights and well being of older workers in the workforce as older workers and less educated tend to have less bargaining power as compared to younger and education workers.

Having an active pool of mature workers in both the service and production line (or even managerial) of retail and F&B is going to become the norm of the future given Singapore's low birth rate and

---

[11] Available at: www.cedefop.europa.eu/files/3045_en.pdf.

increasing silver population. It is imperative for companies to re-look their HR practices and policies in terms of their working environment so as to see how they will be able to engage an active pool of mature workers in the near future. With the right support and job design, mature workers can be a valuable resource that Singapore can tap on to solve its labor crunch in areas such as retail and F&B. There needs to be more creativity in re-designing and engineering a job environment for these matured workers that goes beyond merely run of the mill benefits such as shift work and part-time work.

References

Australia Institute of Management (2013). Engaging and Retaining Older Workers, AIM NSW and ALT Training Centre, Australia.

Bell, D. and Alasdair, R. (2013). Older workers and working time. IZA Discussion paper no 7546, Germany.

Bertschek, I. and Jenny, M. (2008). Do older workers lower IT-enabled productivity? Firm-level evidence from Germany. DRUID working paper no 08-17, Denmark.

Gielen, A.C. (2009). Working hours flexibility and older workers' labor supply. *Oxford Economic Papers*, 61(2), 240–274.

Haoxiang, C. Older workers getting fair or raw deal. *The Straits Times*, July 9 2011. Available at: http://www.healthxchange.com.sg/News/Pages/Older-workers-getting-fair-or-raw-deal.aspx [Accessed July 7, 2015].

Jianye, X. Hiring of women, older workers hits high amid labor crunch. TODAY, November 29 2014. Available at: http://www.todayonline.com/singapore/hiring-women-older-workers-hits-high-amid-labor-crunch [Accessed 5 July 2015].

Kroeger, J. (2010). Organizational Benefits of Training of Older Workers, The Graduate School of Wisconsin-Stout, US.

Lahey, J. (2006). State age protection laws and the age discrimination in employment act. Working Paper w12048, National Bureau of Economic Research.

Maestas, N. and Xiaoyan, L. (2006). Discouraged Workers: Job Search Outcomes of Older Workers, WP 2006-133, MRRC, US.

Meadows, P. (2003). Retirement Ages in the UK: A Review of the Literature, Employment Relations Research Series No. 18. Department of Trade and Industry, London.

McCartney, C. and Worman, D. (2014). Age Diversity in SMEs. CIPD.

MOM. (2007). Firms adoption of Age-Positive Human Resource Practice, Ministry of Manpower, Singapore.

Ranzijn, R., Carson, E. and Winefield, A. (2004). Barriers to mature aged re-employment: perceptions about desirable work-related attributes held by job-seekers and employers, *International Journal of Organisational Behaviour*, 8(7), 559–570.

Ranzijn, R. (2005), Discrimination against the older worker: Psychology and economics. Human Rights Commission. Available at: www.humanrights. gov.au/age/workingage/speeches/ranzijn.html.

Ryan, S. (2012). Demography is not destiny: age discrimination and the economy. Available at: www.humanrights.gov.au.

Sarros, J., Pirola-Merlo, A. and Baker, R. (2012). Research Report: The Impact of Age on Managerial Style, Department of Management Monash University and Australian Institute of Management QLD/NT.

Taylor, P. (2011), Ageism and Age Discrimination in the Labor Market and Employer Responses, In Griffin, T. and Beddie, F. (Eds.) Older Workers: *Research Readings*. NCVER, Adelaide.

Tripartite Alliance for Fair Employment Practices (TAFEP), (2013). The value of mature workers to organization in Singapore, survey report, May 2013.

van Loo, J. (2011). Making the Most of Mature Minds: Issues, Trends and Challenges in Making Active Ageing a Reality, In Griffin, T. and Beddie, F. (Eds.) Older Workers: Research Readings, NCVER, Adelaide.

Appendix

WorkPro Scheme

Grant/Incentive	Funding Amount	Description
Age Management Grant	Tranche 1 is worth $5,000 and Tranche 2 is worth $15,000 Up to $20,000 per company	Helps you acquire the necessary skills and knowledge on age management practices such as good re-employment practices and performance management to better manage and sustain a multigenerational workforce.
Job Re-design Grant	Projects that benefit mature workers: cap of $150,000 Projects that benefit back-to-work locals: cap of $150,000 Up to $300,000 in total per company	Defrays your cost of redesigning your workplace to improve productivity, and helps you to recruit and retain mature workers and back-to-work locals.
Work–Life Grant	Up to $160,000 per company	Supports you in implementing and sustaining work–life strategies, particularly flexible work-arrangements (FWAs). You may tap on the Developmental Grant and/or FWA Incentive under the Work–Life Grant.
(a) Developmental Grant	One-time grant of up to S$40,000 to defray the developmental costs of implementing work–life strategies, particularly FWAs	Co-funds: • Up to 80% for items such as work–life training and work-life consultancy, and • Up to 50% for infrastructure and selected employee support schemes.
(b) FWA Incentive	Up to S$120,000 per company (disbursed in tranches of up to S$40,000 over three years)	Rewards you for providing and sustaining work–life friendly workplaces.

(Continued)

WorkPro Scheme: (*Continued*)

Grant/Incentive	Funding Amount	Description
On-the-Job Training Allowance	Up to $2,000 per newly-hired back-to-work local. Based on 50% of salary, capped at $1,000 per month for two months. Maximum $50,000 per company	You can receive an On-the-Job (OJT) training allowance to partially defray salary costs of training newly-hired back-to-work locals and newly-hired mature workers on a new job scope for the first two months. The newly-hired workers must be hired on permanent full-time or part-time, or contract positions for at least 12 months. They must also be placed on a structured OJT programme.
New Hire Retention Incentive (NHRI)	Up to $2,000 per newly-hired mature worker or back-to-work local who meets the criteria. Based on 50% of salary, capped at $1,000 for retention over six months, and another 50% of salary, capped at $1,000, for retention over the next six months. Maximum $50,000 per company	You must first tap any of the following: the Age Management Grant, Job Redesign Grant or Work–Life Grant to be eligible for NHRI. Receive funding to retain back-to-work locals or newly-hired mature worker who: • are hired on permanent full-time or part-time, or contract full-time positions for at least 12 months; • draw a monthly gross salary of not more than $4,500 per month; and • Have been hired through WorkPro's Programme Partners (NTUC, e2i and SNEF), or referred by WDA Career Centers and CaliberLink.

(*Continued*)

WorkPro Scheme: (*Continued*)

Grant/Incentive	Funding Amount	Description
Mentorship Allowance	$100 per mentor	You must assign a mentor for each back-to-work local or newly-hired mature worker. You must also award the mentor with a mentorship allowance of at least $100 after three months of mentorship. Employers are also encouraged to provide a higher mentorship allowance where possible. WDA will subsidize $100 mentorship allowance for every mentor.
Candidate Referral Service		You can approach NTUC/ SNEF to refer suitable candidates (mature workers or back-to-work locals) for your job openings at no cost.

Source: Ministry of Manpower, Singapore.

Chapter 7

Usage of Social Media to Raise Productivity in the Food & Beverage Sector

1. Introduction

In the past few years, millions of people have joined online communities and started using online social platforms. Popular social media channels in Singapore include Facebook, YouTube and Twitter. It is expected that nearly 1.5 billion members are likely to join social media through information technology (IT). This growth indicates the importance of social technologies, which bring the speed and scale of the internet to social interactions.

Social media has become ever more prevalent and is used pervasively in social interaction and business transactions, which has significantly influence on quality of life and decision making in both the private and public sectors. The government has already recognized its importance by encouraging the public sector to use social media as part of policy management in the economy (Tan, 2013). The increasingly significant role of social media has become too large to ignore.

In *The Social Economy: Unlocking Value and Productivity Through Social Technologies*, the McKinsey Global Institute (MGI) examined the economic impact of social technologies.[1] It identified value-creating

---

[1]McKinsey Growth Institute (2012) *The Social Economy: Unlocking Value and Productivity Through Social Technologies* <http://www.mckinsey.com/insights/mgi>.

'levers' that can be used across value chain, from product development through after-sale customer services. Customers have the ability to advertise for or against merchants, and merchants have to get on par in the use of social media. The use of social media will provide F&B merchants with the ease of reaching their target audience at a relatively lower cost compared to traditional advertising. The correct usage of social media will be important to enhance customers' satisfaction beyond the food and service activities in the retail sectors and food sectors.

Research Objectives

In 2014, more than 50% of Singaporeans post about their food experiences on social media (Fast Forward Trends Report 2014, 2014). Social media has become part of modern Singaporeans' lifestyle. Thus it is important that food and beverage (F&B) merchants do not neglect social media as a crucial means of improving their business viability and profitability.

In this chapter, we will focus on the three main social media sites, namely Facebook, Twitter and Instagram. The purpose of this research is to analyze how social media can increase productivity through interacting constructively with customers. The main objectives of this study:

a. To evaluate the state of social media usage among players in the F&B industry.
b. To discern the successful action or steps adopted in making social media a positive contributor to business expansion and productivity.
c. To propose further measures to enable the potential of social media be tapped to meet the business expansion and productivity upgrading needs of the enterprises in the F&B sector.

2. Literature Review

Social media is computer-mediated tools that allow people to create, share or exchange information, ideas, and pictures/videos in virtual communities and networks. Specialized companies, such as Facebook and Twitter, have been set up to provide such social networking services. Although traditional social media offer a variety of opportunities for companies in a wide range of business sectors, internet-enabled entrepreneurs can makes use of the location- and time-sensitivity aspects of mobile social media in order to engage into marketing research, communication, sales promotions/discounts, and relationship development/loyalty programs.

Several studies have highlighted the importance of social media. Some examples include how consumer behaviour can be affected by a community on social media (Goh *et al.*, 2013), how social media can influence users (Kerin *et al.*, 2010), how social media is susceptibly influential on the newer generation (Skoric and Poor, 2013), how social media is valuable for businesses (Carr, 2012) and how social media can be used to increase awareness of topics and facilitate communication (Leow *et al.*, 2012). Besides engaging consumers through social technologies, merchants can listen in on unfiltered conversations and soak up huge amounts of data on consumer behavior (Manyika *et al.*, 2012).

Furthermore, social media will also address customer satisfaction issues. Customer relationship management and competitive advantage are strongly intertwined. It is essential for merchants to provide service quality, satisfy their customers and build loyalty for long-term customer value in the virtual environment (Bai *et al.*, 2008). Empirical studies have suggested that online satisfaction was found to have a direct and positive effect on purchase intentions. Providers must respond effectively to customers' current expressed needs (Narver *et al.*, 1998) because being responsive to customer requests plays a critical role in satisfying customers (Blocker *et al.*, 2011).

2.1. *Situation in Singapore*

Since Singapore is reputed for being a "food paradise" (Teo, 2013), the F&B industry is highly competitive, especially when local and foreign entrepreneurs can participate in the sector freely. Using Porter's Five Forces, intensity of rivalry is high. Local F&B merchants face competition from well-established overseas franchises, cheap food courts and convenient fast food restaurants. While capital outlay can be sizeable and expertise (e.g. chef) can be scarce, the F&B is one sector with the highest business formation. Bargaining power of buyers is high as customers have low switching costs due to high price elasticity of demand for food. The bargaining power of suppliers is low due to large number of suppliers. Lastly, threats of substitute products are high with availability at food courts and fast food restaurants.

One possibility that might be holding F&B merchants back from using social media might be the lack of knowledge and fear of cost (Bosua *et al.*, 2013). These are reasonable beliefs, but unsubstantiated. This chapter attempts to collate relevant information that will help to support or debunk the prior hypotheses.

3. Methodology

As social media is a relatively new occurrence, this study adopts a qualitative approach by first analyzing the social media sites used by selected F&B merchants. It is supplemented by conducting a survey on consumers who had patronized the F&B outlets and have made remarks or comments using social media. In this way, the interrelationships between the usage of social media and the revenue and productivity of F&B outlets can be discerned.

A total of 88 F&B outlets are being included in the current study. These outlets are founded by Singaporean and are relatively well known. They can be classified into two groups. The first group consists of 59 F&B outlets which are relatively large in scale, and belong to some nine major chains or consortiums. An example is the Bread Talk Group Limited. They are involved as niche dinning enterprises as well as eateries and restaurants catering to the mass. They are usually the fore-runners in the use of social media. The second group consists of the remaining 29 single-brand F&B outlets. Examples of such outlets include Fish & Co and Paradise Inn.

A survey of consumers who had patronized F&B outlets is conducted. The participants for this study are residents of Singapore. They are partitioned broadly into three groups: people who are active on social media sites of the 88 F&B establishments (21); people who patronize these 88 F&B establishments (40) and lastly people who have social media accounts but have not yet patronize the 88 F&B establishments (5). In total, we analyzed data collected from 66 anonymous participants.

We dispensed identical surveys to all those of the first two groups, with a slightly different one for the third group. For the first and third group, they were delivered electronically and administered to the participants over Facebook private message using Google Forms. For the second group of consumers, the interviews were done during visits to more than 10 establishments. They are interviewed in person before they left the restaurants. In order to solicit participation, a token sum of $2–$4 is given to each respondent in appreciation of the participation in the survey.

The survey has provided interesting findings on how well the local F&B establishments made use of social media. The participants' interaction with the employees of those establishments through Facebook posts, wall comments, tweets and photos provide useful platforms to observe how the usage of social media facilitates marketing efforts and bringing more customers to the restaurants. The information can be better understood and analyzed coherently if it can be supplemented by other relevant information such as news articles, annual reports, spokesperson speeches, forums and blogs.

Basic information about the main form of social media will help in better understanding the survey results and its relevance to the stakeholders:

a. Facebook has 1.28 billion monthly active users in March 2014, and in Singapore alone, more than 2.8 million users as of 2012 (five important statistics about Facebook users in Singapore, 2012).
b. Twitter has about 400,000 users in Singapore (Kerin *et al.*, 2010).
c. As for Instagram, many restaurants have been trying to connect to younger users by launching their own Instagram feeds, or hiring Instagrammers with large, deeply engaged followings to capture photos that showcase the brand (Hempel, 2014).

We are interested in the number of fans they have, their online rating, the frequency and content of their posts, analytics results, how they respond to Facebook posts and the promptness of their replies. Additional information such as whether they participate in group-voucher certificates and the response rates were also collected.

4. Social Media Presence

Out of the 88 merchants included in the sample, only 4 have accounts in all 3 main channels: Facebook, Twitter and Instagram (5%); 6 have accounts in Facebook and Twitter; 3 have accounts in Facebook and Instagram; 28 only have a Facebook page; 3 only have an Instagram accounts; and 1 only has a Twitter account.

As indicated in Table 1, 41 F&B Merchants have a Facebook page as of 25 July 2014, making it close to 47%. For more in-depth analysis, 11 restaurants with interaction using Facebook are chosen. These are restaurants who have posted at least once in the month of July 2014, with more than 30 posts by customers altogether since joining Facebook. Among them, the number of queries in 2014 added up to 138, replies to queries added up to 127 with an average response rate of 86%. The number of complaints recorded is 149, and the replies responding to these complaints amounting to 144, giving an average response rate of 92%. Finally, the last category of interaction concerns review. The number of reviews posted is 88, and this has resulted in 53 responses to the reviews, giving an average response rate of 72%. This reflects merchants are more focused

Table 1:   Summary of Social Media Presence

	Facebook Page	Twitter Profile	Instagram Account
(a) Number of restaurants with	41	12	11
(b) Active users	11	4	3
(a) As % of total sample of 88	47%	14%	13%
(b) As % of total sample of 88	13%	5%	3%

on clarifying customer doubts and appeasing them. Not responding to a complaint or a query could have more serious repercussions than not responding to a good review which usually does not require a reply.

Twelve of the 88 restaurants sampled have Twitter accounts as of 25 July 2014. This constitutes almost 14% of the restaurants sampled. Out of the 12, 4 of the more active accounts were chosen for analysis. These are accounts that have interacted at least weekly in the 2014 month of July, with the number of followers not less than 208, the average number of Twitter followers per user (Gilbert, 2013).

Eleven of the 88 restaurants sampled have Instagram accounts as of 25 July 2014, making it close to 13% of all restaurants under study. Out of the 11, 3 of the more active accounts were chosen since they have updated at least weekly in the 2014 month of July, with more than 100 followers.

5. Social Media Content Analysis

To better analyze the relationship between social media and productivity, we have also made reference to the annual reports of the restaurants where available.

5.1. *Facebook*

Facebook is an online social networking services website launched on 4 February 2004 with headquarter in California, USA. After registering to use the site, users can create a user profile, add other users as "friends", exchange messages, post status updates and photos, share videos and receive notifications when others update their profiles.

In the current study, the selected Facebook pages are grouped according to their management focus. The first group is more focused on clarifying doubts of customers. This corresponds to the Management and Message in the 8M framework (Chapter 2). During the past one year, selected restaurants with Facebook have responded more than 30 times to in relation to that focus. Their Facebook pages are as informative as their websites, with email address; location and phone numbers all conveniently included. The second group of restaurant Facebook users include those that use Facebook as low cost advertising platform, focusing on attracting customers with interesting content to promote their brand. There is a third group of restaurant Facebook users that treats the objectives pursued in the first and second groups of Facebook users as equally important. A sample of 30 customer posts covering the first six months of 2014 was taken and they include: queries, complaints and feedback.

The Cable News Network (CNN), an American basic cable and satellite television channel, had conducted a survey on how quickly business enterprises response to its wall post on Facebook. It was reported that the fastest business responds to its wall post takes about 2 minutes. At the opposite end of the spectrum, there were merchants that did not respond to a post until some two days later. This is much in contradiction to the expectation of customers who would expect retailers using Facebook platform to respond faster than interaction using traditional emails; and about as quickly as a phone call (Gross, 2012).

Peach Garden and Toast Box are our examples of the first group of restaurant Facebook users. The team managing Peach Garden Facebook page responds to queries promptly and makes it a practice to ask customers for their emails so they can actively add customers to their mailing list. This helps in retaining customers and references for future marketing efforts.

BreadTalk Group Limited's Toast Box replied every single post within one working day, though they do not update their Facebook content daily. BreadTalk Group Limited's 2013 Annual Report reported seeing an increase in customer engagement (BreadTalk Group Limited, 2013). This augurs well for the objective of building a good customer base and retaining current customers.

The second group of restaurant Facebook users include Botak Jones, The Soup Spoon, Dancing Crab, Fish & Co and Uncle Leong Seafood. They have been using Facebook for marketing and advertising.

Botak Jones' Facebook page is updated daily. Being current and up-to-date with its content and information is the key strategy of Botak Jones to inform and attract fans to its Facebook page. It actively solicit the views of customers and use the information for product development. For example, in apparent imitation of the page post by Walmart, it has included in its post a "product preference question", asking their fans to choose which part of the chicken they like best (see Figure 1).

The Botak Jones' page also includes photos of their menu and any new items they offer. The layout is clean and professional, showing their distinct brand attitude (Liem, 2010).

Another example of a restaurant using Facebook to promote its image is The Soup Spoon. After joining Facebook in 2009, The Soup Spoon (Leow) reported a 21.8% improvement in customer satisfaction and 24.8% increase in revenue. Their average sales also grow at 20–25% every year, and the number of stores is expected exceed 20 by the end 2014.

Its posts include information about opening of new outlets, vouchers that will be given out to viewers who responded with correct answers to quiz. Involving fans in games and contest has helped to increase visitation and interaction with the customer base.

TungLok Group's Dancing Crab started its Facebook page quite recently. The number of fans to the Facebook page has been growing rapidly, though it was reckoned that the 30% discount on the dining bill will be given when people liked its Facebook page is a contributing factor for the rapid growth. It also illustrates a way to use incentive to build a big fan base which hopefully will translate into a customer base for actual business and dining experience. To be one of the top 20 most liked merchants in the world on Facebook, a minimum of 13 million likes is required (Felix, 2012). Taking into account Singapore's population relative to that of the world's, a register of 9,000 likes is sufficient to qualify for that status. For merchants that have just started using Facebook, Dancing Crab's success is encouraging and remarkable.

Fish & Co Facebook page has more than 50,000 likes. Unofficially, it is one of the top Facebook pages in the F&B industry. Managers

Figure 1: A Screenshot of Botak Jones's Facebook Post with Strategies Similar to Walmart's

Figure 2:   Uncle Leong Seafood's Facebook Conducting Polls

of the Fish & Co Facebook page have been very adventurous in trying new presentation styles and are extremely versatile with their combination of contents. Its experience also has lessons for other users experimenting in new contents. Not too long ago, Fish & Co had posted an insensitive advertisement (Singapore: Fish restaurant apologises for riot advert, 2013) on its Facebook page, resulting in a barrage of negative comments and bad publicity. By promptly apologizing and modifying its content, Fish & Co has recovered quickly from the negative publicity and the fan base reached 50,000 fans not long after.

A final example of the second group of restaurant Facebook users is Uncle Leong Seafood which posts polls almost weekly (Figure 2). They prefer to post polls to receive many likes, comments and sharings from fans, achieving an engagement rate of 4%, comparable to that of Target which is an international retail enterprise, ranked 36th on the Fortune 500 list. Thus, it appears that conducting polls using the Facebook page can be an effective way to enlist, engage and interact with fans who may subsequently become customers patronizing the restaurant. Indeed, an active Facebook page with high interactive content is one of the main criteria that helps Uncle Leong Seafood to clinch its first Singapore Quality Brand Award.

Pastamania, Standing Sushi Bar, Sushi Tei, and The Connoisseur Concerto belong to the third group of restaurant Facebook users. They focused on using Facebook to retain old fans (customers) as well as to attract new ones with their interesting and creative contents.

To attract customers, Pastamania focused on a good visual branding with impressive cover photos. It has successfully changed the brand logo color to one that is more eye-catching. It has also not forgotten about responding to customers' queries and comments by providing replies to almost every post within one day. It has also used the social media (screenshots shown in Figure 3) to project an image of a caring employer. This has attracted the attention of the main media such as newspapers (Chin *et al.,*), which helped to boost their brand image further and free of charge. The active use of social media like Facebook since 2010 has helped Pastamania in expanding its business. Enhanced capability to retain old customers and to attract new customers has encouraged and facilitated Pastamania to open about two new outlets per year.

Equally savvy in using the Facebook post to promote its business is Standing Sushi Bar, a chain of restaurants offering Japanese cuisine since 2009. In particular, the Facebook posts are used extensively to highlight all the discounts customers can enjoy if they were to join the several social media platforms initiated by the restaurant. Standing Sushi Bar Facebook posts are not shy to ask for more 'like' votes from customers and fans (Figure 4). It has been able to capitalize on topical events in the community to promote its image. The screenshot in Figure 5 uploaded the photo of an interview of new entrants into the political arena held in the restaurant has gained publicity beyond the social media when items were being consumed

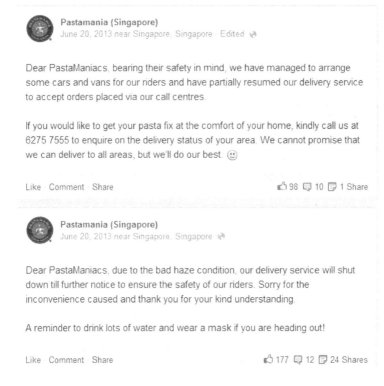

Figure 3:   Pastamania's Facebook Post Appeared in the Newspaper

during the interview became opportunities to advertise and promote products. The team managing the Facebook posts is able to handle the large volume of posts and respond to most of them quickly. The successful use of Facebook posts could be attributed to the leadership and experience of the restaurant founder who used to be active in the Technology industry.

Figure 6 shows the Facebook post by the restaurant, Sushi Tei. It looks ordinary, but it illustrates another productive use of the Facebook post. Sushi Tei has made use of Facebook to give coupons to customers. The restaurant is willing to pay for features and specialized services such as deals coordinated or operated by other companies. Such features and specialized services are integrated into the restaurant's Facebook page. Sushi Tei has actively explored

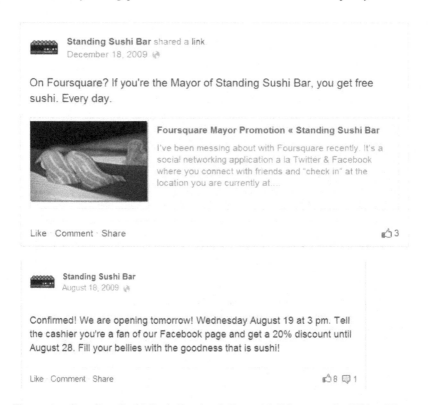

Figure 4: Standing Sushi Bar's Facebook Post with Discounts for Liking Them

Facebook's new features, such as the highlight feature on Timeline to respond to the queries and suggestions of fans. This makes their page more dynamic as Sushi Tei is able to visually highlight contents that fans want to engage with (Gaspar, 2012).

Figure 7 provides another example of a creative use of Facebook post. The Connoisseur Concerto (TCC) is the leading chain of art boutique cafès boasting a comprehensive selection of gourmet food and creative beverages. TCC has managed to attract many new fans by creating and introducing games on the Facebook app platform. The promise of an immersive game experience has sharply increased TCC engagement rate to 4.6%, and through continuously improving their technical and communicative skills, TCC has been able to respond quickly to fans. It has helped to expand its customer base and maintain its competitiveness in the industry.

Standing Sushi Bar
May 12, 2011

SSB's manager Crystal conducting the Chinese interview for Channel 8 about the Nicole Seah and Tin Pei Ling sushi rolls. Her first time speaking to the media!

Like · Comment · Share   👍 11 💬 7

Figure 5:   Standing Sushi Bar's Facebook Post Being Featured in the Newspaper

Sushi Tei Singapore commented on a link.
July 30, 2012

1-for-1 deal at our Tampines 1 outlet from 27 July to 6 Aug 2012!

http://www.facebook.com/hot-deals-details.aspx?id=69
www.facebook.com

Like · Comment · Get Notifications   👍 9 💬 6

Figure 6:   Sushi Tei's Facebook Post which Offers Deals on Facebook

Figure 7: The Connoisseur Concerto's Facebook and Gaming Apps Strategy

5.2. *Twitter*

Twitter is an online social networking service that enables users to send and read short 140-character messages called "tweets". Twitter is a social media like Facebook, but is quite different in at least two ways. Firstly, Twitter is mainly text-based with a character limit which focuses on convenience and ease of use. Secondly, Twitter is known as "the SMS of the Internet" (Curtis, 2013), which emphasizes interaction with each other using features such as Re-tweet (@) to reply to each other's tweets and hashtag (#) to tag tweets so that strangers or newcomers can search for topics and can be made aware of issues people are talking about. However, the level of Re-tweet is relatively low across all four Twitter using merchants in the current study.

Restaurant Botak Jones has posts in both Twitter and Facebook. In fact, it links the Twitter posts with the Facebook posts. While this appears as a strategy to cast the net as wide as possible to engage more potential customers, it may not be an effective approach in practice. This is especially so when the contents posted in the two networks are the same. Customers and fans will have little or no motivation to follow them on both media. It is important for content providers to understand the characteristics and idiosyncrasies of the users of each media and tailored the contents accordingly to achieve their business objectives.

In Figure 8, Botak Jones posted several tweets to solicit for response from fans/followers. However, there is hardly any response. One possible explanation may be that Botak Jones approach with

Figure 8:   Botak Jones' Twitter Profile which Shows No Interaction Despite Many Followers

colored photos to profile its image is better served by Facebook in contrast to the 'text-only' option used in Twitter. The fan base of Botak Jones Twitter post could be miniscule or simply fans are thinking that Botak Jones is more active on Facebook and so they do not actually log into Twitter to response (Heitz, 2013).

Sakae Sushi's effort in the use of Twitter to introduce its product is commendable but may frustrate some potential customers yearning for more detail. In Figure 9, the Tweets put up by Sakae Sushi are curtailed or ended abruptly due to the limitation of 140 characters allowed for each tweet.

An example of restaurant Twitter post using features like Re-tweet "@" or hashtag "#" is that of the TungLok Group. Usage of such features, such as the hashtags has the advantage of reaching out to people who are not their followers, because hashtags messages

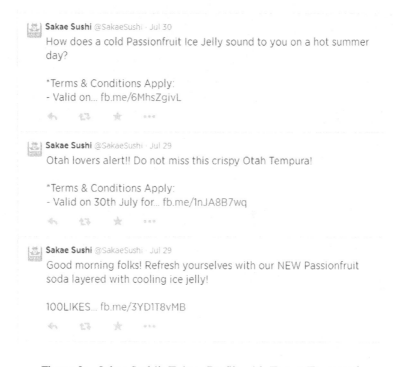

Figure 9: Sakae Sushi's Twitter Profile with Tweets Truncated

can be read by everyone with access to Twitter. The use of hashtags for Twitter marketing purposes has increased steadily in the last few years.[2] Marketing gurus like Mark Burgess claims that *"hashtags function like a lighthouse to attract Twitter users to content that may be of interest."*

Standing Sushi Bar, an avid Facebook user alluded to in the previous section is also an adept user of Twitter in building up a large number of followers. This is in contrast to Botak Jones which also has posts in both Twitter and Facebook. As a means of overcoming the restriction on number of characters in each tweet, Standing Sushi Bar has stood out by not referencing itself directly but still subtly influencing its followers with its interesting and thought-provoking content (Zarrella, 2012). For example, in the month of June 2014, 3 out of 7 posts do not contain any reference to the restaurant. This has the effect of arousing curiosity of followers and fans to find out who is behind the posts and eventually achieving a higher 'hit' rate than otherwise.[3] Standing Sushi Bar also introduces 'unusual phrase' in the tweets and resulting in higher number of re-tweets. An example of this is in Figure 10.

Standing Sushi Bar @standingsushi · Aug 29

Hmm, someone just made reservations with the name Monica Lewinsky and a clearly fake email address. I wonder who (if anyone) will show up.

Figure 10:   Standing Sushi Bar's Tweet Containing Unusual Phrase or Words

---

[2]A good review can be found in Blakley, J. (2012). 12 Tips for effective twitter hashtag marketing. *POSTANO*. Available at: http://www.postano.com/blog/12-tips-for-effective-twitter-hashtag-marketing.

[3]According to past research, there is a negative correlation between self-reference and number of followers (Zarrella, 2012). Also, uncommon words in the tweets would get re-tweet more often (Stelzner, 2009).

This example contains the unusual words like "Monica Lewinsky" and it garnered five re-tweets. The more they are being re-tweeted, the more likely that the re-tweets will be re-tweeted. This set up a chain reaction which multiplies its exposure in the media for greater marketing benefits.

5.3. Instagram

Instagram is an online mobile photo-sharing, video-sharing and social networking service that enables its users to take pictures and videos, and share them on a variety of social networking platforms, such as Facebook and Twitter.

Instagram is different from Facebook, because 50% of the photos uploaded by Instagrammers are those on food instead of self-portraits (Thomas, 2013). Thus, Instagram is definitely a network in which F&B merchants should pay more attention. Currently Instagram is actually the least common among F&B merchants. Compared to Twitter, Instagram is similar with @ and # functions, except Instagram is not text-based. One notable strength of Instagram is its role in keeping F&B merchants on the ball. Photos of the same product can be posted on Instagram daily by various consumers. Discrepancies in look and lack of uniformity in quality will be noticed quite quickly. Thus, Instagram not only fulfills the marketing function, but also ensures the Make (excellent products) is maintained.

In this study, the experiences of the Restaurant Division of the BreadTalk Group Limited, and the Paradise Group, in the use of Instagram are considered.

BreadTalk Group Limited's Restaurant Division, which consists of Din Tai Fung (offering mainly Dim Sum) and RamenPlay (rice and noodle), opened 10 stores in 2013. Din Tai Fung enjoys strong patronage with 18 outlets in Singapore and the one outlet in Thailand. RamenPlay has 11 outlets in Singapore in 2013. The quick pace in business expansion is part of the action plan initiated after a thorough business review and re-positioning exercise.

Table 2:   Financial Information on BreadTalk Restaurant Division

	2011	2012	2013
Growth in Operating profits	—	11.76%	21.01%
New outlets	17	21(13 Din Tai Fung, 8 RamenPlay)	29 (18 Din Tai Fung, 11 RamenPlay)
Profitability ratio	—	4.34%	4.46%
Restaurant sales	$77 million	$102.6 million	$122.2 million

Source: Annual Reports, BreadTalk Group Limited, 2014.

In particular, the re-positioning exercise involves the use of Instagram as the key on-line social media to promote the two restaurants. RamenPlay created an Instagram account in 2014, while Din Tai Fung started in 2013. Din Tai Fung appeals to the young customers, and is able to get them feel connected to the brand, largely due to its continual use of social media such as Facebook, Instagram and Weibo, to engage and interact with them. The good experience for Din Tai Fung in the use of Instagram has encouraged the replication of the same approach for RamenPlay. Favorable financial performance has been registered. As indicated in Table 2, the combined sales revenue has increased by 19.1% increase in 2013 to reach S$122.2 million, accounting for 22.8% of Group's revenue. In 2012, the profitability ratio[4] is close to the 4% average profitability ratio in the restaurant sector in 2012 (DOS, ESS 2012).[5] It has managed to sustain and improve its profitability performance in 2013.

Figure 11 provides an example of the typical RamenPlay's Instagram post. In the design of the post, it has used colour combination that is proven to be effective in encouraging higher shopping rates (Gillett, 2014). Besides the usual marketing pronouncements, it strives to engage customers and followers to provide feedback on recipes. It has helped to garner many followers by investing efforts

---

[4]Profitability ratio is operating profit divide by operating expenses.
[5]Department of Statistics, *Economic Survey of Services: Food and Beverage Sector*, 2012.

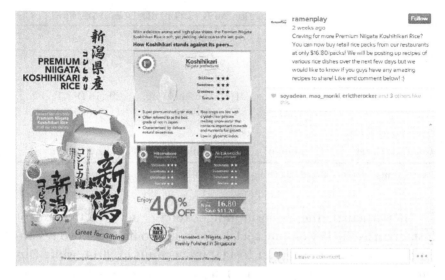

Figure 11: RamenPlay's Instagram Post with Call-to-Action

into writing descriptions about each photo uploaded and nudge followers to take action to respond with 'likes' and comments.

Engaging the drawing power of celebrities to raise the awareness and popularity of the restaurant is also practiced in the posting of Instagram. In Figure 12, Din Tai Fung has engaged celebrities such as Tosh Rock from the film *Ah Boys To Men* to take Instagram photos with their food. Din Tai Fung and RamenPlay have won the 2013 Top Brand Restaurant award. The victory is no less due to their accessible and creative Instagram and Facebook pages. Their spokesperson also concurred that strong social media presence and frequent engagement with online media are important contributing factors for winning the award (Boh, 2013).

Another example of a restaurant using Instagram in promoting its business and customer base is the Paradise Group. The Paradise Group uses a lot of hashtags (#) in the Instagram posts. Instagram hashtags do not just stay within the platform. When someone shares the Instagram content to Facebook, the Instagram hashtag is published along with it. This means the content has a better chance of being discovered by other fans who may not have originally seen the

Figure 12: Din Tai Fung's Instagram Post with Publicity by Celebrities

image or who are searching for the hashtag with Facebook's Graph Search. As alluded to in the section on Twitter, the use of hashtags can possibly help to increase brand recognition and extent the restaurant reach to a wider base of customers. Small business owners who are new to Instagram tend to make two mistakes when it comes to using hashtags: using too many hashtags and using irrelevant hashtags.[6]

Figure 13 shows an example of the Paradise Group Instagram post with hashtags. There is perceptible increase in the revenue of the Paradise Group, but that cannot be solely attributed to the use of Instagram. The performance could possibly be better if Paradise Group can complement its use of social media by having a Facebook account. This would enable it to monitor and evaluate the effectiveness of the hashtags strategy based on Instagram.

---

[6]For a good introductory review, see Sornoso E. 2014 How to use instagram hashtags to expand your reach. Available at: http://www.socialmediaexaminer.com/instagram-hashtags/.

Figure 13: Paradise Group's Instagram Post with #

6. Results & Findings of a Consumer Survey

The consumer survey contains the responses of 66 people based on their visitation or awareness of the above 88 F&B establishments. By virtue of being relatively more active using social media, students make up 59% of the total respondents.[7] Working adults constitute 38% of the total and homemakers make up the remaining 3%.

Each of the 66 respondents has a Facebook account. In addition to Facebook, respondents can be subscribers to other social media. 53% of the respondents have Google+ accounts; 44% have Instagram accounts; 26% have Twitter accounts; and 21% do engage in blogging. 9% of the respondents do visit '*Hungrygowhere*', a popular food-related website. Some 8% of the respondents do have Forum accounts to read and voice their opinions.

The duration in which respondents made use of the social media (Facebook, Twitter and Instagram) is shown in Figure 14.

---

[7] *Singapore Business Review*, (5 important statistics about Facebook users in Singapore, 2012). 17 September 2012. Available at: http://sbr.com.sg/leisure-entertainment/news/5-important-statistics-about-facebook-users-in-singapore.

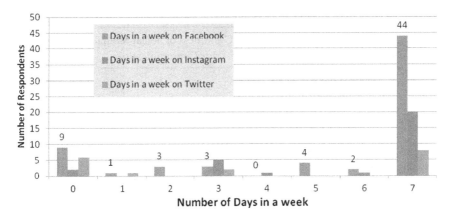

Figure 14:   Time Spent on Social Media

About 67% of the respondents use Facebook daily. Almost similar percentage (69%) is recorded for Instagrammers. In contrast, only 47% of the Tweeters access their Twitter account daily.

The respondents are divided broadly into three groups. Group 1 includes people who are active on social media sites of the 88 F&B merchants (21); Group 2 includes people who had patronized one or more of these 88 F&B establishments (40) and lastly Group 3 which includes people who have social media accounts but have yet to patronise the 88 F&B establishments (5). All respondents are asked to rate the usefulness of social media as a platform for communication on a scale of 1 (least important) to 10 (most important). Table 3 presents the results. It indicates that people who are already members in the communication circle or have visited the selected restaurants give a relatively higher score of importance for social media for interaction. As such restaurant social media users have to accord them with due attention and efforts in addressing their complaints and suggestions. In short, it shows social media do influence customer satisfaction and return visits.

Figure 15 provides information on how satisfied are the consumers with the response furnished by the restaurants using social media for interaction and communications. Only 19% of the respondents give a score 8 or higher (Maximum is 10). There is still

Table 3:   Usefulness of Social Media

	Usefulness of Social Media for Communication
Groups 1 & 2 (61)	7.1
Group 3 (5)	5.4
Average	7

Note: Scores between 1 and 10 with 10 representing maximum level of usefulness.

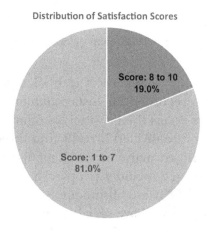

Distribution of Satisfaction Scores

Figure 15:   Level of Satisfaction Relating to Restaurants' Responses to Queries and Complaints Posted on Social Media

Note: Scores between 1 and 10 with 10 representing the highest level of satisfaction.

room for improvement if the target is to have four out of five consumers give a score of eight and higher.

Probing into the reasons for being dissatisfied reveals a few issues worthy of attention: (1) slow response by restaurants to queries and comments. Not directly related to the issue of satisfaction but relating to the effectiveness of social media in expanding business, are the issues: (2) lack of awareness about F&B presence in social media; (3) lack of appropriate skill and strategies in attracting and retaining customers. We shall consider each of the issues in greater depth.

Issue #1: Merchants are slow to react to feedback provided by customers on Facebook, which reflects the importance of Management of the 8Ms. This does not contribute positively in the building of a strong and large consumer base and may adversely affect the revenue stream in the long run.

Empirical Supports
We draw on the data from the consumer survey to discuss and validate this issue. (a) Among the 21 respondents who have posted on Facebook pages, 11 remembered getting a response from the restaurants. Out of these 11, only 5 received a reply within one day; and one day is the expected time for customers. Some had waited a week to get a response from merchants; (b) Response times are not uniform for different kinds of questions; (c) there are 10 cases of no response, or 48% of the total queries that expect replies.

Possible reasons
There could be valid explanations for the slow response. (a) Popular merchants have many fans on Facebook, and hence they were unable to respond to all questions, complaints and feedback promptly. Thus, customers were unhappy about the slow reply if they do ultimately receive response, or may be utterly upset if no response at all.

(b) Due to changes in Facebook features, some merchants might not know how to use the new features resulting in delayed response. Some technical competence is required in understanding the features and using them effectively in the social media platform.

(c) Due to the variety of posts such as complaints, queries or reviews, different posts may require different methods of handling and some are more time-consuming.

Possible remedies
Some suggestions can be made to address the issue.

(1) F&B merchants can allocate more employees to take care of Facebook replies and Twitter replies (@). Using social media is

a relatively cheaper means to attract and retain customers; a successful social media presence is worth the additional manpower investment.

(2) Trade associations, training providers, and vendors can organize courses on customers' relationship management- handling feedback from Facebook and Twitter.

Issue #2: Customers are not aware of F&B merchants' presence on social media sites, which means the Messages that merchants want to carry across did not reach their target readers and followers. This is a 'leakage' that should be plugged if merchants' investments in social media are not wasted.

Empirical Supports
Satisfaction Level about F&B presence in social media; Considering the responses of the 40 people in Group 2, 20 of them who are on Facebook and patrons of local F&B establishments, are unaware that the establishments they patronized do have webpages on social media sites. This is ironic when the majority of people in Groups 1 & 2 believe in the importance of social media and are active on social media (Refer to Figure 16), yet were unaware of the social media presence of the restaurants reflect the low level of publicity and visibility efforts made by the F&B owners in the social media.

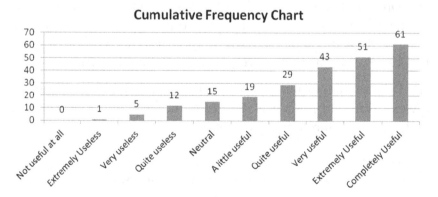

Figure 16: Survey Results from Group 1 & 2 Respondents on Usefulness of Social Media

Possible reasons

The level of sophistication in the use of social media in the F&B industry in Singapore is still relatively low. Despite frequent updates and professional layout, most of the posts on the social media is simply information for dissemination, the publicity and marketing perspective is weak.

Possible remedies

(1) Merchants should visit successful Facebook pages and Instagram accounts of other merchants to learn from them.

(2) Merchants could attend relevant training courses or engage the right expertise to assist them with making better use of social media.

Issue #3: Related to the previous issue on publicity, merchants after making forays into social media, they lack skill and strategies in retaining the attention of the followers.

Generally, the incentives offered by the restaurants are not generous enough. There is uncertainty and ambivalence in the business

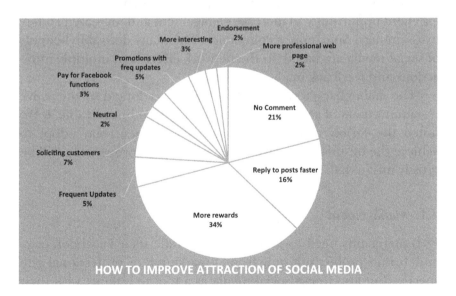

Figure 17:   Survey Results on Features/Contents on Social Media Attract Customers

strategy of treating the participation in the social media as a form of advertisement (hence a cost incurring activity) or social media as a long term revenue generating channel.

Empirical Support
Gleaning on the information from the survey on what features will improve the contact rate with customers (Figure 17). 34% of the respondent would like to do so if more tangible benefits are being offered by merchants using the social media.

Possible reasons
Local F&B merchants face are still experimenting with how to use social media effectively (Kotler and Armstrong).

Possible remedies
The remedies suggested for Issue #2 are equally relevant for Issue #3.

7. Recommendations

In summary, social media can be a powerful media to provide an excellent opportunity to increase engagement and increase productivity amongst Singapore's companies. The many derivable benefits of social media are based on the network effects and multiple interactions and feedback made possible.

The main characteristics of the strategies adopted by the active restaurant users of social media are summarized in the Table 4. We noted the variety of approaches an establishment may adopt to achieve the business objective. A 'one-size fit all' proposition will be grossly misguided.

7.1. Management

F&B merchants need to know how to handle their Facebook page and Twitter profile, not only from a marketing or professional perspective but also to use social media as a tool to interact with their fans and followers. There exist also pitfalls in the use of social media.

Table 4: Main Features Adopted in the Social Media Use by F&B Enterprises

	F&B Enterprise	Social Media	Characteristics/Key features
1	Peach Garden	Facebook	Prompt response; customers contact (emails); obtained to expand consumer base.
2	Toast Box	Facebook	Reply every single post within one working day.
3	Botak Jones	Facebook	Solicit views of customers and use the information for product development.
4	The Soup Spoon	Facebook	Hosting contests to interact with customers/fans.
5	Dancing Crab (TungLok Group)	Facebook	30% discount on the dining bill when 'like'.
6	Fish & Co	Facebook	Trying new presentation styles and are extremely versatile with their combination of contents.
7	Uncle Leong Seafood	Facebook	Conducting polls almost weekly. Able to maintain customers' interest.
8	Pastamania	Facebook	Good visual branding with impressive cover photos. reply to almost every post within one day.
9	Standing Sushi Bar	Facebook	Highlight all the discounts customers can enjoy. Opportune use of topical events.
10	Sushi Tei	Facebook	Give coupons to customers; willing to pay for features and specialized services such as deals coordinated or operated by other companies.

(*Continued*

Table 4: (*Continued*)

	F&B Enterprise	Social Media	Characteristics/Key features
11	The Connoisseur Concerto (TCC)	Facebook	Attract many new fans by creating and introducing games on the Facebook app platform.
12	Botak Jones	Twitter	Many tweets but shows no interaction despite many followers.
13	Sakei Sushi	Twitter	Twitter profile with Tweets truncated due to limitation of 140 characters per tweet.
14	Dancing Crab (TungLok Group)	Twitter	Use of hashtags (#); possibilities of post messages reaching out to people who are not their followers.
15	Standing Sushi Bar	Twitter	Circumvent limitation on 140 characters in each tweets by not referencing itself directly and use of thought-provoking content, unusual phrase or words.
16	BreadTalk Group (Din Dai Fung & RamenPlay)	Instagram — emphasis on photos	— Good color combination that encourage higher shopping propensity; — engage customers and followers to provide feedback on recipes; — writing descriptions about photos uploaded; — engaging the drawing power of celebrities.
17	Paradise Group	Instagram — emphasis on photos	uses a lot of hashtags (#) in the Instagram posts.

Online interactions can violate professional boundaries, and depending on the indiscretion could potentially result in disciplinary action and loss of business (Mansfield *et al.*, 2011).

Gleaning from the analysis of the social media practices of restaurants considered in the current study, the general level of sophistication of social media usage among restaurants is not high. It will be a beneficial investment by the restaurant owners to upgrade the skills of their workers engaged in maintaining the restaurant social media page or websites. Media consultants or mentors can be engaged to give advice to restaurants using social media as a tool for business expansion and productivity improvement. To facilitate improvement, the government in collaboration with private training institutions, could design relevant courses for workers to develop, train and upgrade social media application skill. The relevant agencies could also provide guidelines and supporting policies for the use of social media.

Social media presence does provide opportunities for F&B enterprises to improve productivity. Infrastructure for social media is already in place an Internet-ready economy of Singapore and thus the cost of linking up to social media is relatively low. Social media would be able to improve productivity through:

- *Management*: Merchants could set up a Facebook Page for the purpose of answering customers promptly and updating them with news daily. Thus, they either have to hire the right people or owners will have to teach themselves about functions on Facebook such as private messaging and posts. If done correctly, adopting the appropriate strategies that suit the resources available, merchants can quite quickly reach a pool of fans and customers. Merchants can also set up a Twitter profile, to find out what people are saying about them and to analyze their performance. Trade associations could also do their part, such as organizing courses on customer relationship management-handling feedback from Facebook and Twitter.
- *Money*: Facebook, Twitter and Instagram are relatively cheaper, unlike expensive ads in traditional media like newspapers or

televisions. Anyone with a mobile device and Internet connection can see whatever message SMEs want to broadcast to fans and customers. Facebook pages, Twitter profiles and Instagram accounts are also easy to set up, with updates being shown more clearly. Using social media can allow SMEs to circumvent the cost of publicity through traditional media (Skoric and Poor, 2013). The Government could alleviate the cost of training with subsidies and grants depending on scale of program and affordability of enterprises and workers.

- *Message*: Messages must be timely and relevant. With traditional media, there can be extensive time lags of days or even months. But with Facebook and Twitter, content is instantaneous and there is immediate dispensing of information. Merchants can look forward to connecting their brand with their fans in a continuous manner. Information management is not a trivial matter. Over the internet, news travel at the speed of light. When an image enhancing page, post or video went viral, it will be welcomed with much joy. However, an inadvertent mistake can also go viral threatening costly public image disaster. Hence, there is a need to cultivate a pool of loyal customers who will speak up for the restaurant in time of negative publicity or crisis. Social media can dissipate attention away from bad reputation and negative publicity submitting supportive testimonials help to dispel allegations of poor hygiene at the restaurant.

The advantages of the social media in fostering business expansion and productivity improvement are many. However, to enjoy the benefits, efforts have to be made, financial resources have to be allocated and users have to be willing to learn the new skill and techniques and apply them appropriately. We suggest that a more concerted effort be made by the merchants and government agencies to have intensive and intelligent use of social media to achieve objectives of business viability and productivity upgrading.

References

A Performance Guide on Singapore's 'Groupon clones' scene — Part 2 of 2 (2010, October 29). Available at: http://www.youngupstarts.com/2010/10/29/a-performance-guide-on-singapore%E2%80%99s-%E2%80%98groupon-clones%E2%80%99-scene-%E2%80%93-part-2-of-2/.

asiaone. (2011, March 17). *The Straits Times*, 17 March. Available at: http://news.asiaone.com/News/AsiaOne+News/Singapore/Story/A1Story 20110316-268495.html.

Bai, B., Law, R. and Wen, I. (2008). The impact of website quality on customer satisfaction and purchase intentions: Evidence from Chinese online visitors. *International Journal of Hospitality Management*, 27(3), 391.

Blocker, C.P., Flint, D.J., Myers, M.B. and Slater, S.F. (2011). Proactive customer orientation and its role for creating customer value in global markets. *Journal of the Academy of Marketing Science*, 39(2), 216.

Boh, S. (2013). *Din Tai Fung among top brands with Gen Y.* 28 November. Available at: http://mypaper.sg/news/din-tai-fung-among-top-brands-gen-y-20131128.

Bosua, R., Evans, N. and Sawyer, J. (2013). Social networks, social media and absorptive capacity in regional Small and Medium Enterprises (SMES) in Australia. *Australian and International Journal of Rural Education*, 23(1), 117.

BreadTalk Group Limited (2011). *Annual Report.*

BreadTalk Group Limited (2012). *Annual Report.*

BreadTalk Group Limited (2013). *Annual Report.*

Carr, D.F. (2012). McKinsey's Trillion-Dollar Social Prediction. *InformationWeek*, 10, 3 August.

Chan, D. (2014, May 30). *Higher impairment charge worsens losses of Tung Lok Restaurants. Available at: http://www.straitstimes.com/news/business/companies/story/higher-impairment-charge-worsens-losses-tung-lok-restaurants-20140530#sthash.3KKai1Or.dpuf;* http://www.straitstimes.com/news/business/companies/story/higher-impairment-charge-worsens-losses-tung-lok-restaurants-20140530.

Chin, D., Wong, L. and Ong, A. (2013, June 21). *Haze update: Firms provide help for employees working outdoors. Available at: http://www.straitstimes.com/breaking-news/singapore/story/haze-update-firms-provide-help-employees-working-outdoors-20130621?itemid=630#sthash.8Y6ArsiW.dpuf;* http://www.

straitstimes.com/breaking-news/singapore/story/haze-update-firms-provide-help-employees-working-outdoors-20130621?itemid=630.

Cohen, D. (2013, September 25). *STUDY: How Fortune 500 Companies Use Instagram.* Available at: http://allfacebook.com/trackmaven-study-for-tune-500-instagram_b125447.

Curtis, S. (2013). *Twitter claims 15m active users in the UK.* The Telegraph, 6 September. Available at: http://www.telegraph.co.uk/technology/twitter/10291360/Twitter-claims-15m-active-users-in-the-UK.html.

Eat the Nicole Seah Sushi Roll at this sushi bar (2011, April 27). Available at: http://news.asiaone.com/News/AsiaOne+News/Singapore/Story/A1Story20110427-275981.html.

(2014). *Fast Forward Trends Report 2014.* Singapore: Weber Shandwick.

Felix, S. (2012). *The 20 Most-Liked Facebook Companies Ever. Businessinsider* 7 August. Available at: http://www.businessinsider.com/the-20-most-liked-companies-on-facebook-2012-8?IR=T&op=1.

Food & Beverage Services (2012). *Services Survey Series,* 4.

Gaspar, M.A. (2012, March 13). *5 Facebook Timeline Features that Drive Better Engagement.* Available at: http://blog.himss.org/2012/03/13/five-facebook-timeline-features-driving-better-engagement/.

Gilbert, J. (2013, September 13). *Twitter, by the numbers.* Retrieved from News Yahoo: http://news.yahoo.com/twitter-statistics-by-the-numbers-153151584.html.

Gillett, R. (2014, April 22). *How The Most Successful Brands Dominate Instagram, and You can Too.* Available at: http://www.fastcompany.com/3029395/bottom-line/how-the-most-successful-brands-dominate-instagram-and-you-can-too.

Goh, K.-y., Heng, C.-s. and Zhijie, L. (2013, March). Social media brand community and consumer behavior: Quantifying the relative impact of user- and marketer-generated content. *Information Systems Research,* 24(1), 88–107.

Gross, D. (2012). *Which companies respond quickest (or not at all) on Facebook?* CNN, 27 March. Available at: http://edition.cnn.com/2012/03/27/tech/social-media/retailers-facebook-questions/.

Groupon and its Competitors in Singapore (2011, April 11). Available at: http://www.incitez.com/blog/daily-deal-websites-singapore.

Heitz, B. (2013, November 19). *Why You Shouldn't Link Your Company's Facebook Account to Twitter.* Available at: http://www.socialmediatoday.com/content/why-you-shouldnt-link-your-companys-facebook-account-twitter.

Hempel, J. (2014, July). Instagram is ready to take its shot. *Fortune*, 10, 40–44.

Ho, V. (2014). *Groupon clones ditch business model*. The Business Times, 25 February. Available at: http://mypaper.sg/top-stories/groupon-clones-ditch-business-model-20140225.

5 important statistics about Facebook users in Singapore (2012). *The Straits Times*, 17 September. Available at: http://sbr.com.sg/leisure-entertain-ment/news/5-important-statistics-about-facebook-users-in-singapore.

Interview: Eldwin Chua CEO, Paradise Group (2012). *Biz Daily*, 30 May. Available at: http://bizdaily.com.sg/newsite/biz-interview-eldwin-chua-ceo-paradise-group/.

Jackson, L. (2014). *Retailers With the Most Facebook and Twitter Followers*. Wall Street, 1 April. Available at: http://247wallst.com/retail/2014/04/01/retailers-with-the-most-facebook-and-twitter-followers/.

Kerin, R., Lau, G. T., Hartley, S. and Rudelius, W. (2010). *Marketing in Asia, 2nd Edition*. McGraw Hill, New York.

Kotler, P. and Armstrong, G. (n.d.). *Principles of Marketing: Global Edition* (15e ed.). Pearson, New Jersey.

Kwong, C. (2014). *Waiter, There's a Roach in My Soup*. The New Paper, 31 January. Available at: http://news.asiaone.com/news/soshiok/waiter-theres-roach-my-soup.

Leiker, M. (2011). When to 'friend' a patient: Social media tips for health care professionals. *Wisconsin Medical Journal*, 110(1), 42–43.

Leow, B. (n.d.). *The Soup Spoon*. Available at: http://www.alplayservice.com/soup-spoon.html.

Liem, D. (2010, September 14). *5 Great Facebook Page Examples from Singapore*. Available at: http://www.happymarketer.com/5-great-facebook-page-examples-singapore.

Lo, H. (2012, July 11). *For brands, Groupons can mean bad reviews*. Available at: http://www.zdnet.com/for-brands-groupons-can-mean-bad-reviews-7000000631/.

Mansfield, S. J., Morrison, S. G., Stephens, H. O., Bonning, M. A., Wang, S. H., Withers, A. H., *et al.* (2011). Social media and the medical profession. *Medical Journal of Australia*, 194(12), 642–644.

Manyika, J., Chui, M. and Sarrazin, H. (2012). Social media's productivity payoff. *Harvard Business Review*, 21 August.

Mershon, P. (2012, September 6). *Top 10 Small Business Facebook Pages: 2012 Winners!* Available at: https://www.google.com.sg/url?sa=t&rct=j&q=&e src=s&source=web&cd=1&cad=rja&uact=8&ved=0CBsQFjAA&url=http

%3A%2F%2Fwww.socialmediaexaminer.com%2Ftop-10-small-business-facebook-pages-2012-winners%2F&ei=YxnWU5_qIcS9uASG4YLw DQ&usg=AFQjCNG8qeV0HLmyxQkiKK4digrCg.

Mokhtar, M. (2013). *Three hurt in JEM mall ceiling collapse. The Straits Times*, 18 September. Available at: http://www.straitstimes.com/breaking-news/singapore/story/three-injured-after-first-floor-ceiling-jem-mall-collapses-20130918.

Narver, J.C., Slater, S.F. and & Tietje, B.C. (1998). Creating a Market Orientation. *Journal of Market Focused Management*, 2(3), 241–255.

Ng, T. (2011, June 1). *Actress Walks Out on Restaurant, Wait Staff Applauds. Available at: http:// news.asiaone.com/News/Latest+News/SoShiok/Story/ A1Story20110601-281946.html#sthash.V0kpo74b.dpuf*; http://news.asiaone.com/News/Latest+News/SoShiok/Story/A1Story20110601-281946.html [Accessed on 2 August 2014].

Pastamania's recipe for success (2012). *Business Times*, 12 Febraury. Available at: http://www.valuebuddies.com/thread-1834.html.

Rezab, J. (2012, June 20). *70% of Fans Are Being Ignored By Companies — Now what?* Available at: http://www.socialbakers.com/blog/655-70-of-fans-are-being-ignored-by-companies-now-what.

Sakae Holdings Ltd. (2011). *Annual Report*.

Sakae Holdings Ltd. (2013). *Annual Report*.

Select Group Ltd. (2011). *Annual Report*.

Select Group Ltd. (2013). *Annual Report*.

Seow, B.Y. (2014). *3-D art Wows Visitors. The Straits Times*, 13 June. Available at: http://www.straitstimes.com/lifestyle/visual-arts/story/3-d-art-wows-visitors-20140613.

Shetty, D. (2013). *An Hour @ The Museum. The Straits Times*, 15 March. Available at: http://www.stschoolpocketmoneyfund.org.sg/web/media-coverage-article78.php.

Singapore: Fish restaurant apologises for riot advert (2013). *BBC*, 12 December. Available at: http://www.bbc.com/news/blogs-news-from-elsewhere-25335636.

Skoric, M. M., & Poor, N. (2013, April). Youth engagement in Singapore: The interplay of social and traditional media. *Journal of Broadcasting & Electronic Media*, 57(2), 196.

SME One Asia Awardees. (n.d.). Available at: http://www.sme1.asia/paradise-group-holdings.

Soh, A. (2012). *Searching for a 'Souper' Model. The Business Times*, 21 August. Available at: http://bschool.nus.edu/LinkClick.aspx?fileticket=OoJ%2 BTGAADDM%3D&tabid=1771&mid=5732.

Stelzner, M. (2009). *The Marketing Power of the Retweet: An Interview With Dan Zarrella. Socialmediaexaminer,* 12 October. Available at: http://www. socialmediaexaminer.com/the-marketing-power-of-the-retweet-an-interview-with-dan-zarrella.

Tan, K. (2013). *Singapore's Experience Initiatives to Promote e-Participation.* Singapore: Infocomm Development Authority.

Teo, C.W. (2012). *Singapore eateries draw queues in KL suburbs. The Straits Times,* 30 April. Available at: http://www.asianewsnet.net/news-30056. html.

Teo, E. (2013). *ST100: International Food Paradise. The Straits Times,* 31 December. Available at: http://www.straitstimes.com/the-big-story/goodbye-2013-hello-2014/story/st100-international-food-paradise-20131231.

Thomas, O. (2013). *Here's A Delicious Way Facebook Could Profit From Instagram — And Destroy OpenTable And Yelp. Business Insider,* 30 January. Available at: http://www.businessinsider.com/instagram-food-photos-are-a-phenomenon-2013-1?IR=T&.

TungLok Group. (2013). *Annual Report.*

Zarrella, D. (2012). *A Tested Social Media Success Formula: Talk as Yourself, Not About Yourself. Copyblogger,* 9 January. Available at: http://www.copyblogger. com/social-media-success-formula.

Chapter 8

Sufficiency of Marketing Efforts by Singapore SMEs in Retail and Food & Beverage Sectors

1. Introduction

Countries worldwide are pursuing higher economic growth in order to improve the standard of living of their citizens. Singapore is no exception to the rule. Small and Medium-sized Enterprises (SMEs), which make up 99% of the enterprises in Singapore and contribute to nearly half of its GDP,[1] are crucial in improving the growth of the economy. To ensure a sustainable economic growth, firms, including micro-SMEs, have to invest in improving the productivity of their labor and capital. However, it is estimated that about 70% of Singapore's enterprises are micro-SMEs which have a turnover of less than $1 million[2] (The Straits Times, 2014). Thus, majority of local businesses face a resource constraint and thus are unable to invest in improving the productivity of their firms.

Thus, before addressing the issue of productivity, it is foremost that micro-SMEs improve their profitability. With higher profitability, they would have more resources to invest in productivity. One way in which micro-SMEs can improve their profitability is through a

---

[1] Available at: http://www.spring.gov.sg/Pages/Homepage.aspx.
[2] Available at: http://www.straitstimes.com/singapore/some-micro-smes-gradually-restructuring.

refinement of their marketing practices which will result in greater competitiveness. It has been found in past research that SMEs abroad tend to neglect the marketing function in their organizations (Yola Emeksiz and Fatmagul, 2009). Few resources are allocated to the marketing function and marketing often relies on the intuition of the owner–manager. However, marketing is as important to small firms as it is to larger firms in terms of improving financial performance. It is therefore important to examine the gaps in the marketing management of Singapore micro-SMEs before further steps can be taken to improve the productivity of these firms.

1.1. *Objectives*

In this chapter, we will focus on Singapore-based micro-SMEs in the Food and Beverages (F&B) and Retail Sector. The chapter will be exploratory in nature and seek to uncover the existing marketing practices of micro-SMEs. These are the main objectives in this paper:

(a) To determine the common marketing practices of micro-SMEs in the F&B and Retail sector.
(b) To identify the common marketing management gaps present among micro-SMEs in the F&B and Retail sector.
(c) To propose further steps that could be taken to improve the marketing abilities of these firms.

We hope that the findings provide greater insight into the current marketing practices of micro-SMEs in the retail and F&B sector in Singapore and allow us to identify areas in marketing management which can be improved upon. From there, recommendations can be made to encourage the adoption of more effective marketing practices, resulting in an improvement in the competitiveness of firms.

2. Definition of Marketing

Marketing can be defined as managing profitable customer relationships by creating value for customers and capturing value from customers in return (Kotler *et al.*, 2011). To do so, marketers have to understand the market and identify consumers' needs and wants. Consumers' needs and wants are then satisfied through a market offering.

To design a market offering, companies have to first decide which consumers it will serve by dividing the market into segments and selecting one or more segments to target. This is known as market segmentation and targeting. After deciding on its target segment, the company must also decide how it should position itself in the market in order to differentiate itself from its competitors. The positioning of a company is reflected in its value proposition, which is a set of benefits the company promises to deliver to consumers to satisfy their needs. Thus, a unique value proposition will differentiate one company from others in the mind of consumers.

In order to deliver on its value proposition, the company must decide on its marketing mix which comprises of product, price, place and promotion. In other words, the company must create a need-satisfying market offering, decide how much to charge for the marketing offering, decide how it will make the market offering available to its target consumers and communicate with its target consumers about the offering. This is known as the 4Ps of marketing.

Finally, given the central role consumers play in marketing, customer relationship management (CRM) is a crucial aspect of marketing. CRM is the process of the building and maintaining of profitable customer relationships by delivering customer value and satisfaction. More recently, CRM began to involve the management of detailed information about individual customers using sophisticated software and analytical tool in order to maximize customer loyalty.

3. Literature Review

A review of past literature is conducted to understand the general characteristics of SMEs, unearth marketing management gaps that have been found in SMEs located in other countries as well as identify recommended marketing strategies for SMEs. The findings from the literature review will be used to determine the hypotheses of the chapter.

3.1. Characteristics of SMEs

It is widely acknowledged in past literature that SMEs have unique characteristics that set them apart from larger enterprises and thus, they cannot be seen as merely miniature versions of large companies. SMEs are very close to their markets, have a lot of flexibility, have the capacity to operate on slim margins and can make the decisions quickly (Awan and Hashmi, 2014). However, they are characterized by three main limitations, limited resources in terms of financial situation, time and marketing skills, manager's lack of expertise in marketing and the low visibility and impact of the SME in the marketplace (Gilmore, *et al.*, 2001).

As a result of these limitations, SMEs tend to give marketing a low priority (Yolal *et al.*, 2009). In a study of small and medium hotel enterprises (SMHEs) in Turkey (Yolal *et al.*, 2009), it was found that majority of SMHEs (68.9%) plan their general activities such as finance, human resources and production. When marketing planning is analyzed, the rate drops to 47.9%. In addition, research indicates that small firms typically spend modestly on marketing expenditure and utilize few of the available marketing techniques (Marjanova and Stojanovski, 2012). Entrepreneurs also tend to underestimate the importance of marketing (Marjanova and Stojanovski, 2012). Instead, SMEs tend to be focused on sales as a firm's survival is highly dependent on its sales (Awan and Hashmi, 2014). This is supported by a study done by Reijonen (2009) which found that the ultimate aim of marketing for SMEs seemed to be making a sale.

When marketing is carried out in SMEs, it often relies on the intuition and energy of the owner–manager (Yolal *et al.*, 2009). According to literature, marketing in small firms is related to the owner–manager's attitudes, experience of and expertise in marketing (Reijonen, 2009). Thus, small firm marketing is described to be haphazard, informal, loose, unstructured and spontaneous (Reijonen, 2009).

However, marketing is just as important to SMEs as it is to larger firms as Siu *et al.* (2004) found that marketing in the higher performing Taiwanese SMEs seem to enjoy a higher priority than other business functions in corporate planning. The importance of coordinated marketing efforts to SMEs is further highlighted by Fuller (1994) which found that the larger, more profitable firms practice "explicit-sophisticated" marketing which is described as a coordinated program with a clear purpose and objective. However, the smaller, less profitable firm practiced "instinctive-simple" marketing. In addition, Simpson *et al.* (2006) found that "Marketing-Led" SMEs, which are characterized by marketing having a major role in the company and marketing having a major relevance to the company, seemed to have more employees and had significantly greater turnover than other companies. This suggests a positive relationship between marketing activity and financial performance and growth of the companies.

3.2. Marketing management gaps found in SMEs

To begin, it has been suggested in past literature that there is a lack of understanding of marketing among SMEs. In a study conducted by Reijonen (2009), it was found that a little less than a half of the respondents thought that they had enough knowledge about marketing and only a half thought they exploited marketing sufficiently. The respondents also had ambivalent views regarding the scope of marketing as marketing is perceived to comprise solely of promotion and advertising.

There is also consensus among literature that small firms find conducting market research difficult (Marjanova and Stojanovski, 2012) and the market research efforts of SMEs are inadequate. It was found that it was difficult for SMHEs in Turkey to conduct market research due to costs and lack of time (Yolal *et al.*, 2009). In addition, although many SMEs are interested in information on their customers and competitors, only the highly entrepreneurial SMEs are active in information acquisition and utilization (Reijonen, 2009). Most of the SMEs are opportunistic in their information seeking behavior and the main sources of market intelligence appear to be informal (Reijonen, 2009). Gathered data was also not necessarily thoroughly analyzed or shared with personnel within the companies (Reijonen, 2009). Similarly, Parrott *et al.* (2010) argued that even though most SMEs do use information, information was drawn from a very narrow set of sources such as associates and acquaintances and was not in the format to be used effectively. Thus, market information gathered were largely inadequate (Parrott *et al.*, 2010). However, a market-driven approach is needed in order to identity other actors on the market that constitute a threat as well as help small enterprises develop a competitive advantage through increased customer knowledge (Marjanova and Stojanovski, 2012). With extensive market research, firms are better able to understand the market and identify market wants and needs. At the same time, firms are also able to anticipate and react to market competitors to protect and expand market share. Thus, given the benefits of market research to businesses and the potential difficulties small businesses face when conducting market research, it is important to focus our attention on market research as a method of improving the profitability of SMEs.

From the previous chapter, we learnt the advantages of active social media account for businesses. The focus on social media is especially relevant in this time and age, when technology and social media has a significant influence on marketing and the interaction between the company and the consumer. Through a study of local F&B businesses, it was found that many merchants are slow to embrace social media and only certain merchants with tech-savvy owners are able to use social media correctly without guidance (Toh *et al.*, 2014).

3.3. *Recommended marketing strategies for SMEs*

A review of past literature found that innovative marketing is an effective marketing strategy for SMEs. Through a study of 13 SMEs in Multan *et al.* (2014) found that these SMEs achieved success through innovations. Innovative Marketing in SMEs is defined to be much wider than simply product innovation. It covers the whole spectrum of marketing activity within an SME (Awan and Hasmi, 2014). Other than product innovation, innovative marketing may also include innovative pricing tactics, innovative promotional methods and offering an innovative retail environment. The importance of innovative marketing to SMEs is further supported by Siu *et al.* (2004) who found that higher performing Taiwanese SMEs tend to be more innovative than their lower performing counterpart in terms of developing and marketing new products and introducing new ways of doing business. Since the performance of firms sampled by Siu *et al.* (2004) were evaluated based on their profit, sales volume, market share and return on investment, this study implies that innovative marketing improves the competitiveness of a firm and enhances business performance. The importance of innovative marketing is also pointed out in an article published by McKinsey & Company.[3] It is highlighted that consumers will now seek out retailers that provide value in new and different ways. Thus, it is believed that retailers will need to offer consumers an innovative retail experience such as deep product expertize and a unique product education. Additionally, retailers must do these things in an environment that is increasingly experiential.

In addition, it emerged in past literature that relationship marketing is important in improving the performance of small firms. Relationship marketing is defined by Morgan and Hunt as "all marketing activities directed towards establishing, developing and maintaining successful relational exchanges (Palmatier *et al.*, 2006). The focus of relationship marketing is to achieve customer loyalty (Hanley, 2008) which is described by Lovelock *et al.* (1999) as a customer's willingness to continue patronising a firm over the long-term, purchasing and using its goods and services on a repeated and preferably exclusive basis and voluntarily recommending the firm's products to friends and associates. Thus, it can be seen that there is an association between relationship marketing and Word-of-Mouth.

---

[3]Available at: http://www.mckinsey.com/insights/consumer_and_retail/how_retailers_can_keep_up_with_consumers.

Although relationship marketing may consist of different strategies such as store loyalty programs and customer service, it was found that not all RM strategies are equally effective for building relationships (Palmatier *et al.*, 2006). Overall, Palmatier *et al.* (2006) found that expertise and communication are the most effective relationship-building strategies while conflict has the largest absolute impact on customer relationships. This finding supports the importance of resolving problems and disagreements to prevent relationship-damaging conflicts. To add on, in a study of department stores, Hanley (2008) found that consumers place more importance on customer service from friendly and effective staff than on store loyalty schemes. The main reason for customer service having a significant influence on consumers' decision to shop in a store is that it is part of human nature for individuals to be sensitive to the treatment received from others (Hanley, 2008).

Through a study of small retailers in Spain and the UK, Coca-Stefaniak *et al.* (2010) found that these retailers placed a strong emphasis on relationship marketing. It was found that the development of interpersonal relationships between the customers and the shop owners, which can also be seen as part of a relationship marketing strategy, play a vital role as an element of marketing competitiveness for these small retailers (Coca-Stefaniak *et al.*, 2010). Such a relationship marketing strategy is argued to provide small retailers with a sustainable competitive advantage as it would not be easily replicated by larger or global retailers (Coca-Stefaniak *et al.*, 2010).

A review of literature on relationship marketing highlights that it can benefit small retailers to build high quality relationships with customers as relationship quality built with customers can be leveraged to increase a small retailer's market responsiveness when competitive intensity is high (Adjei *et al.*, 2009). Small retailers with high quality customer relationships are more able to identify and match customer demand shifts in a speedy manner. This is supported by Harrigan *et al.* (2009) who argue that SMEs' primary activity in the pursuit of competitive advantage is the development of strong customer relationships. Thus, relationship marketing efforts have been found to have a significant influence on seller objective performance (Palmatier *et al.*, 2006). This finding is supported by a research study of 24 firms from the Danish food catering sector, the Danish dairy sector, the Danish bacon sector and the New Zealand wine sector which gave evidence that relationship quality translates into first customer retention and then shareholder value creation (Lindgreen, 2001). Thus, relationship marketing can be seen to have a positive impact on the business performance of small firms. However, over-reliance on relationship quality creates an inertia effect when market practices are changing by hindering a retailer's ability to adapt to changing market practices (Adjei *et al.*, 2009).

Coca-Stefaniak *et al.* (2010) also found that small retailers in Spain and the UK rely heavily on Word-of-Mouth marketing by satisfied customers. Most small retailers studied viewed Word-of-Mouth marketing as a process leading to sustainable competitive advantage (Coca-Stefaniak *et al.*, 2010). Similarly, a survey ran by Linkdex in the UK and USA[4] found that the most important marketing tool for SME businesses is Word-of-Mouth, with 81% of the companies polled indicating that referrals and recommendations were the most important marketing method. Because Word-of-Mouth is a form of communication initiated by independent actors, it is perceived to be more trustworthy and thus, has a strong influence on consumer decision making (Bulearca and Bulearca, 2010). The business impact of Word-of-Mouth is investigated by WOMMA in a study[5] of top brands such as Frito-Lay and PepsiCo. It was found that Word-of-Mouth is responsible for 13% of all consumer sales, which equates to $6 trillion of annual consumer spending. This highlights the importance of Word-of-Mouth in driving business performance.

Finally, market segmentation is found to be an essential marketing strategy, especially for SMEs. In an interview with Lorraine Twohill,[6] Google's senior vice-president for global marketing, she

---

[4] Available at: http://www.marketingdonut.co.uk/blog/2011/05/word-mouth-tops-survey-sme-marketing.

[5] Available at: http://www.womma.org/ReturnOnWOM.

[6] Available at: http://www.mckinsey.com/insights/marketing_sales/how_google_breaks_through.

highlighted that marketing is about "knowing the user, knowing the magic, and connecting the two" (McKinsey and Company, 2015). Knowing the user means understanding who your consumers are, who your customers are, what they need, and understanding how the company can help them. Marketers should also understand what the company's engineers and product managers are building and thus, bring the company's products to consumers in a relevant, meaningful and compelling manner. What Lorraine Twohill is referring to is the process of market segmentation, targeting and positioning. As customers become increasingly diverse due to variations in customer needs and buying behaviour (Dibb, 1998; Dibb and Simkin, 1991), companies have found it essential to move away from a mass marketing approach to a target marketing strategy. Customers are first segmented according to their needs and buying behavior. Choices about which segments are the most appropriate to serve can then be made, thus making the best of finite resources (Dibb, 1998). Careful and creative segmentation of the market can enable companies to identify market opportunities. Thus, market segmentation can be used by minor players in the market to gain a foothold in a particular niche (Dibb and Simkin, 1991). For market segmentation to be most effective, firms should identify segments using basis variables such as customer needs and benefits sought which describe why customers respond differently (Lilien *et al.*, 2013). In addition, marketers should also ensure that segments choose are identifiable, large enough to be profitable, accessible and stable (Dibb and Simkin, 1991).

The usefulness of market segmentation to small businesses to enter a market is well supported in past literature. The niching strategy, which refers to the concentration of resources to fulfill the unmet needs of a particular market segment, is a widely recommended strategy for SMEs as SMEs will be able to avoid competitive reaction from bigger firms (Lee *et al.*, 2001). Through a study of small local grocery retailers in China *et al.* (2015) showed that the Chinese latecomers' success in the grocery retailing market relies on their effective strategy to target the niche market, hence, helping them to avoid head-on competition with their foreign counterparts.

However, evidence of how market segmentation works in practice raises two fundamental concerns: businesses which believe they are applying a market segmentation approach may not necessarily be doing so and marketers who are following the prescribed steps may not be achieving results which can be implemented (Dibb, 1998). First, marketers may fail to consider that segments must be meaningful to customers and not just to the business (Dibb, 1998). This may result in the formation of customer segments that do not consist of customers with homogeneous needs and buying behavior. The second problem associated with market segmentation is that in the collection of segment data and the development of suitable marketing programmes for the segments, marketers may overlook the attractiveness of the customer segments to the company (Dibb, 1998). Thus, it is helpful to maintain an awareness of segmentation success factors (Dibb, 1998). In addition, market segmentation advocates insist that like any marketing planning activity, segmentation analysis should have a long time horizon (Dibb, 1998). Thus, segmentation should begin with a clear analysis of customer needs and buyer behavior, examine the competitive and wider trading environments and result in consistent marketing programs that are implemented over time.

4. Hypotheses

The list of hypotheses outlines the potential marketing management gaps that may exist among Singapore micro-SMEs in the Retail and F&B sector, given findings uncovered in past literature. This chapter will adopt a two-pronged approach. On one hand, we will explore whether deficiencies in marketing practices of SMEs in other countries are also present among Singapore micro-SMEs. On the other, we will also look into whether Singapore micro-SMEs are lacking in undertaking recommended marketing strategies for SMEs. Each of these hypotheses is chosen due to the potential each marketing strategy holds in improving the profitability of micro-SMEs.

4.1. *Hypotheses*

H1. Singapore micro-SMEs in the retail and F&B sector have a poor understanding of marketing.

Past literature suggests a lack of understanding of marketing among SMEs. A more thorough understanding of marketing among SMEs will allow them to better exploit marketing to improve their profitability.

H2a. Singapore micro-SMEs in the retail and F&B sector find conducting market research difficult.

H2b. Singapore micro-SMEs in the retail and F&B sector do not conduct market research.

Conducting market research is defined as the active collection of information about customers and competitors. Past literature suggests that SMEs find conducting market research difficult and thus are largely opportunistic in gathering information. Gathered data was also not necessarily thoroughly analysed or shared with personnel within the companies. However, a market-driven approach is important to improve performance of a firm through better understanding of the opportunities and threats in the market.

H3a. Singapore micro-SMEs in the retail and F&B sector do not offer innovative products. Innovation refer to offering creative, novel or unusual solutions to consumers' problems and needs. In the case of SME retailers, innovative products may be a result of the retailer's new-product development or sourced from suppliers.

H3b. Singapore micro-SMEs in the retail and F&B sector do not have innovative ways of doing business that cater to customers' needs. Examples of innovative business practices include offering deep product expertise or offering an experiential retail environment.

In a review of past literature, it was found that an innovative marketing strategy, which comprises of product innovations and innovative marketing practices, can enable an SME to achieve success. Innovative marketing is associated with better performance for Taiwanese SMEs.

H4. Singapore micro-SMEs in the retail and F&B sector do not place a high emphasis on building relationships with customers. Building relationships with customers refers to the development of long-term working relationships with customers through methods such as loyalty programs, building interpersonal relationships between shop personnel and customers and providing good customer service.

H5. Singapore micro-SMEs in the retail and F&B sector do not view Word-of-Mouth as being important in improving sales.

In this study, relationship marketing is defined as the building of customer relationships in order to foster customer loyalty. SMEs should exploit their closeness to the market by building high quality relationships with their customers. In addition to increasing their market responsiveness and therefore being able to better customise the 4Ps to the market, relationship marketing is found to have a positive impact on business performance. Such a strategy will also allow SMEs to utilize WOM as a promotion tool. Word-of-Mouth has been noted to provide SME businesses with a sustainable competitive advantage.

H6a. Singapore micro-SMEs in the retail and F&B sector do not have social media accounts for their business.

H6b. Micro-SMEs in the retail and F&B sector have social media accounts for their business but they encounter problems when managing their social media accounts.

Although it has been found in past literature that SMEs are more reluctant to adopt social media as a marketing tool as compared to larger companies due to certain barriers to adoption, social media remains extremely relevant to SMEs. Social media marketing can be a tool for SMEs to improve customer service, increase brand awareness, improve communication with customers and improve communication and marketing of products/services. It has also been found that social media is important in terms of driving sales.

H7. Singapore micro-SMEs in the retail and F&B sector adopt a mass market approach whereby they aim to target the whole market with one offer.

A market segmentation strategy allows a small business to survive in the market against bigger players by gaining a foothold in a particular niche. By segmenting the market and targeting one or more segments, a company can design its marketing mix to better meet the needs of a group of consumers.

5. Methodology

To affirm or reject the hypotheses listed in Section 4, a total of 30 Singapore-based micro-SMEs operating either in the Retail or F&B sector are individually interviewed in a face-to-face and/or telephone interview. This is to ensure that further elaboration can be provided by the interviewer in the event whereby the respondent does not fully understand the questions. Care is also taken to ensure that the respondents are either the owner or manager of the company, and thus, have a clear understanding of the company's marketing function. Respondents should also have a significant influence over the company's marketing decisions before the interview is conducted. This is to ensure the validity of the data collected.

6. Findings

This section explores how the data collected using the methodology described above lends support to the hypotheses put forward in Section 4. Findings are broken down by company size and industry as doing so will make the results more quantitatively distinguishing (see Tables 1 and 2). In the event whereby results are not broken down by

Table 1: Breakdown of Companies Interviewed by Size

Number of Employees	Number of Companies Interviewed	% of total
1–10	19	63.33
11–20	8	26.67
21–30	3	10
Total	30	100

Table 2: Breakdown of Companies Interviewed by Industry

Industry	Number of Companies Interviewed	% of total
Retail	20	66.67
F&B	10	33.33
Total	30	100

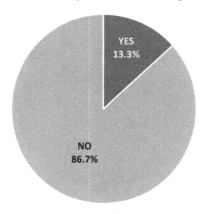

Figure 1:   Percentage of Respondents with Previous Experience in Marketing

company size or industry, it may be assumed that results are consistent among companies.

6.1. *Micro-SMEs' understanding of marketing*

The percentage of respondents with previous marketing experience is shown in Figure 1. Among the sample of 30 micro-SMEs, only 13.3% of the respondents provided feedback that they had previous marketing experience. It is observed that none of the respondents from a company with 10 or less employees have previous marketing experience while 36.36% of the respondents from a company with more than 10 employees possess previous marketing experience. This shows that the lack of previous marketing experience is a more prevalent issue among companies with 10 or less employees.

Figure 2 shows the percentage of respondents with prior marketing training. Similarly, only 20% of the respondents expressed that they have prior marketing training. When the sampled companies are broken down by size, we see that only 12.50% of the respondents from companies with 10 or less employees have prior training in marketing. On the other hand, 36.36% of the respondents from larger companies have undergone prior marketing training.

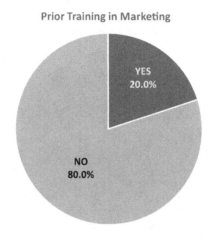

Figure 2: Percentage of Respondents with Prior Training in Marketing

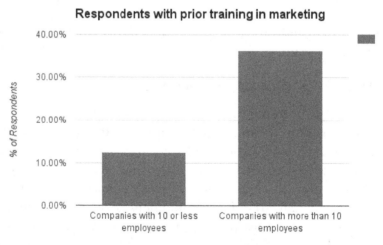

Figure 3: Percentage of Respondents with Prior Training in Marketing by Company Size

To gain a better understanding of the respondents' grasp of marketing, respondents are also asked to describe the activities that marketing include. It was found that 16.67% of the respondents are unable to list any marketing activities while 30% of the respondents thought that marketing consisted solely of advertising and promotion. While the remaining respondents demonstrated their understanding that marketing comprises of more than advertising and promotion, none of the respondents were able to pinpoint market segmentation, which is widely acknowledged to be a crucial aspect of marketing, as a marketing activity. It can be concluded that although some micro-SMEs have a better understanding of marketing than others, most have a narrow understanding of marketing. This stems from the lack of exposure of owners and managers to marketing as it was found that majority of the owners and managers of micro-SMEs do not possess previous marketing training or experience. This is especially true of SMEs with 10 or less employees. This may be traced back to micro companies lacking the resources to hire more skilled employees and provide job training. Thus, the findings from this study supports the hypothesis that Singapore micro-SMEs have a poor understanding of marketing and this may hinder them in exploiting marketing sufficiently.

6.2. *Market research in micro-SMEs*

It was found that 56.7% of the micro-SMEs studied do not collect consumer information. As for the remaining 43.3% of micro-SMEs which expressed that they gather information on their consumers such as the current market trends and customer feedback (see Figure 4). Companies gather information on their consumers from existing customers, non-commercial online sources, friends and acquaintances and through observation of the market. An overwhelming 84.62% of micro-SMEs that gather consumer information highlighted that they collect such information from their existing customers. Out of the 13 respondents found to collect consumer information, 69.23% of them use customers as their only source of information.

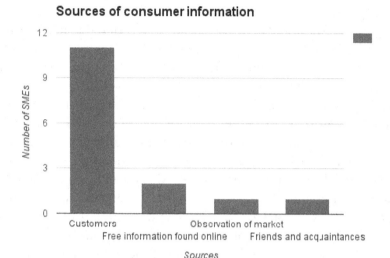

Figure 4:   Sources of Consumer Information

Furthermore, it was also found that 53.3% of the respondents do not collect information on their competitors. This result is consistent among companies from both the retail and F&B sector. From the remaining 46.7% of micro-SMEs which collect competitor information, their sources of competitor information is investigated and shown in Figure 5. Apart from observing and monitoring the market, micro-SMEs also collect competitor information from non-commercial online sources, magazines and newspapers, existing customers and friends and acquaintances. It can be seen that 78.57% of the respondents which collect information on competitors do so by observation of the market. For instance, a representative from an ice cream shop expressed that the business owner and employees will periodically visit competitors to taste their products. In contrast, only 21.43% of micro-SMEs which collect competitor information make use of free information posted online.

The difficulties that companies face in collecting market information are summarized in Figures 6 and 7. It can be seen that smaller companies typically face more problems when collecting market information as only 15.79% of companies with 10 or less

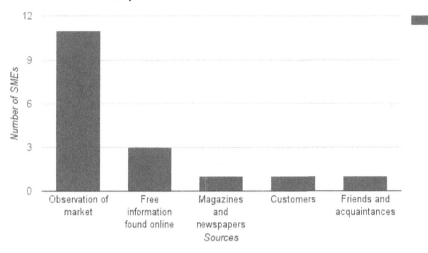

Figure 5: Sources of Competitor Information

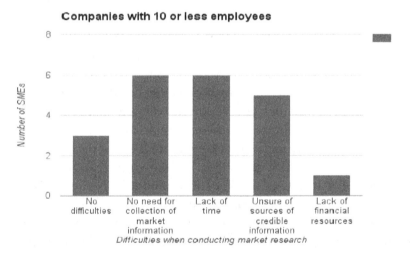

Figure 6: Difficulties When Collecting Market Information for Companies With 10 or Less Employees

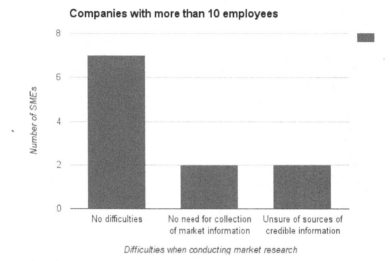

Figure 7: Difficulties When Collecting Market Information for Companies With More than 10 Employees

employees reported facing no difficulties as opposed to 63.64% of larger companies reporting having no difficulties collecting market information. It was also found that a significant 26.67% of total companies sampled felt that there was no need for the collection of market information. Uncertainty about sources of credible information is a common issue faced by both smaller and larger companies while smaller companies also reported facing a lack of time and a lack of financial resources when collecting market information.

It can be seen from the interview findings that a significant number of micro-SMEs do not collect market information. Even for micro-SMEs that collect market information, information is gathered from a very narrow set of sources. It can thus be concluded that the market research efforts of many Singapore merchants could still be further improved upon. In addition, from the number of respondents claimed that market research is irrelevant to their businesses, it can be inferred that a pressing issue micro-SMEs face is the lack of understanding of how market research can be utilized to improve sales. Finally, we see that smaller companies find conducting market research difficult as they reported facing difficulties such as a lack of time, uncertainty about sources of credible market information and a lack of financial resources.

6.3. *Innovative marketing in micro-SMEs*

To determine the innovative marketing efforts of local micro-SMEs, sampled companies are asked to describe how their companies differentiates themselves from companies through offering innovative products and/or having innovative ways of doing business. A score of 1–4 is then awarded to each company by the interviewer based on the interviewer's judgement of the company's innovative marketing efforts. Companies which described themselves to be similar to competitors and thus, are deemed to not practice innovative marketing are given a score of 1 while companies which are found to practice innovative marketing extensively are given a score of 4. Figure 8 shows the scores received by sampled companies.

It was found that 53.3% of the micro-SMEs do not engage in any form of innovative marketing are thus receive a score of 1. While 46.7% of sampled micro-SMEs are found to engage in innovative marketing, only 6.7% of the respondents practice innovative marketing extensively. An example of the innovative marketing efforts of sampled companies is a furniture and furnishings retail business

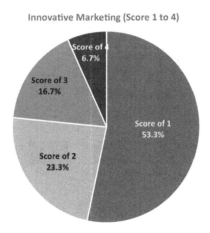

Figure 8:   Scores Received by Companies for Innovative Marketing

offering customers the option of customization. Another ice-cream shop sampled also engages in innovative marketing by providing customers with a unique dining experience through the creative Brighton beach-themed store decoration.

From the interview findings, it can be seen that although approximately half of the sampled companies practice innovative marketing, the innovative marketing efforts of these companies are largely insufficient. Thus, it holds true that the lack of innovative marketing is a common marketing management gap among Singapore micro-SME retailers.

6.4. Relationship marketing in micro-SMEs

Relationship marketing is defined as the building of high quality relationships with customers in order to create value for the business. The efforts of micro-SMEs to build and maintain relationships with their customers are represented in Figure 9. As seen, 86.67% of the sampled micro-SMEs engage in some form of activity to develop

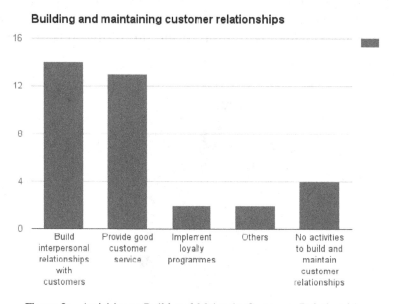

Figure 9: Activities to Build and Maintain Customer Relationships

and sustain customer relationships. 43.33% of merchants aim to build and maintain customer relationships by providing good customer service. To add on, the most commonly cited method to build and maintain customer relationships, as revealed by 46.67% of the sampled micro-SMEs, is to develop interpersonal relationships with customers. One way of doing so is through the exchange of contact numbers between the business owner or sales personnel and the customer. It is found that only 13.33% of the sampled micro-SMEs do not engage in any activities to build and maintain customer relationships.

From the above findings, it can be concluded that Singapore micro-SME retailers generally place a high emphasis on building and maintaining customer relationships in order to develop long-term working relationships with customers. Moreover, methods most commonly used by local SMEs are found in past literature to be effective for relationship building. Hence, it does not hold true that there is an absence of relationship marketing among Singapore micro-SMEs in the retail and F&B sector, given the closeness of micro-SMEs to their market.

6.5. *Reliance on Word-of-Mouth by micro-SMEs*

Figure 10 shows the importance of different promotion methods to micro-SMEs in term of boosting their sales performance. It was found that micro-SMEs rely the most heavily on Word-of-Mouth as a promotion method, with 96.67% of the companies sampled agreeing that Word-of-Mouth is important in contributing to the company's sales. On the other hand, paid advertising is found to be the least relevant promotion method for micro-SMEs, with only 13.33% of the companies sampled agreeing that it is important in contributing to the company's sales.

The interview findings do not support the hypothesis that Singapore micro-SME retailers do not view Word-of-Mouth as being important in improving sales. On the contrary, it is found that Word-of-Mouth is the most important promotion method. This is because micro-SMEs tend to have less resources to spend on marketing.

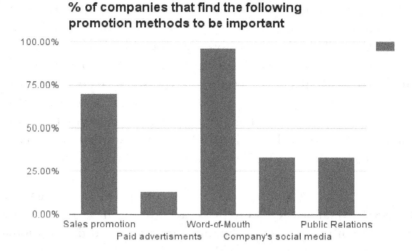

% of companies that find the following promotion methods to be important

Figure 10: Companies that Find the Following Promotion Methods to be Important

Thus, Word-of-Mouth, being a free promotional method, would appeal to micro-SMEs greatly. Given that it has been found in past literature that Word-of-Mouth marketing provides small retailers with a sustainable competitive advantage, the reliance of local micro-SMEs on Word-of-Mouth marketing is desirable. However, businesses should be mindful not to place over reliance on Word-of-Mouth marketing to improve sales as this may result in companies narrow-casting and overlooking many potential customers (Parrott *et al.*, 2010).

6.6. Market segmentation strategy of micro-SMEs

Figure 11 shows the percentage of micro-SMEs sampled which practice market segmentation. To determine whether a company practices market segmentation, each respondent is asked to describe the characteristics of the company's target group of customers. From the respondent's answer, the interviewer will judge if the company has a clearly defined target segment or chooses to target the entire market. It was found that 30% of the respondents are able to clearly describe the group of customers that the company is targeting and

Do Companies Practise Market Segmentation?

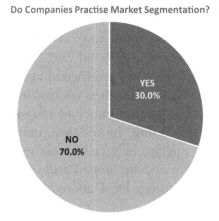

Figure 11:   Companies that Practice Market Segmentation

thus, 30% of the sampled companies are found to practice market segmentation. It was also found that most of the companies currently practicing market segmentation use age as a variable to segment the market. Since variables used to segment the market should describe why customers respond differently to a market offering and directly reflect customers' underlying needs, using age as the only segmentation variable may not be an effective method of market segmentation. For instance, a clothing retailer may describe its target market to be women from their 30s to 50s. However, such a market segmentation method does not reflect the underlying needs of each customer. A more effective method of segmenting the market will be to target women with moderate to high purchasing power, who value a comfortable shopping environment and quality over price.

From the findings, it can be concluded that majority of the micro-SMEs in the Retail and F&B sector that do not practice market segmentation. In addition, the market segmentation efforts of merchants currently practicing market segmentation are largely unsophisticated and thus, may be ineffective. Hence, the findings in this study support the hypothesis that Singapore micro-SMEs in the retail and F&B sector adopt a mass market approach by which they aim to target the whole market with one offer. Furthermore social media users can be developed and targeted as another market segment.

7. Conclusion and Recommendations

In summary, the common marketing management gaps present among local micro-SMEs in the Retail and F&B sector are a poor understanding of marketing and insufficient market research due to the difficulties micro-SMEs face when conducting market research. Another problem is the large number of micro-SMEs that do not practice innovative marketing. In addition, majority of the micro-SMEs either do not engage in social media marketing or do not utilize it sufficiently. Finally, the limited and unsophisticated use of market segmentation among local micro-SMEs is also a gap that should be addressed.

7.1. *Training*

First, to address micro-SMEs' lack of understanding of marketing and suitable marketing strategies for small businesses, relevant marketing courses could be designed and targeted at micro-SME business owners and managers. The courses should provide participants with a more in-depth understanding of marketing and increase awareness of recommended marketing strategies for small businesses such as innovative marketing and market segmentation. This would motivate companies to adopt more effective marketing strategies in order to improve their business performance. In addition, there should also be workshops to cover the importance of market research and how market research can be utilized to improve business performance. This is to address local micro-SMEs' perception that market research is irrelevant to their businesses. Since micro-SMEs face limited resources, subsidies can be provided for such training.

The lack of understanding of marketing is likely to be a problem faced by only micro-SMEs as it was found that the lack of exposure to marketing is a more prevalent issue among companies with 10 or less employees. This is because larger companies often have the resources to employ managers with specialized knowledge in marketing while micro-companies are usually run by the owner–manager.

Thus, training should only be open to micro companies with a greater need for such training.

In addition, it was found that a barrier to adoption of social media marketing for micro-SMEs with 10 or less employees is the lack of expertise in social media. To address this issue, merchants should be encouraged to send their employees to workshops which will provide training on how to use social media such as Facebook and Instagram for marketing purposes. As this is an issue faced by only smaller companies, the government can subsidize training for employees from companies with 10 or less employees to encourage participation from smaller companies.

7.2. Guidance

In addition to providing training, certain guidelines can also be provided to micro-SMEs to steer them in the right direction in the execution of marketing strategies. For instance, guidelines on effective social media marketing can be developed to help micro-SMEs make more effective use of social media. While market segmentation is an useful strategy for small businesses, it may be challenging for firms with a low level of marketing expertise to execute. Hence, consultants can be engaged to provide guidance to micro-SMEs in the execution of their market segmentation strategy. Consultants can help merchants to determine their target market as well as advise them on how to customize their marketing mix to meet the needs of their target market. This recommendation is more relevant towards micro-SMEs, and especially SMEs with 10 or less employees as smaller SMEs tend to lack marketing knowledge and experience. On the other hand, larger SMEs often have employees which are trained in marketing and thus do not require external help or guidance in the execution of marketing strategies.

7.3. Sharing of information

Since it has been found that the lack of time and lack of financial resources are problems SMEs with less 10 employees face when conducting market research, trade associations can facilitate the partnering of small businesses in the same industry to share market research findings. The exchange of market information between partnered firms will allow businesses to make more effective use of time and resources put into market research. Moreover, trade associations or other similar organisations can also publish industry-specific market information such as consumer surveys, market trends and general information about market players. Such information can be released annually on trade associations' webpages for SMEs' reference. In addition to publishing collated market information, links to government reports, commercial market research sites and other sources of market information can also be provided for companies that are interested in conducting more market research but are unsure of sources of credible market information.

While the partnering of businesses should only apply to small companies which face a greater resource constraint in conducting market research, the publication of market information material will serve to benefit all firms in the industry regardless of the company size. This is because the published market information will be a public good, where it is difficult to limit certain companies from obtaining and using the published information and the information is non-rivalrous.

7.4. What individual SMEs can do?

To increase the adoption of innovative marketing among SMEs, firms should be encouraged to be open to novel and creative ideas. Micro-SMEs should be receptive towards recommendations and suggestions from company employees and customers and take up ideas that can allow the firm to offer customers greater value. On way firms can do so is to encourage customers to share ideas with the company through crowdsourcing activities. Firms can also generate a culture of innovation within the company by rewarding employees who have contributed good ideas.

The above recommendations are aimed at bridging the gaps in marketing management of local micro-SMEs in the Retail and F&B

sector in order to improve their competitiveness. With better sales performance, micro-SMEs will be able to enjoy higher profits which can be invested in improving the firm's productivity. It was found that the productivity of a firm is affected by factors that operate within the firm as well as elements of the market environment that are external to the firm. Managerial talent, the quality of general labor and capital inputs and the use of Information Technology and Research and Development are recognised to be factors that directly impact productivity at the micro level (Syverson, 2010). Thus, with greater profits, firms will be able to invest in recruiting managerial talent and improving the quality of the firm's inputs. Firms will also be able to invest in Information Technology and R&D which can be extremely costly. It is to be noted that SMEs and in particular, micro-SMEs, are characterised by a limitation in financial resources and thus, without an improvement in the firm's performance, they will lack the resources necessary to invest in improving productivity.

Finally, it is to be highlighted that the above recommendations are targeted at micro-SMEs which are closer to the market and have more flexibility as compared to their larger counterparts. However, they are also be constrained in terms of their resources. Thus, some of the above recommendations are irrelevant to larger SMEs which have greater access to financial resources and marketing skills. However, some of the recommendations, such as the publication of market information by trade associations and encouraging companies to be open to novel ideas, remain relevant to larger SMEs.

References

Adjei, M. T., Griffith, D. A. and Noble, S. M. (2009). When do relationships pay off for small retailers? Exploring targets and contexts to understand the value of relationship marketing. *Journal of Retailing*, 85(4), 493–501.

Aileron. (2013). Why Your Small Business Needs CRM. Available at: from http://www.forbes.com/sites/aileron/2013/05/01/why-your-small-business-needs-crm/ [Accessed on 16 June 2015].

Alshawi, S., Missi, F. and Irani, Z. (2011). Organisational, technical and data quality factors in CRM adoption — SMEs perspective. *Industrial Marketing Management*, 40(3), 376–383.

Bulearca, M. and Bulearca, S. (2010). Twitter: A viable marketing tool for SMEs. *Global Business and Management Research: An International Journal*, 2(4), 296–309.

Coca-Stefaniak, A., J., Parker, C. and Rees, P. (2010). Localisation as a marketing strategy for small retailers. *International Journal of Retail & Distribution Management*, 38(9), 677–697.

Dibb, S. (1998). Market segmentation: Strategies for success. *Marketing Intelligence & Planning*, 16(7), 394–406.

Dibb, S. and Simkin, L. (1991). Targeting, segments and positioning. *International Journal of Retail & Distribution Management*, 19(3).

Durkin, M., McGowan, P. and McKeown, N. (2013). Exploring social media adoption in small to medium-sized enterprises in Ireland. *Journal of Small Business and Enterprise Development*, 20(4), 716–734.

Fox, N. (2014). Singapore SMEs and their challenges in the Second Half of 2014. Available at: http://sbr.com.sg/economy/commentary/singapore-smes-and-their-challenges-in-second-half-2014 [Accessed on 30 July 2015].

Fuller, P. B. (1994). Assessing marketing in small and medium-sized enterprises. *European Journal of Marketing*, 28(12), 34–49.

Ghosh, B. C. and Taylor, D. B. (1995). Marketing practices among SMEs: a cross national study of Singapore and New Zealand organizations. *Journal of Small Business & Entrepreneurship*, 12(3), 40–49.

Gilmore, A., Carson, D. and Grant, K. (2001). SME marketing in practice. *Marketing Intelligence & Planning*, 19(1), 6–11.

Gordon, J. (2015). *How Google breaks through*. Available at: http://www.mckinsey.com/insights/marketing_sales/how_google_breaks_through [Accessed on 30 July 2015].

Hanley, S. and Leahy, R. (2009). The effectiveness of relationship marketing strategies in department stores. *International Journal of Business and Management*, 3(10), 133.

Harrigan, P., Ramsey, E. and Ibbotson, P. (2009). Investigating the e-CRM activities of Irish SMEs. *Journal of Small Business and Enterprise Development*, 16(3), 443–465.

Lee, K. (2014). *The Social Media Frequency Guide: How Often To Post To Facebook, Twitter, LinkedIn, and More*. Available at: http://www.fastcompany.com/3029019/work-smart/the-social-media-frequency-guide-how-often-to-post-to-facebook-twitter-linkedin-a [Accessed on 30 July 2015].

Lee, K. S., Lim, G. H., Tan, S. J. and Wee, C. H. (2001). Generic marketing strategies for small and medium-sized enterprises — conceptual framework and examples from Asia. *Journal of Strategic Marketing*, 9(2), 145–162.

Lorenzo-Romero, C. and Constantinides, E. (2013). Social media as marketing strategy: an explorative study on adoption and use by retailers. *Social Media in Strategic Management*, 11, 197.

MacKenzie, I., Meyer, C. and Noble, S. (2014). *How Retailers Can Keep Up with Consumers*. Available at: http://www.mckinsey.com/insights/consumer_and_retail/how_retailers_can_keep_up_with_consumers [Accessed on 30 July 2015].

McCann, M. and Barlow, A. (2015). Use and measurement of social media for SMEs. *Journal of Small Business and Enterprise Development*, 22(2).

Megicks, P. (2001). Competitive strategy types in the UK independent retail sector. *Journal of Strategic Marketing*, 9(4), 315–328.

Nakara, W. A., Benmoussa, F. Z. and Jaouen, A. (2012). Entrepreneurship and social media marketing: evidence from French small business. *International Journal of Entrepreneurship and Small Business*, 16(4), 386–405.

O'Dwyer, M., Gilmore, A. and Carson, D. (2009). Innovative marketing in SMEs: an empirical study. *Journal of Strategic Marketing*, 17(5), 383–396.

Özgener, Ş. and İraz, R. (2006). Customer relationship management in small–medium enterprises: the case of Turkish tourism industry. *Tourism Management*, 27(6), 1356–1363.

Palmatier, R. W., Dant, R. P., Grewal, D. and Evans, K. R. (2006). Factors influencing the effectiveness of relationship marketing: a meta-analysis. *Journal of marketing*, 70(4), 136–153.

Parrott, G., Azam Roomi, M. and Holliman, D. (2010). An analysis of marketing programmes adopted by regional small and medium-sized enterprises. *Journal of Small Business and Enterprise Development*, 17(2), 184–203.

Reijonen, H. (2009). *Role and Practices of Marketing in SMEs*. Available at: http://epublications.uef.fi/pub/urn_isbn_978–952-219-306-3/index.html [Accessed on 16 July 2015].

Shi, J. and Au-Yeung, A. Y. S. (2015). An innovation perspective on Chinese retailers' competitive advantage. *The International Review of Retail, Distribution and Consumer Research*, 25(2), 120–144.

Simpson, M. and Taylor, N. (2002). The role and relevance of marketing in SMEs: towards a new model. *Journal of Small Business and Enterprise Development*, 9(4), 370–382.

Simpson, M., Padmore, J., Taylor, N. and Frecknall-Hughes, J. (2006). Marketing in small and medium sized enterprises. *International Journal of Entrepreneurial Behavior & Research*, 12(6), 361–387.

Siu, W. S. (2005). An institutional analysis of marketing practices of small and medium-sized enterprises (SMEs) in China, Hong Kong and Taiwan. *Entrepreneurship & Regional Development*, 17(1), 65–88.

Siu, W. S., Fang, W. and Lin, T. (2004). Strategic marketing practices and the performance of Chinese small and medium-sized enterprises (SMEs) in Taiwan. *Entrepreneurship & Regional Development*, 16(2), 161–178.

Straw, J. (2011). *Word of Mouth Tops Survey of SME Marketing*. Available at: http://www.marketingdonut.co.uk/blog/2011/05/word-mouth-tops-survey-sme-marketing [Accessed on 16 July 2015].

Syverson, C. (2010). *What determines productivity?* (No. w15712). National Bureau of Economic Research.

Walsh, M. F. and Lipinski, J. (2009). The role of the marketing function in small and medium sized enterprises. *Journal of Small Business and Enterprise Development*, 16(4), 569–585.

Yolal, M., Emeksiz, M. and Cetinel, F. (2009). Marketing of SMHEs in Turkey: A comparative analysis. *Journal of Hospitality Marketing & Management*, 18(4), 372–385.

Chapter 9

Cost Control and Accounting Practices: Impact on and Improvement of Productivity in Singapore Food & Beverage Enterprises

1. Introduction

Singapore's food and beverage (F&B) services industry has been lagging behind other industries in terms of productivity growth. The stark difference between productivity levels of businesses that compete at the international level and those that focus on the domestic market, has been acknowledged in the 2015 Budget Speech by Deputy Prime Minister and then-Finance Minister, Mr Tharman Shanmugaratnam. Domestic-oriented industries experienced an annual productivity growth of 1%, compared to 5% in the outward-oriented industries (Ministry of Finance, 2015), thus raising concerns over the performance of several industries such as the F&B industry.

Recent productivity efforts in Singapore's F&B industry tend to concentrate on the front-of-house and back-of-house innovations to enhance operational efficiency of F&B establishments (SPRING Singapore). However, relatively less emphasis was placed at the headquarters or the management capabilities of these enterprises.

An important component of the proposed 8M Productivity Framework is the Management, and to enhance productivity, managers of the establishments need to be equipped with effective management techniques. Furthermore, to attain the organization's goals and objectives, the management needs to evaluate important information about the firm's internal and external environment. To do so, managers need to employ some form of managerial accounting practices, as these practices have a critical role to play in assisting the managers to measure, manage and improve operational activities (Hilton, 1994), which will eventually lead to higher productivity. In addition, the advance of information technology has led the development of various accounting information systems, making it easier for managers to integrate and have access to reliable, accurate and timely information. The management can leverage on the information to assess operational efficiency, improve resource utilization and make strategic decisions to achieve the goals of the organization.

This chapter focuses on two key aspects of the 8M Productivity Framework, namely, Management and Money. It covers the findings of a study carried out to:

(a) Examine how enterprises in the F&B industry can enhance productivity by using appropriate accounting methods to monitor costs or operations, especially in areas such as costing, budgeting and performance evaluation;

(b) Determine the current cost control and accounting practices adopted by F&B enterprises in Singapore;

(c) Identify the common financial and accounting management gaps that may impede productivity, and the challenges faced by enterprises in implementing the best practices to control costs and enhance productivity and

(d) Provide recommendations on how enterprises can enhance productivity via effective cost control and management accounting practices.

2. Research Methodology

Two approaches were adopted in the study:

(a) A literature review was conducted on major findings in previous work in Singapore and/or other countries; and an
(b) Evidence-based research was carried out in Singapore through:
(i)   Secondary data, reports and published papers;
(ii) Interviews or surveys with the management of F&B enterprises and
(iii) Case studies of F&B enterprises.

Data was gathered from a range of F&B enterprises to reflect the diversity of the industry in Singapore. They include restaurants, food caterers, cafes, coffee houses and pubs.

3. Literature Review

3.1. *Management accounting*

According to Hilton (1994), managerial accounting is the process of identifying, measuring, analyzing, interpreting, and communicating information in pursuit of an organization's goals. In addition, Hilton (1994) states that managerial accountants have the ability to add value to the organization by pursuing five main objectives, which are:

(a) Providing information to decision making and planning and proactively participating as part of the management team in the decision making and planning processes.
(b) Assisting managers in directing and controlling operational activities.
(c) Motivating managers and other employees towards the organization's goals.
(d) Measuring the performance of activities, subunits, managers, and other employees within the organization.
(e) Assessing the organization's competitive position, and working with other managers to ensure the organization's long-run competitiveness in its industry.

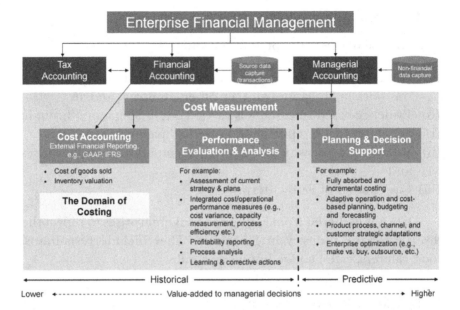

Figure 1: Enterprise Financial Management

Source: Professional Accountants in Business Committee, 2009.

The five objectives are summarized in Figure 1. Performance Evaluation and Analysis and Planning and Decision Support are significant aspects of cost measurement. These areas relate to internal management decision making and have wide-ranging impact on a firm's productivity level.

A model was also developed by the International Federation of Accountants (IFAC) to describe the development and progress of management accounting through various stages (Figure 2). As organizations adopt more sophisticated management accounting practices to suit the ever-changing business environment, they can ultimately benefit from such practices by value creation through effective use of resources. In this time and age where firms face intense global competition, new management techniques have been introduced and the focus of management accounting has shifted to value creation, using technology to identify drivers of customer and shareholder value.

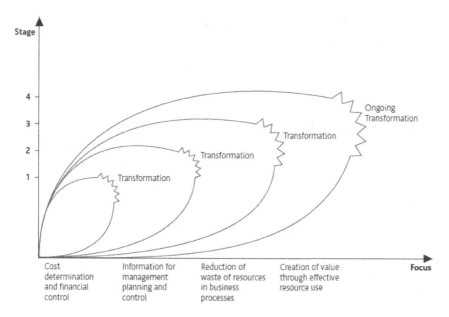

Figure 2: Evolution of Management Accounting

Source: International Federation of Accountants, 1998.

3.2. *Use of accounting information and degree of market competiveness*

Mia and Clarke (1999) identify that the degree of market competitiveness is a significant push factor for business unit managers to utilize information generated by accounting systems. In Singapore's context, F&B is recognized as being highly competitive (Economic Review Committee, 2002; Think Business, 2013) with approximately 6,751 establishments as of 2013 (Department of Statistics Singapore, 2014). With such intense rivalry and competition amongst different players in the industry, the management of various establishments can consider making effective use of the available accounting data by processing it into relevant and useful information. Besides allowing the enterprises to thrive in this environment, this move can have a positive impact on productivity, and potentially raise the overall level of productivity.

3.3. Impact of accounting information on performance and productivity

Several studies were conducted to analyze the impact of the use of accounting information and performance. For instance, Mia and Clarke's (1999) study finds evidence that greater use of information by managers is related to improved business unit performance.[1] In addition, the feedback provided by accounting information has been found to be positively related to managerial motivation, attitude and performance (Mock, 1973; Kenis, 1979).

3.4. Application of accounting information and common accounting practices

Management accounting systems have the ability to provide management with useful information for benchmarking competitors and monitoring strategies (Bromwich, 1990). Such information is able to equip the management with important knowledge to deal with threats and identify opportunities to increase customer value (Mia and Clarke, 1999). With respect to a firm's internal environment, the utilization of accounting information can offer feedback and insights on various performance areas, which include cost structures, sales volume, profitability, and productivity (Kaplan, 1983). Mia and Clarke's (1999) interviews with 90 Australian manufacturing firms reveal that business unit managers use accounting information for decision making in areas such as product costing, forecasts, purchasing and productivity.

Based on in-depth interviews with 21 senior executives and questionnaires completed by 65 marketing directors and 55 finance directors in the Australian Food industry, Ratnatunga *et al.* (1990) found that while marketers do acknowledge the potential contribution of accountants in their decision making process, the involvement of accountants in this aspect is lower than expected. Hence, this may

---

[1] Mia and Clarke (1999) measure business unit performance as the extent to which the business unit is successful in realizing its planned performance targets such as targeted level of productivity, costs, profit, sales volume, etc.

suggest that greater integration of management accounting in decision-making can enhance corporate effectiveness. Furthermore, Asquer's (2003) paper on the food industry acknowledges that many firms do not adopt most of the management accounting innovations such as activity-based costing (ABC) systems and management systems. This suggests that more effort can be focused on increasing the take-up of management accounting innovations by firms.

In Singapore' context, there are limited studies on the adoption of management accounting practices amongst firms. The most prominent study is by Ghosh and Chan (1997) and the results show that a greater number of firms have employed various accounting practices in order to run the business more efficiently. Furthermore, newer accounting innovations are slowly gaining attention by local companies. Finally, the authors find that multi-national companies are ahead of local companies in employing management accounting practices.

A study by Abdel-Kader and Luther (2006) focuses on identifying the frequency of implementing various management accounting practices in the British Food and Drinks industry. According to the study, management accounting practices can be classified into five broad categories: Costing systems, Budgeting, Performance evaluation, Information for decision making and Strategic analysis. This Chapter will focus on costing systems, budgeting and performance evaluation.

3.4.1. Costing systems

Abdel-Kader and Luther's (2006) results reveal that 48% of the surveyed companies either "often" or "very often" differentiate between fixed and variable costs in decision making. Furthermore, 83% of the respondents rate this costing technique as either "moderately important" or "important", signaling its importance. The study also finds a relatively low usage of absorption costing, such as ABC even though approximately half of the respondents perceive such methods as either "moderately important" or "important".

The low usage of ABC also corroborates with the results of other studies. For instance, Groot's (1997) research on the American and

Dutch food industries shows that the adoption rate was only 18% and 12% in the US and Dutch food sectors respectively, contrary to the expectation of a widespread adoption.

Raab's (2003) study on the application of the ABC method finds that common reasons why restaurants do not adopt ABC include a lack of awareness of the concept, the perception that this method is not beneficial due to its complexity, expensive implementation process and resource constraints. The unfamiliarity with the ABC method is also commonly cited as a reason for not adopting ABC in Groot's (1997) research.

Despite the low adoption rate amongst firm, the ABC method does possess several advantages over traditional costing methods. For instance, this method helps to minimize cost distortion that is commonly associated with traditional, volume-based costing systems (Hilton, 1994). In addition, ABC is able to provide a clear understanding of how products and services generate revenue and consume an organization's resources (Cooper and Kaplan, 1991), which is essential in managerial decision making. Hence, ABC analysis can be viewed as a "guide to profitability" (Cooper and Kaplan, 1991).

Raab's (2003) study also reveals that this costing method is feasible for attaining overall menu profitability. A subsequent study by Raab *et al.* (2005) on the application of this method in a Hong Kong buffet restaurant, reveals favorable results and allows operation managers to identify inefficiencies. Hence, this costing system can be recommended to establishments in the F&B sector to boost productivity.

3.4.2. Budgeting

A budget details how resources will be acquired and used over a specific period. In essence, budgeting allows managers to plan ahead of time and is an important means of allocating resources. In addition, a budget serves as a benchmark, against which actual performance can be compared to, thus evaluating the firm's and managers' performance and incentivizing managers to improve performance (Hilton, 1994).

Abdel-Kader and Luther's (2006) survey results reveal that 48% and 73% of the respondents either "often" or "very often" use budgeting for planning and cost control respectively. In terms of the specific budgeting techniques, 32% of the respondents use flexible budgeting "often" or "very often", compared to only 19% for activity-based budgeting (ABB). Furthermore, what if analysis is perceived to be very important, but is only used from time to time. Finally, zero-based budgeting is viewed as largely unimportant by approximately 58% of the respondents.

Despite being perceived as largely unimportant in Abdel-Kader and Luther's (2006) study, zero-based budgeting has been implemented in several large firms in the F&B industry. For instance, Joshua Kobaz, the Chief Financial Officer of Restaurant Brands International Inc., which is the parent company of Tim Hortons, mentioned to analysts that zero-based budgeting has been implemented in Tim Hortons and this has enabled the firm to "achieve savings and refocus on the organization and (its) resources on the real key priorities" (Strauss, 2015). In addition, zero-based budgeting has also been introduced in other companies bought over by 3G Capital Partners LP, such as H. J. Heinz Co. and Burger King and it is expected to be adopted in Kraft Foods Group Inc. According to David Kincaid, the founder of Consultancy Level5 Strategic Group, this budgeting method has helped to increase the profits of Heinz and Burger King (Strauss, 2015). These case studies demonstrate the potential benefits that this budgeting method can offer.

3.4.3 *Performance evaluation and productivity measurement*

Performance evaluation also plays an important role in aiding the management to increase productivity levels. By increasing awareness about productivity and the firm's performance, the management can identify areas to enhance productivity and direct the performance of the organization's personnel.

In the aspect of performance evaluation measures, Abdel-Kader and Luther (2006) find that a large majority (78%) of the respondents view financial measures as "important" and a similar percentage utilize such measures. In relation to non-performance measures, 38% of the respondents either "never" or "rarely" adopt such measures, even though more than 75% rated these forms of measures as at least "moderately important". In addition, approximately 41% of the respondents "never" use employee-related measures. Their results also reveal that economic-value added and benchmarking are yet to gain traction in the British Food and Drinks industry.

An important tool used in performance evaluation is the Balanced Scorecard (BSC), which was introduced by Kaplan and Norton (1993). BSC incorporates both financial and non-financial aspects of the organization. Financial performance measures have received criticisms due to the promotion of short-termism amongst managers (Wilson and Chua, 1993; Doyle, 1994), inability to reflect managerial efforts (Emmanuel *et al.*, 1990) and the lack of balance between operational and financial indicators (Kaplan and Norton, 1993). The BSC provides managers with four different measurement perspectives (Figure 3). In addition to the traditional financial performance measures, it incorporates non-financial measures in areas such as customers, internal processes and innovation and improvement activities. Unlike financial measures of performance,

Figure 3: Balanced Scorecard

non-financial measures focus on current activities, which serve as drivers of future financial performance. Hence, it is important for managers to adopt a balanced perspective when measuring performance (Hilton, 1994).

In the context of Singapore, there have been calls for more targeted measurements of productivity in our F&B sector. For instance, during the Committee of Supply debate in Parliament on the issue of productivity, nominated Member of Parliament (MP) Mr Randolph Tan proposed for the Ministry of Trade and Industry to monitor productivity levels of firms. This may translate into benchmarks for other businesses and can also serve as a form of performance evaluation (Lee, 2015). In addition, MP for Choa Chu Kang GRC, Mr Zaqy Mohamad called for "clearer (and) more specific productivity goals" as a single productivity measure is too broad (Lee, 2015). For instance, he recommended that table turns can serve as a possible productivity measure in the F&B sector. This is also closely related to the idea of performance measurement, where firms can make effective use of accounting and finance information to devise key performance indicators that are relevant to their industry and operations.

The Integrated Management of Productivity Activities (IMPACT) framework developed by SPRING Singapore highlights the importance of accounting and financial information in managing and enhancing productivity (SPRING Singapore, 2011). The key contribution of managerial accounting lies in assisting the management in setting the overall productivity goals, assessing and monitoring performance. The definition of productivity adopted by SPRING Singapore is a measure of the "effectiveness and efficiency of (the) organization in generating output with (the) resource available" (SPRING Singapore, 2011). Hence, existing data from an organization's accounts can be translated into useful information for the management to monitor productivity levels.

3.5. *Productivity indicators*

According to SPRING Singapore, value added is an important and widely-used measure of output as it reflects the amount of wealth created by the enterprise through its production of goods and/or services. It is defined as the difference between sales and the cost of goods and services purchased. This indicator has the advantages of measuring the real output of the business and is able to capture the intangible aspects of value creation (SPRING Singapore, 2011). There are two main methods of calculating value added, namely, the addition and subtraction method illustrated below (Figure 4).

Profit and loss statement		Value added statement	
	$		$
Sales	450,000	Sales	450,000
		Less: Change in inventory level	
Less: Cost of sales		Opening stock	(200,000)
Opening stock	200,000	Closing stock	120,000
Purchases	300,000	Gross output	370,000
Less: Closing stock	(120,000)		
	380,000	Less: Purchase of goods and	
		services	
Gross profit	70,000	Purchases of stock	(300,000)
Non-operating income	10,000	Services and administrative	
		expenses	(27,700)
Less: Operating expenses			
		Value added	42,300
Advertising and marketing	5,000		
Audit fees	8,000		
Depreciation	2,000	Distribution of value added:	
Directors' fees	5,000		
Rental	8,000	Staff costs and other benefits	45,000
Repairs and maintenance	500	Depreciation	2,000
Staff costs	36,000	Interest	2,000
Staff welfare and development	4,000	Tax	300
Foreign worker levy	300	Profit before tax	2,000
Interest	2,000	Less: Non-operating income	(10,000)
Office and other supplies	800	Add: Non-operating expenses	1,000
Utilities	3,200		
Transport, postage &		Value added	42,300
communications	2,000		
Other operating expenses	200		
Total operating expenses	77,000		
Non-operating expenses	1,000		
Profit before tax	2,000		
Income tax expense	(130)		
Profit after tax	1,870		

Figure 4: Profit and Loss Statement and Value Added Statement

Source: SPRING Singapore, 2011.

Addition method:

Value added = Labor cost to employees + Interest to lenders of money + Depreciation for re-investment in machinery and equipment + Retained Profits + Other distributed costs

Subtraction method:

Value added = Sales — Cost of purchased goods and services.

To further leverage on the profit and loss statement that companies use for reporting purposes, a value added statement can be easily derived from the available numbers. With a value added statement, firms can then easily monitor the amount of value generated from its operations and use it to identify areas for improvement.

SPRING Singapore also suggests that an integrated approach should be undertaken when measuring productivity, as reflected in Figure 5.

Management accounting and control systems will be essential in the development of indicators at varying levels, such as activity and operational indicators, to provide the upper management with a comprehensive understanding of the firm's performance. Tables 1 and 2 depict the 10 common key management and productivity indicators used in the services sector:

According to a Retail and Food Services Productivity Benchmarking study conducted by the Singapore Productivity Centre (SPC) in 2014,

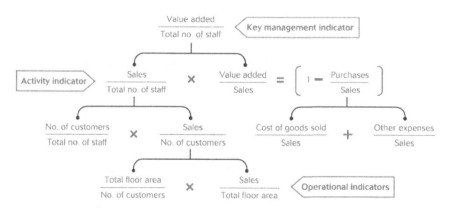

Figure 5: An Integrated Approach to Productivity Measurement

Source: SPRING Singapore, 2011.

Table 1:   Common Key Management Indicators

No.	Indicator	Formula
1.	Labor productivity	Value added/number of employees
2.	Sales per employee	Sales/number of employees
3.	Value added-to-sales ratio	Value added/sales
4.	Profit margin	Operating profit/sales
5.	Profit-to-value added ratio	Operating profit/value added
6.	Labor cost competitiveness	Value added/labor cost
7.	Labor cost per employee	Labor costs/number of employees
8.	Sales per dollar of capital	Sales/fixed assets
9.	Capital intensity	Fixed assets/number of employees
10.	Capital productivity	Value added/fixed assets

Source: SPRING Singapore, 2011.

Table 2:   Common Productivity Indicators in the Services Sector

No.	Indicator	Formula
1.	Sales per customer	Sales/number of customers served
2.	Waiting time per meal or customer served	Time taken from point of entering the outlet to the point an order is filled
3.	Compliment to complaint ratio	Number of compliments/Number of complaints
4.	Cost per customer	Operating expenses/number of customers served
5.	Inventory turnover ratio	Cost of sales/average inventory held during period
6.	Employee to customer ratio	Number of employees or servers/number of customers
7.	Investment in training per employee	Amount of training expenses/number of employees
8.	Equipment efficiency	Number of jobs done by equipment /total working hours
9.	Income or expenses per square metre	Income or expenses/total floor area
10.	Customer-to-seat ratio	Number of customers/total number of seats

Source: SPRING Singapore, 2011.

approximately one-third of the F&B enterprises do not measure their productivity levels. This is partially contributed to a lack of "a culture of continual improvement". Hence, with the accounting information and proper control systems in place, F&B enterprises are well equipped to constantly monitor their productivity levels. This research will also go further to document the most common indicators used by firms as well as the challenges faced when implementing productivity management practices.

3.6. Productivity efforts by firms in Singapore

A survey on 550 senior finance executives from four jurisdictions, namely, Singapore, Hong Kong, China and Japan, was conducted by the Institute of Singapore Chartered Accountants (ISCA) and Robert Half with the goal of understanding productivity efforts in the accounting and finance functions. The key results from this study indicate that organizations tend to focus on employee-related initiatives such as motivating employees and improving staff's performance evaluation, in contrast to process-related initiatives such as streamlining business processes and outsourcing functions (Goh, 2014). Furthermore, the study finds that firms are placing greater emphasis on improving productivity, which can be attributed to the restriction on foreign Labor as well as government initiatives to boost productivity. Goh (2014) also acknowledges that technology adoption is an important aspect that firms should consider when implementing initiatives to enhance productivity. According to The Global Information Technology Report by the World Economic Forum, despite ranking 4th with respect to information and communications technology development, Singapore's businesses are ranked relatively lower when it comes to their ability to use technology to achieve productivity gains.

3.7. Accounting information systems, business processes and intelligence tools

Accounting information systems such as Enterprise Resource Planning (ERP) can improve the efficiency of organizations by allowing businesses to effectively collect, store and manage data arising from various business activities. By having an integrated database that captures all aspects of the business, the management will be able to monitor operations and make decisions more effectively. Having proper control systems in place to collect and transmit real-time data will also provide management with the necessary information to make well-informed decisions and to identity key areas for productivity improvement.

Leveraging on technology to enhance the effectiveness of business processes and systems have been cited as some of the key ways to enhance productivity by some of the firms in Singapore, such as Deloitte & Touche, KPMG and DBS (Suwardy, 2012). The implementation of ERP at Micro-Mechanics Holdings has enabled the firm to standardize business processes and workflow, and integrate information from various departments. In addition, the firm has adopted business intelligence tools, instead of the old practice of using spreadsheets. This has saved valuable time and enhanced the decision-making process (Suwardy, 2012). Research has also shown that the adoption of technology and accounting information systems can raise productivity. Finally, Medina-Quintero *et al.* (2015) study shows that information management derived from the use of accounting information systems, is able to increase productivity of small and medium-sized (SMEs) in Mexico, especially in areas such as improving administrative activities, decision making and the usage of information generated.

4. Survey Findings

4.1. *Characteristics of respondents*

Fifty-two responses were obtained via online questionnaires and door-to-door surveys with the management of F&B enterprises in Singapore. Figures 6–8 illustrate the demographics of these enterprises in terms of their dining concept and size.

44% of the respondents belong to the "Restaurants" category, which is generally in line with the composition of the F&B sector in Singapore where "Restaurants" remains as one of the most significant segments (Department of Statistics Singapore, 2014).

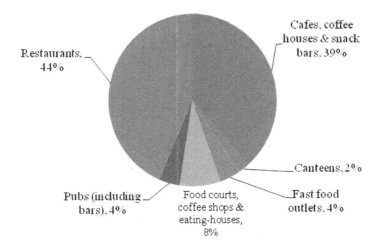

Figure 6: Type of Establishment

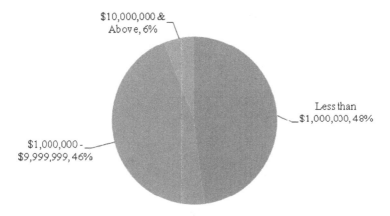

Figure 7: Size of Operating Receipts

Majority of the enterprises surveyed are smaller enterprises, in terms of operating receipts and number of outlets, indicative of their relatively smaller scale of operations.

4.2. *Overall adoption and perception of management accounting*

This section presents the results for the overall adoption and perception of management accounting and cost control practices. These results reflect the overall situation of management accounting practices and set the stage for discussion in the subsequent sections.

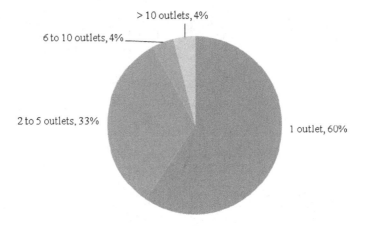

Figure 8: Number of Outlets

Use of Accounting Information for Decision-Making

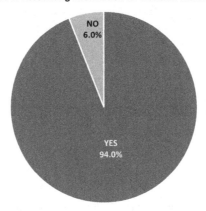

Figure 9: Use of Accounting Information for Decision-Making

As illustrated in Figure 9, a large majority (94%) of the surveyed enterprises use accounting information for decision making and/or to monitor operations and performance, in addition to reporting purposes. This indicates that the various enterprises do utilize and transform available financial information into useful data. However, this result does not reveal the extent and the effectiveness of their practices, which are difficult to measure.

A large majority (78%) of the enterprises either "strongly agree" or "agree" that cost control practices and management accounting techniques can improve operational efficiency and increase productivity. This reflects a general consensus that such practices can be potentially beneficial to the company.

Upon further analysis, it appears that larger enterprises (i.e. those with a greater number of outlets) tend to either "strongly agree" or "agree" that such practices can enhance productivity. In contrast, the enterprises that either "strongly disagree" or "disagree" comprise those with only one outlet. While these associations may not be statistically significant (p-value = 0.55), it is useful to note that the perceived usefulness of management accounting seems to be positively correlated with the scale of operations of businesses. This suggests that economies of scale may be a significant factor in this area.

Similar to the trend observed in Figure 10, approximately 7 in 10 (72%) enterprises are either "very receptive" or "receptive" towards implementing such techniques (Figure 11). Likewise, the larger ones tend to be more receptive towards the implementation of cost control and management accounting techniques. This is in line with the trend observed in Figure 10. However, it should be noted that this relationship is not statistically significant (p-value = 0.36).

6 in 10 (64%) enterprises use cost control and management accounting techniques on a rather frequent basis, either "very often" (e.g. daily/weekly) or "often" (e.g. monthly). However, there still exists a significant proportion, some 37% of the enterprises that utilize these techniques on a less than preferred frequency. This signals that there is still room for improvement. In addition, there is a disparity between the beliefs of the management and the actual implementation. While 78% of the respondents either "strongly agree" or "agree" that these practices are beneficial (Figure 10), only 64% of the enterprises employ these practices frequently. This difference in percentages can be attributed to the challenges faced by the enterprises in the implementation process.

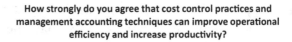

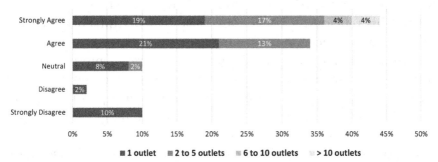

Figure 10: Level of Agreement on that Cost Control Practices and Management Accounting Techniques can Improve Operational Efficiency and Increase Productivity

Note: Number in horizontal bar denotes percentage share of companies having outlets classified.

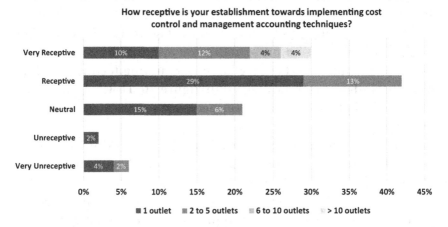

Figure 11: Receptiveness towards Implementing Cost Control and Management Accounting Techniques

Note: Number in horizontal bar denotes percentage share of companies having outlets classified.

Further analysis of the results reveals that there is a statistically significant (p-value = 0.08) difference in the frequency of employing such techniques across merchants that belong to different operating receipts categories. As illustrated in Figure 12, those enterprises that indicate "rarely" or "never" are those that belong to the smaller categories.

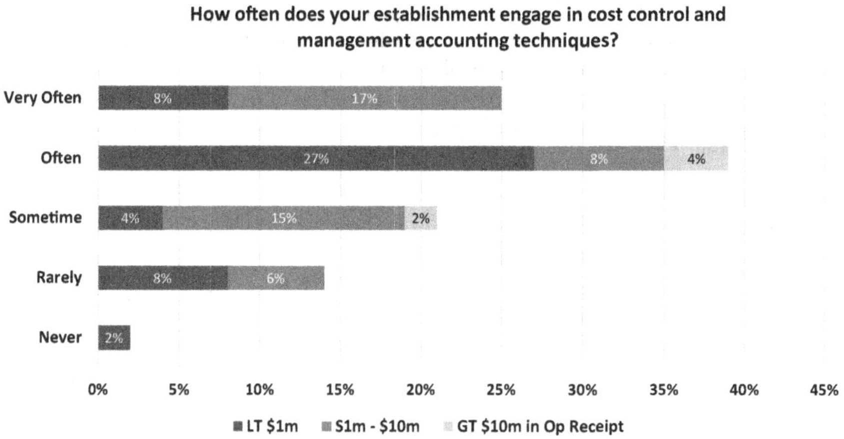

How often does your establishment engage in cost control and management accounting techniques?

Figure 12: Frequency of Engaging in Cost Control and Management Accounting Techniques

Note: Number in horizontal bar denotes percentage share of companies having operating receipts classified.

4.3. *Specific management accounting practices*

This section of the report focuses on the specific management accounting practices, namely, costing, budgeting and performance evaluation. It also documents the common techniques adopted by the F&B enterprises surveyed (Figure 15).

4.3.1. *Importance and frequency*

8 in 10 (81%) of the F&B enterprises rank "Costing Systems" as either "very important" or "important". In contrast, 77% rank "Budgeting" as either "very important" or "important". Finally, 7 in 10 (71%) rank "Performance Evaluation" in the same manner. The mean scores for "Costing Systems" and "Budgeting" are the same at 4.06 out of 5, while the mean score for "Performance Evaluation" is 3.96. This indicates that the merchants perceive "Performance Evaluation" to be slightly less important as compared to "Costing Systems" and "Budgeting".

As reflected in Figure 14, the proportion of merchants indicating that they adopt "Costing Systems", "Budgeting" and "Performance

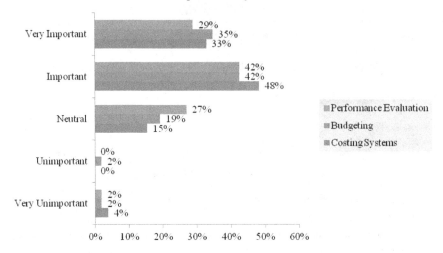

Figure 13:   Importance of Management Accounting Techniques in Decision Making and Enhancing Productivity

Evaluation" either "very often" or "often" are 59%, 55% and 50%, respectively. This decreasing frequency of adoption across the various categories is similar to the trend observed in Figure 13.

4.3.2. Costing systems

The top three common costing method employed by F&B enterprises are "Breakdown of costs by menu category and/or individual outlets", "Separate between variable and fixed costs" and "Traditional cost plus method", with 63%, 42% and 33% of the respondents, respectively indicating that they use these techniques.

Figures 16 and 17 below show an example of how an actual F&B establishment does its costing by menu category and menu items. This is an extract of the costing template used by Cafe A (Anonymous Name), which operates as a single outlet.

How often does your establishment use the following management accounting techniques?

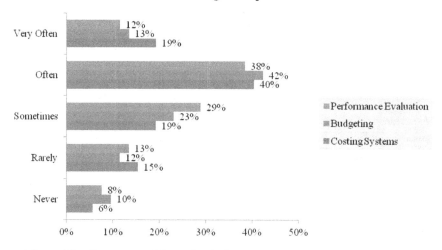

Figure 14: Frequency of Engaging in Management Accounting Techniques

Which of the following costing system does your establishment use?

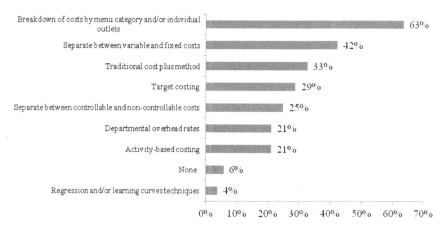

Figure 15: Common Costing Systems Utilized by Establishments

Dish	Recipe Portion	Unit/portion	Cost/portion	Wholesale Price	Unit	Remarks
Beef Brisket						
Frozen Beef Brisket/Shin						
Salted Soya Bean (Tau Cheau)						
Red Salted Bean Cake						
Ginger						
Garlic						
Star Anise						
Carrot						
Fresh Coriander						
Salt						
Sugar						
Pepper						
Sesame Oil						
Cornflour						
Light Soya Sauce						
Black Soya Sauce						
Potatoes						
Cost						
Suggested Retail						
Retail (Final)						
Discounted (Community - 20%)						
Babi Chin						
Frozen Pork Belly						
Shallots						
Garlic						
Salted Soya Bean (Tau Cheau)						
Sugar						
Black Soya Sauce						
Salt						
Ground coriander						
Oil						
White Rice						
Cost						
Suggested Retail						
Retail						
Discounted (Community - 20%)						
Smoked Salmon						
Smoked Salmon						
Cream Cheese						
Dill						
Romaine Lettuce						
Tomato						
Doritos						
Ciabatta						
Cost						
Suggested Retail						
Retail						
Discounted (Community - 20%)						

Figure 16: Food Costs Template of Cafe A (Simplified Version)

In addition, interviews conducted with the management of other enterprises reveal a similar situation at these businesses. One of them mentioned that costing has to "go down to the smallest detail", such as "number of man hours to process" to obtain the "most accurate costing of items per menu".

Besides menu costing, enterprises also use some form of costing method to keep track of business expenses. An example is shown in Figure 18 below, where Cafe A monitors its expenses by categorizing them according to the different aspects of its operations. Thus, the trend is that these SMEs tend to use a simple and direct costing

Drink	Price/unit	Unit
Coffee		
Roasted Coffee Beans		
Roasted Decaf Coffee		
Green Coffee Bean		
Sencha Tea		
Lychee Tea		
Darjeeling Tea		
Ceylon Tea		
Englisth Breakfast		
Earl Grey		
Mint Tea		
Garam Masala		
Decaf Tea		
Milk		
Coke		
Sprite		
Kickapoo		
Nutella		
Peanut Butter		
Strawberry Jam		
Horlicks		
Rose Syrup		
Peanut Butter		
Vanilla Ice Cream		

Figure 17: Beverage Costs Template of Cafe A (Simplified Version)

method, which will eventually help in menu pricing. While new accounting methods such as ABC have been deemed beneficial in various academic articles, such methods are not popular amongst these merchants. In fact, ABC is one of the least common techniques, with only 1 in 5 (21%) of the respondents indicating that they use such techniques. A respondent cited the lack of manpower and knowledge as the key reasons for not implementing more sophisticated costing methods. In addition, the nature of operations is such that there is no need to use ABC unless the establishment expands further.

Item	Startup Amt	Supplier	Oct-14	Nov-14	Dec Sub	Dec-14	Jan-15	Qty
Incorporation, Permits, Licenses & Business Ops Related								
ACRA Incorporation								
Food Handler Licence								
Banking and Finance								
Loan - Valuation Cost								
Corporate Account Fees								
Debt Financing								
Renovation								
Residence								
Fans								
Equipment								
Espresso Machine								
Grinders, Coffee Brush, Cleaning Tablet								
Barista Tools & Accessories								
Chocolate shakers								
Espresso machine cleaners								
Utensils and Cutlery								
Dinner and tableware, glasses, utensils, knifes								
Interior Decorations								
3-seat sofa								
Cafe tables & chairs								
Information Technology								
Website domain								
Email hosting								
Shopify								
Marketing								
Website development & marketing								
Cleaning & Sanitation Equipment								
Dishwashing detergent								
Paper Towels								
Operating Expenses of Premise								
Rental								
Equity Loan								
Stamp Duty								
Utilities (water, gas, electricity)								
WIFI, TV cable, digi phone lines								
Salaries								
Salary & CPF								
Barista Salary & CPF								
Employee Benefits								
Medical								
Dental								
Materials to Sell Food & Drinks								
Packaging Materials								
Napkins								
Disposable cutlery								
Carrier bags								
Food & Beverages								
Roasted beans								
Full cream fresh milk								
Skimmed milk								
Soy milk								
Other drinks								
Nutella								
Food								
Frozen Pork Belly Skin On								
Frozen Chicken Bless Sless Legs								
Frozen Beef Brisket Bless								
Cakes								
Carrot Cake								
Chocolate Cake								
Total								
Projected Expenses 1H2015								

Figure 18: Business Expenses Template of Cafe A (Simplified Version)

4.3.3. Budgeting

In terms of budgeting, the most common technique adopted is simple budgeting, with 54% of the merchants indicating that they utilize this method (Figure 19). Other common forms of budgeting

Which of the following budgeting techniques does your establishment use?

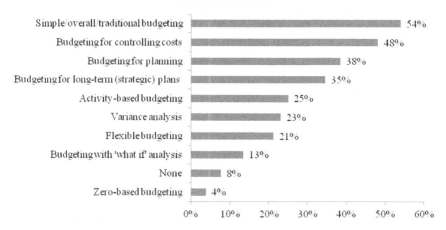

Figure 19:   Common Budgeting Techniques Utilized by Enterprises

include budgeting for controlling costs and for planning, with 48% and 38% of the respondents using these techniques, respectively. Similar to costing systems, more complex techniques such as activity-based budgeting, flexible budgeting and variance analysis are less commonly used. Reasons cited for such practices amongst establishments are similar to those cited for costing systems.

While there may not be a formal budget in place at Cafe A, the directors of Cafe A will do a projection of the volume of F&B to be sold, as illustrated in Figure 20. This allows the management to have a rough estimate of the projected sales and expenses for the following period. As part of the budgeting process, the management of Cafe A will first project the amount of sales, followed by deducting rental expenses and operational costs. Finally, the residual amount will be set aside for salaries for the personnel, as the Cafe is a family-owned business.

In addition, Cafe A closely tracks its cash flow, as seen in Figures 21 and 22. By monitoring its cash receipts and cash payments, the management will be able to make strategic decisions, such as whether to expand the business or invest in equipment.

At one of the enterprise surveyed, budgets are done for marketing expenses, Labor costs and raw materials. As it has several outlets

Projected Volume										
Drink	Volume/wk	Unit	Cost/wk	Drinks/wk	Drinks/day	Cost/mth	Cost/espresso shot Cost/1oz milk Cost/teacup	Cost per drink	Suggested Retail per drink	Retail	Comments
Coffee										
Roasted		kg	$ -							
Green		kg	$							
Decaf		kg	$ -							
			$ -							
Strawberry Shake		kg	$ -							
Nutella Shake		kg	$ -							
Rose Syrup		L	$							
Peanut Butter & Nutella		kg	$ -							
			$ -							
Milk for coffee		L	$ -							
Milk for Nutella shakes		L	$ -							
Milk for Horlicks shakes		L	$ -							
Milk for pink lady		L	$ -							
Milk for tea		L	$ -							
			$ -							
Soft drinks										
Coke		can	$ -							
Sprite		can	$ -							
Sarsi										
			$ -							
Total			$ -							

Figure 20: Projected Volume Template of Cafe A (Simplified Version)

in Singapore, budgeting is conducted for each outlet and it depends on the projected sales volume of each outlet. Interestingly, at another enterprise with one outlet, there is no formal budgeting carried out. Budgeting is done using pen and paper and that it is all "in the boss's mind".

As expected, the three aspects which are of utmost importance when controlling costs and budgeting are food costs, Labor costs and beverage costs, with 98%, 92% and 79% of the businesses indicating so (Figure 23). F&B costs are key concerns as they constitute a significant proportion of business costs. Labor cost is also an important aspect due to the tightening of foreign Labor in Singapore. Aspects that are less important include training and technology, which are actually essential factors in enhancing productivity. However, the management may place less emphasis on these areas due to other pressing segments that are of greater concern.

4.3.4. *Performance evaluation*

As illustrated in Figure 24, the three common performance evaluation techniques are the use of financial measure(s), benchmarks

Figure 21: Cash Flow Template of Cafe A (Simplified Version)

and trend analysis, with 46%, 31% and 27% of the merchants indicating that they employ such methods. While the use of financial measure(s) may be the most common method to evaluate performance, the percentage gathered from the questionnaire results is significantly lower compared to the results obtained in Abdel-Kader and Luther's (2006) and study (78%).

In contrast, the use of non-financial measure(s) is less common amongst the enterprises, with an average of only 15% of the establish-

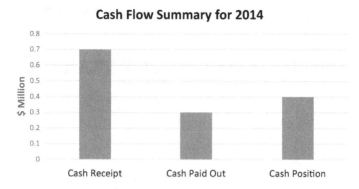

Figure 22: Cash Flow Summary Chart of Cafe A

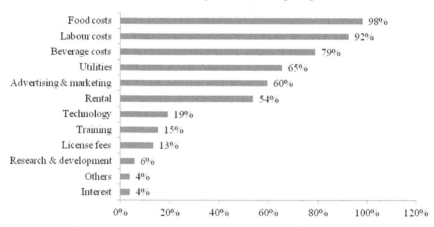

Figure 23: Aspects for Controlling Costs and Budgeting

ments indicating so. A respondent indicated the inability to measure non-financial aspects of the business as a key challenge faced by the restaurant. Further, most of the value created by the business comes in the form of tangibles, which are easier to measure. Hence, such enterprises prefer to use financial measures as the main form of performance evaluation. Additionally, the respondent mentioned that implementing Key Performance Indicators (KPIs) for employees

Which of the following performance evaluation techniques does your establishment use?

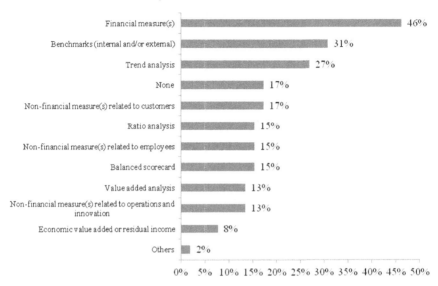

Figure 24: Common Performance Evaluation Techniques Utilized by Establishments

may be counter-productive as it may "chase workers away", especially in a tight Labor market.

It should also be noted that there is a rather significant proportion (17%) of respondents that do not employ some form of performance evaluation. Hence, more resources can be offered to these enterprises so as to encourage them to engage in some form of performance evaluation. It is also interesting to note that despite the efforts of SPRING Singapore to encourage enterprises to calculate value added, only some 13% of the businesses do so.

The management of Cafe A uses the application, Shopify, to monitor the establishment's sales performance. As seen in Figure 25 above (with sensitive financial data removed), Shopify is able to generate sales performance charts over a selected time period. This allows the management to save time and also provides the management with real-time information.

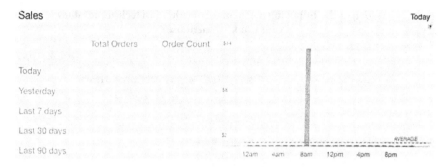

Figure 25: Sales Performance of Cafe A

Figure 26: Top Products of Cafe A

In addition to the above mentioned indicators, the respondents also monitor their products in terms of popularity. In the case of Cafe A, Shopify helps the management to generate the top products for the day, as seen in Figure 26.

This form of evaluation is also used at another one-outlet establishment, where the management does product rationalizing by analyzing the moving items and hot items and conduct in-store marketing when necessary. The point of sales (POS) system also allows the management to track and identify the top selling item and the poor performers.

The most common management indicators used are profit margin, Labor cost per employee and Labor cost competitiveness, with some 71%, 40% and 29% of the merchants indicating that they use

Which of the following management indicators does your establishment use?

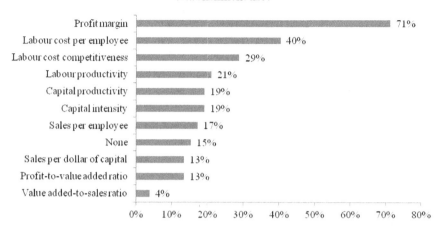

Figure 27:   Common Management Indicators Utilized by Establishments

such indicators (Figure 27). The use and close monitoring of Labor-related indicators is possibly due to the fact that manpower is very tight and manpower is a key resource for service-oriented businesses.

Cafe A also uses the Shopify application to compute management indicators, such as sales per employee, as reflected in Figure 28.

Other enterprises use revenue or sales per employee to measure the value that each employee contributes to the company. One of the respondents does not believe in measuring output or the amount of food produced by employee, for example, the number of items made, as this may not translate into sales. Hence, the top line is an important figure that the management utilizes in the measurement of performance.

As reflected in Figure 29, the most common productivity indicator used by establishments is sales per customer, with 1 in 2 respondents indicating that they employ this indicator. The remaining indicators are less commonly used, with less than 30% of the merchants using them. There is also a significant proportion (27%) of the respondents that do not use any form of productivity indicators to monitor their productivity levels.

Figure 28: Sales per Employee of Cafe A

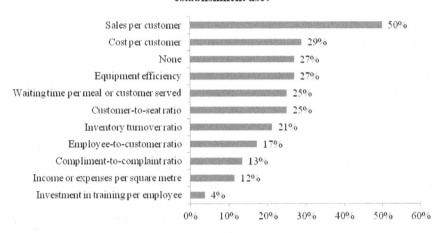

Figure 29: Common Productivity Indicators Utilized by Establishments

4.3.5. Resources for SMEs

Surprisingly, more than half (56%) of the respondents are not aware of the resources made available by SPRING Singapore. The level of awareness of the various resources are rather low, with only less than 1 in 5 respondents who of these resources.

Similar to the trend observed in Figure 30, the use of such resources available for SMEs is very low, with only 10% of the respondents indicating that they have used them. This signals that more can be done to increase the adoption rate of these useful resources by F&B enterprises.

The top three reasons for not utilizing the available resources are the "Lack of resources" (49%), "Have not heard of these

Which of the following resources for SMEs are you aware of?

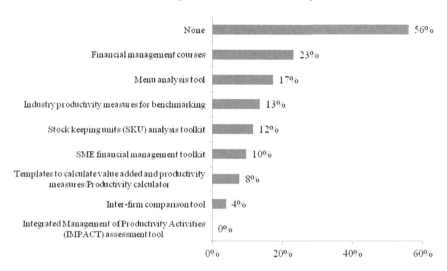

Figure 30: Awareness of Resources for SMEs

resources before" (49%) and "Do not know where to obtain these resources" (42%).

4.4. *Challenges faced by enterprises*

The main challenges cited by enterprises are the "Lack of time" (37%) and the "Lack of resources" (37%). In addition, some 27% of the merchants indicate that they do not have proper control systems to track operations.

The specific challenges faced by the respondents when implementing such practices are listed below:

- Lack of resources and investment in control systems;
- Lack of manpower;
- The whole team must work together to achieve our goals;
- Lack of time and analytics;
- Lack of skilled manpower, and "deep hands on domain expertise";
- Difficult to measure ;

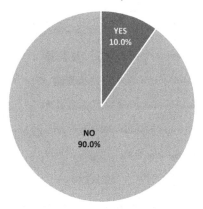

Figure 31:   Usage of SME Resources

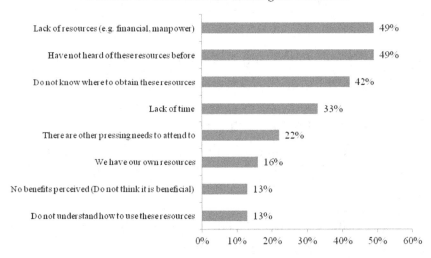

Figure 32:   Reasons for Not Utilizing the Resources

- Need the time and manpower to consistently follow through the practices with commitment and accuracy;
- Staff more concerned with just pushing sales without really giving time to processes;

What are some of the reasons for the low frequency?

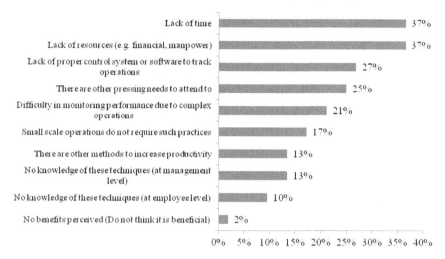

Figure 33:   Challenges Faced by Enterprises

- Difficult to keep up with regulations and trying to meet the requirements for grants by the government;
- Operations are too small to implement these practices and techniques;
- High cost of implementation;
- High staff turnover;
- Lack of control;
- Employees do not see the importance and reasons why we do it;
- Insufficient focus on these techniques by management.

4.5. Accounting software and accounting function

As reflected in Figure 34, a large majority (63%) of the establishments do not outsource their accounting function, rather they have an in-house accountant or personnel in charge of the finance and accounting aspects of the business. Due to the small scale of operations, many of the respondents do not have a full-fledged accounting department. Instead, they tend to have one personnel in-charge of this aspect.

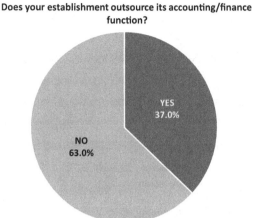

Figure 34: Outsourcing of Accounting Function

8 in 10 respondents (80%) do not use a control system or accounting software (Figure 35). This suggests that small and medium F&B enterprises lack sophisticated programs that can potentially assist them in monitoring performance, costing and budgeting. However, this may be due to the unwillingness to invest in such technology as well as the lack of knowledgeable personnel to operate such systems. Nonetheless, it appears that most of the enterprises have some form of POS system that allows them to track and monitor sales. This may suffice due to the small scale of operations.

Similar to the trends observed in the previous figures, a significant percentage (73%) of the merchants do not have an accounting system that is integrated with control systems (Figure 36). This may hinder the ability of the management to obtain real-time information and that more effort is needed to transfer data from the control system to the accounting system.

As illustrated in Figure 37, approximately 52% of the respondents either "strongly agree" or "agree" that management accounting information is available on a systematic, regular and short-term basis. There is also a significant percentage (19%) of respondents that select otherwise.

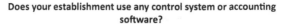

Does your establishment use any control system or accounting software?

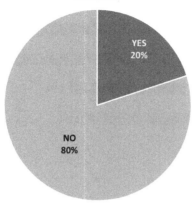

Figure 35: Usage of Control System or Accounting Software

Is the accounting system integrated with other control system used to track operations?

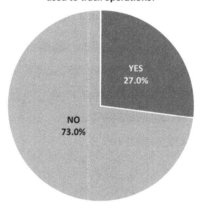

Figure 36: Integration of Accounting System with Control Systems

Close to half (48%) of the surveyed establishments either "strongly agree" or "agree" that information is available on a real-time basis. Not having updated information on hand can hinder the decision-making process as the management or line managers do not have the relevant information to make well-informed decisions.

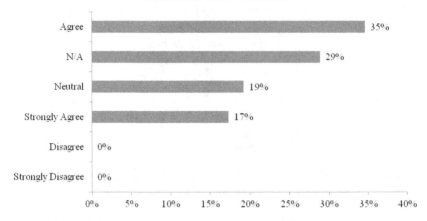

Figure 37: Availability of Information on a Systematic, Regular and Short-term Basis

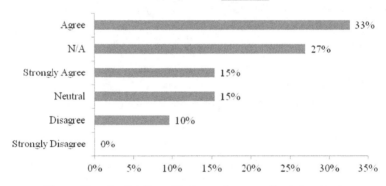

Figure 38: Availability of Information on a Real-time Basis

Approximately half (49%) of the respondents either "strongly agree" or "agree" that the line managers or outlet managers have access to management accounting information. This apparent lack of access to information may affect the degree of empowerment of the managers and their motivation to perform.

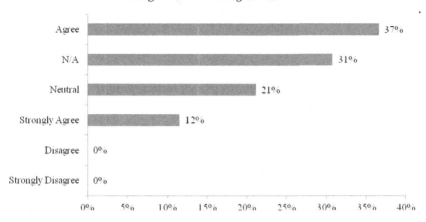

Figure 39: Availability of Information to Line Managers/Outlet Managers

5. Summary of Key Findings

5.1. *Key Finding #1: Disparity between perception and actual implementation*

The survey findings reveal that a large majority (78%) of the F&B enterprises either "strongly agree" or "agree" that management accounting practices are beneficial to the business (Figure 10). However, when asked about whether such practices have been put in place, the percentage of respondents that either "strongly agree" or "agree" fell to just 64% (Figure 12). This was also observed for the three broad management accounting practices; costing systems, budgeting and performance evaluation. The percentage of merchants who believe that costing systems, budgeting and performance evaluation is at least important is approximately 81%, 77%, 71% (Figure 13), respectively and these percentages decrease to 59%, 55% and 50% (Figure 14), respectively, when asked about the frequency of implementation.

As suggested earlier, this decline in the percentages could be due to several constraints or challenges that hinder the actual implementation of such practices. Hence, the proposed recommendations aim to address the challenges faced by enterprises so as to reduce the gap between the management belief and actual implementation.

5.2. Key finding #2: inadequate use of management accounting practices

Even though Figure 9 showed that some 94% of the respondents do use accounting information for decision making and to monitor operations and performance, it appears that the frequency of doing so may not be sufficient. This may reduce the effectiveness of such techniques and prevent the enterprises from effectively enhancing productivity.

According to Figure 14, there is still a significant portion of respondents that only utilize these practices either "Sometimes" (e.g. semi-annually), "Rarely" (e.g. yearly) or "Never". With respect to the individual practices, some 41%, 45% and 50% utilize costing systems, budgeting and performance evaluation at a frequency of semi-annually or less.

In addition, when comparing across the three aspects, performance evaluation fares poorly in terms of perceived importance and actual implementation. This may be because of the difficulty in computing the indicators for performance evaluation and the lack of manpower and/or resources to monitor operations.

Hence, the recommendations should also aim to encourage enterprises to increase the frequency of using such techniques, especially in the area of performance evaluation.

5.3. Key Finding #3: establishments are receptive towards the use of management accounting

The receptiveness of merchants can be seen in Figure 11, where 72% of the respondents are either "very receptive" or "receptive" towards the implementation of such techniques. This significant percentage signals that in general, F&B enterprises have a positive and open mind set towards the use of cost control and management accounting techniques. This also implies that it is easier to obtain buy-in from stakeholders, which are the establishments themselves. Hence, any resources or help provided would be welcomed by the merchants.

Coupled with the fact that a large majority also perceive management accounting techniques to be either "very important" or "important", this shows that recommendations should place less emphasis on educating the management about the importance of management accounting, and instead, focus on equipping the management and personnel with the relevant knowledge and expertise.

5.4. Key finding #4: use of simple and direct techniques

Despite the more complex techniques are deemed to be better than the traditional techniques by academic journals, the common techniques utilized by merchants are the traditional methods, which are simple and direct. These include the breakdown of costs by menu and traditional costing for costing systems, traditional budgeting, and use of financial measures, profit margin and sales per customer for performance evaluation.

Possible reasons for the preference of traditional methods include the lack of knowledge, the small scale of operations, and the impracticality of such techniques after performing a cost–benefit comparison. In a way, the traditional techniques also allow the enterprises to achieve the same objectives as the more complex techniques. Further, complex techniques may require additional manpower or greater investment in software and ultimately, the benefits do not outweigh the costs. Hence, the common practice across SMEs in the F&B industry is to adopt the simpler and traditional techniques as these techniques are sufficient given the nature of their operations.

Hence, recommendations may target the smaller establishments and encourage them to start adopting some of the simpler techniques that are widely practiced by majority of the establishments. As for those enterprises that have already put in practice some of the techniques, more can be done to help them fine tune the techniques or incentivize them to invest in technology so that more complex techniques can be adopted.

5.5. Key finding #5: lack of manpower and resources

The lack of manpower and resources has been cited as a key challenge when implementing management accounting practices. When asked about the reasons for the low frequency of engaging in cost control practices and management accounting techniques, the lack of time and resources are the top two reasons, followed by the lack of proper control systems (Figure 33).

The lack of resources includes skilled manpower as well as proper systems to aid in the implementation of these techniques. The lack of expertise is a key challenge faced by the company as it is difficult for SMEs to hire and retain personnel with the relevant expertise. Hence, proposed recommendations need to address these resource constraints so as to increase the adoption rate of these techniques by enterprises.

5.6. Key finding #6: lack of awareness of available resources

The final key finding from the survey results is that there is an apparent lack of awareness of the available resources for SMEs. Despite the great emphasis on enhancing productivity in the recent budgets as well as the various efforts from government agencies to assist SMEs in this area, some 56% of the surveyed establishments have not heard of any of the resources made available to them (Figure 30).

This lack of awareness of resources may have translated to a rather low utilization rate of these beneficial resources and toolkits, with only a mere 10% of the respondents indicating that they have used these resources before (Figure 31). This lack of awareness of the resources is further supported by Figure 32, where the key reasons include having not heard of the resources as well as a lack of knowledge as to where to obtain them. This suggests that more outreach has to be done, in terms of publicity and promotion of these resources to SMEs.

6. Recommendations

From the discussion above, two main issues have surfaced, namely, the lack of manpower and resources as well as the lack of awareness of available resources. To address these issues, a multi-pronged approach has to be adopted, and different agencies and stakeholders in the F&B industry play a crucial role in this aspect.

6.1. *Increase skilled manpower and resources*

6.1.1. *Recommendation #1: provision of training*

Since the lack of knowledgeable and skilled personnel is one of the main concerns for F&B establishments, industry associations and related organizations can spearhead the provision of seminars and workshops for employees and management of these enterprises, with the support from government agencies. Workshops on financial management and management accounting techniques could introduce some of the common practices adopted by companies in the F&B industry to the management.

In addition, during the interviews with the management of several establishments, the inability of employees to attend the workshops and seminars was highlighted as an issue facing the companies. While many establishments are willing to sign up for such workshops, the management and personnel often are not available to attend the sessions due to the long operating hours. Hence, a respondent suggested that online workshops and seminars can be offered, so that employees of establishments can "attend" these seminars when they are free. Another possible suggestion is that short online videos can be made available on the websites of government agencies, industry and training institutions, to introduce the concepts to employees and teach management the purpose of the resources and how to use them.

Moreover, the training available should also be tailored to the targeted audience. As most of the personnel do not have the necessary expertise and prior knowledge, training provided by the agencies should be easy to comprehend and suited to the needs of the F&B enterprises. This could mean offering the programs in languages other than English.

6.1.2. Recommendation #2: financial analyst services

There could be an online directory or search service to allow SMEs to find and engage financial analyst services at a subsidized rate. This will relieve the burden of those establishments that lack personnel with expertise as well as those that are unable to hire new personnel solely for this purpose. A respondent suggested that additional manpower could be provided to assist SMEs. With this recommendation, establishments will be able to obtain the services of a financial analyst without having to commit much resource.

6.1.3. Recommendation #3: Widen the criteria and scope of grants & vouchers

To relieve the financial burden for local F&B enterprises and to incentivize merchants to adopt such practices and related technology (e.g. data analytic tools), the criteria and scope of current grants and assistance programs for SMEs can be broadened further. The director of the House of Commons mentioned that one key challenge is difficulty in meeting the requirements of grants offered by the government.

Additionally, greater tax incentives can also be offered to establishments for implementing process improvement and control systems.

Since local F&B establishments are facing challenges on many fronts, any form of financial support by the government, agencies or associations will be welcomed by the management of these enterprises.

6.2. Increase awareness of available resources

6.2.1. Recommendation #4: increase outreach

The apparent lack of awareness of resources available for SMEs is worrying. To ensure that the establishments make effective use of these resources, greater outreach and communication with the merchants is needed. Letters and flyers could be sent to every SME to inform them about the help available. In essence, the relevant agencies need to increase outreach and promote these resources. The leveraging of different agencies and associations' networks would be very useful in spreading the message as a wider audience can be targeted.

6.3. Commitment of the management

6.3.1. Recommendation #5: commitment and support from the management

Ultimately, efforts to enhance productivity have to start from the enterprises themselves. Thus, the management has to be proactive and committed in the adoption of management accounting practices. There needs to be a consistent follow through of the practices with commitment and accuracy. Merchants need to commit sufficient resources into ensuring that these techniques are being put in place and that the message needs to be effectively communicated to employees in the organization.

7. Conclusion

While many local F&B operators in Singapore may not have the expertise to implement more sophisticated techniques, the management should work towards having a more intensive and effective use of such practices. In addition, there still remains a rather significant portion of local SMEs that do not adopt such practices. Hence, the proposed recommendations discussed in this chapter aim to equip local SMEs with the relevant expertise and resources for implementing such techniques.

The first step should be to encourage and incentivize establishments to adopt at least some form of costing systems, budgeting and performance evaluation. Moving forward, more resources can be channeled into enhancing and fine-tuning the methods adopted by establishments. Ultimately, the management of the various enterprises have to be willing and committed to adopt such practices and to utilize them appropriately. Only then will establishments be able to reap the benefits that management accounting can offer and achieve the objective of enhancing productivity levels.

References

Abdel-Kader, M. and Luther, R. (2006). Management accounting practices in the British food and drinks industry. *British Food Journal*, 108(5), 336–357.

Asquer, A. (2003). In for a penne.... *Financial Management*, pp. 28–29.

Boon, R. (2015). Many eatery owners fail to do their homework. *The Straits Times*. Available at: http://www.straitstimes.com/the-big-story/budget-2015/story/many-eatery-owners-fail-do-their-homework-20150219.

Bromwich, M. (1990). The case for strategic management accounting: the role of accounting information for strategy in competitive markets. *Accounting, Organizations and Society*, 15(1), 27–46.

Cooper, R. and Kaplan, R.S. (1991). Profit priorities from activity-based costing. *Harvard Business Review*, 69(3), 130–135.

Department of Statistics Singapore (2014). *Key Indicators of Food & Beverage Services 2013*. Department of Statistics Singapore, Singapore.

Doyle, P. (1994). Setting business objectives and measuring performance. *European Management Journal*, 12(2), 123–132.

Economic Review Committee (2002). *Sub-committee on Domestic Enterprises*. Ministry of Trade and Industry Singapore, Singapore.

Emmanuel, Clive R., Otley, D. and Merchant, K. (1990). *Accounting for Management Control*. Springer, US.

Ghosh, B.C. and Chan, Y.-K. (1997). Management accounting in Singapore-well in place? *Managerial Auditing Journal*, 12(1), 16–18.

Goh, C. (2014). Managing the accounting and finance function. *IS Chartered Accountant*, 16–27.

Hilton, R.W. (1994). *Managerial accounting*. McGraw-Hill, London.

International Federation of Accountants (1998). *International Management Accounting Practice Statement: Management Accounting Concepts*. The Federation.

Kaplan, R.S. (1983). Measuring Manufacturing Performance: A New Challenge for Managerial Accounting Research, *The Accounting Review*, 58(4), 686–705.

Kaplan, R.S. and Norton, D.P. (1993). Putting the balanced scorecard to work. *Harvard Business Review*, 134–147.

Kenis, I. (1979). Effects of budgetary goal characteristics on managerial attitudes and performance. *Accounting Review*, 707–721.

Lee, M. (2015). Singapore Budget 2015: MPs call for more clarity and direction in productivity drive. *The Straits Times*. Available at: http://www.straitstimes.com/news/singapore/more-singapore-stories/story/singapore-budget-2015-mps-call-more-clarity-and-directio.

Medina-Quintero, J.M., Mora, A. and Abrego, D. (2015). Enterprise technology in support for accounting information systems. An innovation and productivity approach. *Journal of Information Systems and Technology Management*, 12(1), 29–44.

Mia, L. and Clarke, B. (1999). Market competition, management accounting systems and business unit performance. *Management Accounting Research*, 10(2), 137–158.

Ministry of Finance (2015). *Singapore Budget 2015*.

Mock, T.J. (1973). The value of budget information. *Accounting Review*, 520–534.

Professional Accountants in Business Committee (2009). *Evaluating and improving costing in organizations*.

Raab, C. (2003). *The Feasibility of Activity-based Costing in the Restaurant Industry*. UMI Dissertations Publishing, University of Nevada, Las Vegas, ProQuest.

Raab, C., Mayer, K., Ramdeen, C. and Ng, S. (2005). The application of activity-based costing in a Hong Kong buffet restaurant. *International Journal of Hospitality & Tourism Administration*, 6(3), 11–26.

Ratnatunga, J., Hooley, G. and Pike, R. (1990). The marketing-finance interface. *European Journal of Marketing*, 29–43.

SPRING Singapore (2011). *A Guide to Productivity Measurement*. SPRING Singapore, Singapore.

Spring Singapore (n.d.). *A Recipe to Strengthen Business Capabilities: Improving Productivity for Your F&B Business*. Singapore.

Strauss, M. (2015). Cost-cutting strategy a boost for Tim Hortons, improves operations. *The Globe and Mail*. Available at: http://www.theglobeandmail.com/report-on-business/combined-tim-hortons-burger-king-results-miss-analyst-estimates/article24135140/.

Suwardy, T. (2012). Productivity in Accounting Practices. *In Accounting and Productivity: Answering the Big Questions*. CPA Australia.

Think Business. (2013). Case study: Suki Group serving up success. *Think Business*. Available at: http://thinkbusiness.nus.edu/articles/item/111-case-study-serving-up-success.

Wilson, R.M. and Chua, W.F. (1993). *Managerial Accounting: Method and Meaning* (Vol. 2). Chapman & Hall, London.

World Economic Forum (2011). The Global Information Technology Report 2010–2011.

Chapter 10

Conclusion

Productivity is the key driver of competitiveness and sustainability of any industry. However, as opposed to the manufacturing sector, the sources of productivity growth in the services sector are more difficult to identify largely due to its intrinsic nature of production. Given that services are directly embodied in the activities of providing the service, we do not directly observe the productivity performance of the service sector.

In this book, we address both the intrinsic and extrinsic components of the productive performance of services and the service sector in Singapore. Each chapter is supported by both case studies and qualitative surveys that clearly identify the intrinsic components to improve the productivity and competitiveness of the retail and food & beverage (F&B) sectors in Singapore. This approach of case studies and qualitative surveys enables us to identify the key policies that could be adopted to improve the productivity of the two sectors.

The key conceptual framework for identifying the intrinsic and extrinsic components of competitiveness of the services sector is provided by the 8M framework in the introductory chapter. Based on the 8M framework for productivity improvement, the subsequent chapters explore in greater depth the specific issues relating to entrepreneurship, use of part-time and mature workers, the efficacy of social media, marketing efforts and cost control and accounting practices.

Each chapter is self-contained, together with recommendations made. The salient points and lessons which can be discerned from the chapters are summarized here. Firstly, the 8M framework has been a useful guide and organization platform in developing and implementing the research activities in each of the topics covered. The 8M is an enhanced Total Quality Management (TQM) approach and hence can be easily adapted to accommodate other frameworks such as the Business Excellence Framework. It also provides the basis for formulating a scheme, based on the Data Enveloping Analysis (DEA), for benchmarking individual enterprises against their peers.

Secondly, there are certain key findings from the research studies:

(a) Several studies and projects have been commissioned by SPC to benchmark SMEs in the F&B and Retail Sector. The DEA method in Chapter 3 can be an additional approach such that participating companies can be told of their scores and areas of 'deficiency'. This will enable target improvement measures to be taken and guidance to be provided by consultants where necessary.

(b) The empirical investigation of entrepreneurship and start-ups shows that they adversely affect the productivity of firms if they are "casual" in nature. This is clearly reflected in the allocative inefficiency when resources are not effectively utilized and allocated to key productive activities.

(c) Amidst the tight labor market, companies have resorted to using part-time workers to bridge their manpower requirement gaps. It is important that a pool of loyal "permanent" part-timers be cultivated to ensure that productivity is not adversely affected by casual part-timers.

(d) In the employment of mature workers, their efficiency can be raised if there is a more flexible working environment that could accommodate their intrinsic knowledge and skills. In addition, machine and smart equipment can be deployed to complement them in completing their tasks. For instance, equipment that lighten heavy lifting and magnify visibility for the mature workers will enhance their performance.

(e) Progressive small and medium-sized enterprises (SMEs) are the ones that are continuously seeking for new markets and sources of revenue. The use of social media is a precursor for more intensive involvement in e-commerce. The sharing of information and educating SMEs on the proper management and usage of social media is expected to have productive impact on the performance of SMEs.

(f) There is a lack of effort and understanding on the new marketing techniques in the retail and F&B sectors. Relevant courses for SME business owners and managers can be designed to introduce them to new marketing strategies.

(g) Cost and management accounting practice among SMEs are often viewed as inconsequential to the productivity of the enterprise. In reality, bad cost and management practices can deprive the enterprise of efficiency improvement and saddles it with high production cost, low profit margin and low productivity. Sound management practices can be promoted through financial analyst services, probably at a subsidized fee for a start, to the SMEs.

Index